GREAT GLASGOW STORIES

GREAT GLASGOW STORIES

JOHN BURROWES

MAINSTREAM
PUBLISHING
EDINBURGH AND LONDON

DEDICATION

For Sam, Alex, Evie, Lucy and Sophie – five
great wee Glasgow stories . . .

This edition 2010

Copyright © John Burrowes, 1998

First published in Great Britain in 1998 by
MAINSTREAM PUBLISHING COMPANY (EDINBURGH) LTD
7 Albany Street
Edinburgh EH1 3UG

ISBN 9781845966782

A catalogue record for this book is available from the British Library

Printed in Great Britain by
CPI Cox and Wyman, Reading, Berkshire RG18EX

CONTENTS

ACKNOWLEDGEMENTS

When facts are involved, no book can reach completion without the help of many people. Among those who most willingly assisted me with *Great Glasgow Stories* were those ever-helpful assistants who staff the Glasgow Room of the Mitchell Library, an unsurpassable fount of knowledge of Scotland's greatest city. My thanks must also go to their equally responsive counterparts at the *Daily Record/Sunday Mail*; the *Scottish Catholic Observer*; the Linenhall Library, Belfast; Colette O'Flaherty at the National Library of Ireland in Dublin for finding me my Soggarth Aroon; the Scottish Climate Office, Glasgow; soccer historian Pat Woods; the redoubtable Tufail Shaheen, OBE, for once again pointing me in the right direction in matters Muslim; the ever-exuberant Alex Thomson, formerly of Kearny and now Lakewood, New Jersey, USA; and finally, for reading the chapters with which they had such an intimate knowledge, former colleagues Arnot McWhinnie and John Millar, respectively Scotland's foremost crime and showbusiness journalists.

FOREWORD

Few cities in the world abound with greater stories than Scotland's greatest city, Glasgow. In the last hundred years alone, it has been witness to some of the most significant events of our time – from tremendous triumphs to cataclysmic calamities, amazing achievements to spectacular sensations. They have all been part of the eventful and colourful fabric of the Glasgow story in modern times. Many of them have been dedicated to them while others have been overlooked – and only the most astute researchers can located details of them

The purpose of this book is to assemble for the first time, as far as I can ascertain, a collection of the best of these great Glasgow stories in one book. Each story has been meticulously re-researched and presented with a fresh new slant. For instance, to really understand one of the events of more consequence – the legendary Work-in at the Upper Clyde Shipbuilders – means an appreciation of the unparalleled industrial triumph on the Clyde which came before that celebrated display of worker solidarity. Likewise, to fully comprehend *No Mean City*, that truly sensational novel about Glasgow, you have to know about the man who wrote it and why he did so, as well as appreciate the characters he knew and lived among.

And just who was Maggie McIver, Glasgow's most astute businesswoman, the mother and founder of The Barras ... and who, precisely, is the most famous Glaswegian living today?

The nostalgia of our trams and our cinemas, the memories of our finest stage comics, the terror of the horrific disease that blighted and threatened to wipe out the city, the time when they sent the tanks to tame our workers, the courage of the citizens when their city was the target of the bombers, the people from afar who brought changes to our lives, the most famous name in law dismissed from its lofty post because of a piteous girl from the East End. These are just some of the tales which fascinated me enough to include them in this collection of *Great Glasgow Stories*.

1

NO MEAN CITY

It's the greatest book ever written about Glasgow! Nothing is surer to create a state of near apoplexy among intellectuals and those who merely think they are, than making an observation like the above on the most sensational novel ever written about Glasgow . . . *No Mean City*. But then saying it's our greatest-ever book has that kind of effect on various other people, even ones with no literati or quasi-literati pretensions. Lord Provosts and City Councillors of numerous generations turn all shades at the very mention of it. And yet, if that same novel with the same success had been about an American city, smart people would certainly have capitalised on it to maximum effect.

Take the title for a start. It causes a lot of confusion on its own. Ask six people what it means and you'll get as many different answers. A common consensus is that it has something to do with the city being stingy: that we're perhaps a mean lot; or that maybe we're not a mean lot; or that Glasgow is not a mean kind of city. Actually, it doesn't really qualify for any of these. About the best interpretation of *No Mean City* is what Glasgow really is: an exclamation of just how great a city it is. In other words, *No Mean City* is just like saying, in popular terms . . . Wow! What a place! And isn't Glasgow just that?

Behind the sensationalism and the controversy which *No Mean City* still inspires more than half a century after it made its debut on the literary scene, or, if you prefer, the newsagent and bookstall scene, there lies a bizarre and rather tragic story of one man and his dream to be a great writer. And despite being the linchpin behind one of Glasgow's most read novels, Alexander McArthur was to discover a lamentable truth about himself. For years he had played the role of the observant writer, listening to this, watching that, making a note of everything. His 'garret', a room and kitchen in the Gorbals, was filled with all his notes and jottings, completed manuscripts for future novels, others for short stories and plays he had painstakingly typed out ready for consideration. Despite all of that, the sad reality was that he was never to be considered a writer of any merit whatsoever: he appears simply as A. McArthur, the first named of the two authors' by-lines on the cover of the most famous of Glasgow books.

His full name was Arthur Alexander McArthur, but he was known locally as Alec McArthur in the Gorbals where he was born and bred and which he knew so intimately. It was to the Gorbals that he devoted his writings. The McArthur family were, like so many others in the district, from Highland stock, and Alec was brought up with his brother James in Waddell Street, right in the very heart of the suburb. Like the majority of those who lived there, they went to work in one of the nearby factories or trades places. Alec was to find work and learn his trade in one of these local establishments, as an apprentice in a large bakery factory.

His mother had been widowed when she was still comparatively young and his brother James went off to sea as an engineer. Alec was just in his late twenties when he lost his job at the bakery and joined that vast army of unemployed, an army which at that time amounted to more than 130,000 in the city. Some observed that perhaps he had lost his job through being a heavy drinker, but then there were no hiding places in the Gorbals. Everything was noted about everyone, the most popular pastime of the day being the 'hing', as they called it . . . taking in all the events of the street's daily drama, leaning from your house's opened main window, arms folded on a cushion on top of the sill. Every house had its own 'Lowry' view of the Gorbals street theatre and from that part of Waddell Street, the ones having their 'hing' could see the nearest pub, the Stag, over on the other side of the street from Alec's close, a hundred yards or so down towards the Clyde at the corner of Ballater Street. Alec McArthur had been a regular there and if he was the heavy drinker that some speculated, then that must be viewed in the light of a city that had a tenth of the UK's alcoholics and an alcoholic dependency two to three times as high as any equivalent English city. Whatever the reason for his unemployment, it gave the otherwise industrious McArthur more of an opportunity to concentrate on his favoured pastime of writing and to fulfil his ambition of creating a great book about Glasgow set in his native district, the Gorbals.

The Glasgow of that period, although less than 70 years ago, was a vastly different place from the city we know today. The old suburb of Gorbals was like a city on its own until its demise during the Second World War and the years immediately after it. Until then, it was a self-contained unit of the city unlike anywhere else that is known today. A place where every commodity you could want in life would either be made or made available; where the dominant landscape was that of the tall, belching chimney stacks of busy factories and heavy industrial plants which worked day and night, cheek by jowl to the grim black tenement houses in which their workers lived.

Those pulsating works included all sorts of manufacturing plants, such as clothing factories; bakeries of varied descriptions producing various biscuits, cakes, plain loaves and bagels; jam and sauce factories; wine and cordial producers; a whisky distillery; a cotton mill and calico printers; bottling stores; blacksmiths' forges and horse stables; coachbuilders and cabinetmakers and a huge ironworks; and we mustn't forget the thirteen churches, three chapels, eleven schools, a subway station, a theatre, a varying number of cinemas and a small square with trees and a bandstand. There were also 50,000 people and their tenement homes were all crammed into a tiny area of 272 acres, which is about half the size of an average working farm. That was the Gorbals and there was nowhere else like it in Scotland.

Housing conditions were absolutely atrocious. More than 80 per cent of homes were of two rooms or less and the density of the population was six times greater than that of any other area of the over-populated city. Little wonder those hard-pressed lives needed the cheer of 120 public houses – 14 in one street alone! – which again was more per head than any other part of the city. Times were more than hard-pressed for McArthur, who on being made unemployed at 28 became more convinced than ever that there was a great book to be written about the Gorbals and that he was the one to write it.

For the next four years he was to fill an assortment of notebooks from his readings and writings at the local McNeil Street Library which he was sure would form the novel about Glasgow which everyone would one day read. Alec McArthur was a keen observer of the local scene and in a place like the Gorbals as it entered the new decade of the '30s there was plenty to observe – much more than the average eye or ear could take in. Despite the apparent despair, the squalor, the lack of sanitation and washing facilities, that grim, sepia world of the Gorbals reeked with character and characters. The streets throbbed with a vitality long since vanished from the city scene. Streets were packed with children at play amidst traders of all descriptions noisily plying their wares, heralding their presence with anything that created a din such as bugles and horns and rasping ricketies, or else merely bellowing the type of goods they had for sale.

Groups of men gathered at every street corner to participate in all forms of lively discourse, joking, debating, arguing, agitating, story-telling, sermonising, haranguing . . . and watching. There was no need for the prying eyes of CCTV when you had the corner boys vetting who was who that walked down your street, because if you weren't of their ken, well . . !

Alec McArthur saw and noted it all. He too would mix with the corner boys and listen to their patter. To survive among them, you had to have the patter as well: the patter that showed them that you knew what went on, you knew who was up to this and that (and there was a lot of this and that going on that a nod and a wink told you much about) and who the Busies were after and who they weren't after, and who was going in and who was about to come out of the big house up at Riddrie to which they gave a variety of names, all of them meaning prison.

He was just a young man in his early twenties when all the talk, it seemed, had been about the formation of the big new gangs in the East End, which were much bigger and far more talked about than anything they had at the time in the South Side, the customary way of referring to the Gorbals and adjoining districts at the time. It had begun with the one they called the Billy Boys. The street corners of the Gorbals were buzzing with talk of how it had all begun when that game of football on the pitches at Glasgow Green had gone wrong after that Brigton boy, the one called Billy Fullerton, playing for a scratch team against the Kent Star from the Calton, had scored the winning goal. It was one of those football games which still occur in Scotland, whereby it's not so much the taking part but the winning that's more important than life or death. And when Fullerton scored that victorious goal the Kent Star went for him, and in no way in the sporting sense. As it was called at the time, they had given him 'the hammer'.

But Billy Fullerton wasn't the kind to accept that kind of treatment, and following the game he promptly set about organising a gang of his own which would sort out any future problems, not only with the Kent

Star, but with any others of a similar intention whom the gang considered appropriate to be given 'the message'.

Being one of the Billy Boys had appealed to the young men of the area with Orange sympathies, of which there was no shortage in Brigton. In the years to come the Billy Boy volunteers were to battle it out with their arch rivals, the Norman Conks, led by Bull Bowman of the Abercrombie Street area, hundreds of them being involved in either side in a form of street warfare, the scale of which the city had never experienced before, or thankfully since. Vicious, unmitigated conflicts that they were, involving every and any kind of available weapon, but usually swords, razors, daggers, chains, hammers and knuckledusters; the gangs and their gangfights were to provide an escape for those enduring the unbearable and seemingly endless ennui of unemployment and poverty. And among those who congregated at street corners, the best of the fighters like Fullerton and Bowman and company, were to become living legends, spoken only in the most reverential tones. It was part of your street curriculum that you knew who they were, could relate your own special tale of them and maybe even boast of being on personal terms with them.

McArthur, too, knew who the warriors were among them, whether they were in the Liberty Boys, the Stickers, the Dirty Dozen or the Redskins, all 1930s gangs of the South Side.

They are the stuff of folklore now but they were a very real issue in the streets of the Gorbals that Alexander McArthur knew. For among those who had nothing, the Gorbals *descamisados* were not without their pride, their vanity. And there was no better masculine way of demonstrating that pride than by being what they knew as the hard man. The harder the man, the more that pride was satisfied, the more the vanity gratified. There was nothing like their gang fights and their subculture of conflict to establish reputation, for the gang fight revealed everything about the man: who was first to run; who was second; who was next after that; who was last; who scored the most; who scored the least; and who was the most defiant of them all. It was the latter one they admired most of all, the type that would take anyone and everyone on, single-handed. Johnnie Stark, the Razor King hero of *No Mean City* was that very kind of man. He had pride and vanity. There was no one more defiant. And Alec McArthur must have known him well.

The man who was to become the most talked about writer in the city eventually put together the work of his writing lifetime. Having spent some years as a nightshift baker, he had become used to being awake through the night and that was when the neighbours would hear the peck, peck, pecking of his old typewriter through the thin walls of the room and kitchen in which he lived with his mother at 141 Waddell Street.

He had been out of work for almost five years when he had at last completed the manuscript of his story about life in the Gorbals, centred on a series of very violent events which were by no means atypical of existence there in the '20s and '30s. However, the manuscript which he sent to the well-known Longman publishing house was to be considered unpublishable . . . that is, in the form which the review editors initially read it. But there was something in this rambling story by the Glasgow baker; something evocative of the raw and primitive subculture of Glasgow slumland; something so sordid it would startle; something they thought had great possibilities and might even be a sensational bestseller.

The story of such a grim life in the worst slums in Britain had a compelling fascination. It told the story of a young man, Johnnie Stark ('tall, broadchested and with dark, sullen eyes, he looked like a fighter ...'), and the responsibility he took for his family and home after the death of his violent father, his courtship with a girl some rungs up the social ladder, his wars as the Razor King with his flashing blades on the streets of the Gorbals with other gangs and the shock of his return from prison to find his wife carrying the child of another man.

Being the experienced publishers they were, Longman appreciated that even the worst compilation of words in the hands of the right person could be put into good, readable order.

Well, they had the perfect candidate to do just that, a journalist who worked on a London Sunday newspaper by the name of Charles Kingsley Long. He had done similar work for them in the past and he agreed to take on the Glasgow man's manuscript on a co-authorship basis, his instructions from Longman's being, to make the story readable and, of course, sellable. It was obviously a mammoth task, given the allocation of royalties drawn up by the publishers: the baker was to get a quarter of the monies and the journalist and writer, three quarters. He would be by-lined on the book's cover as C. Kingsley Long, although the first named would be McArthur.

The new novel was christened *No Mean City* by Long, the title, like so many things in life, taken from the Bible. Found in Acts 21, verse 39, it continues on the questioning of St Paul, one of the first of the Christian missionaries to the Gentiles who also died a martyr in Rome. He had been taken prisoner and was under interrogation. When they asked him if he was an Egyptian he replied: 'I am a man which as a Jew of Tarsus, a city in Cilicia, a citizen of no mean city . . .' That answer of

St Paul's, put in modern terms, meant that he was a citizen of no obscure city. Or, in other words, that he came from a great place, which Tarsus, an ancient city in Turkey, was at the time.

You couldn't buy a slogan as good as that in America. If such a book had existed in New York, and with a similar level of success, the chances are you would never have heard of that most celebrated of catchphrases, The Big Apple. The up side of life to them is much more important than the down side. That's why they can capitalise on their gang culture and make wonderful musicals like *West Side Story* and sing the praises of such unlikely places as the Bowery and the Bronx. *No Mean City* would have been a gift of a catch-phrase for selling the dear green place metropolis. And despite the small fortune spent on such advertising agency ephemerals as 'Glasgow Smiles Better' and its accompanying 'Mr Happy', 'Glasgow Alive', and 'Glasgow the Friendly City', all of which have come and gone, it's still the title of that enduring novel which rings the bell loudest.

Right from the start, the book *No Mean City* was to be a sensational success, much of that due to the controversy it was to cause. It was the *Trainspotting* of the '30s, and the opening lines of the *Scotsman*'s review of *No Mean City* remain uncannily appropriate to both books: 'This is an exceedingly sordid novel and it is on account of its very sordidness that it will startle readers.'

They were calling it 'The book that shook the world' and it was with these words under the headline 'Why I Am Publishing *No Mean City*' that the editor of the *Sunday Mail* took the rare step of explaining to his readers his reasons for making the boldest newspaper decision of the day by buying the full serialisation rights of the book.

'The book that shook the world,' he said, 'is a social document of the first importance.' He referred to the reviews it had received in the *Evening News*, the *Glasgow Herald* and *Daily Record*, each commending it as a book that all with a social conscience should read. Emphasising that the serialisation of *No Mean City* was not meant as a slur on the city, his message concluded: 'It may be of more use than 100 Commission (Government inquiry) reports or sermons. I hope it will give a reformative zeal which will remove the whole cancer of slumdom.'

No publisher or writer appreciates anything more than controversy being connected with one of their publications, for nothing sells faster. The *Glasgow Herald* of the day described *No Mean City* as being a book of tremendous power that could hold the reader 'enchained in a shocked fascination from the moment of the drunken father's awakening in the first chapter to the Razor King's death at the iron-shod boots of his supplanters'.

The *Herald* was most sympathetic to McArthur's work, the review appearing under the heading 'Book of the Day'. Looking now at that journal in context, the review was not only generous in its comments, but also in its length which is summarised in the following.

> Novels purporting to deal with life in the slums are usually more picturesque than truthful . . . Their portrayals of violent deeds and brutal passions make the flesh of well-bred readers shudder delightfully . . . McArthur's novel of life in the Gorbals is different from these . . . Only the uttermost sincerity and passionate resolution to expose the beastliness that underlies the false glamour surrounding and distorting 'gangsters' and the 'razor kings' could justify Mr McArthur's manner of writing . . . The result is a novel of tremendous power, a horrible story that holds one enchained . . . But at what cost is the triumph secured? . . . It is a dangerous as well as a salutary book. Its title is unfortunate. If it should, as it may, be accepted as a picture of Glasgow or of working-class Glasgow, we might well complain the city has been travestied. The author of such a book has courage, he also has faith. He is unfalteringly realistic. His characters, vile, pathetic and contemptible, are as real and earthy as a Gorbals tenement. His dialogue would do credit to a veteran dramatist. We hope Mr McArthur will feel sufficiently encouraged by his success to acquire the technique and self-confidence to produce his next novel without the aid of a collaborator, even one as useful and experienced as Mr Long.

As the *Herald* had put it, the tremendous power, the vile, pathetic and contemptible characters, its danger and unfaltering realism were, alas, to prove all too much for the elected incumbents of Glasgow City Chambers who, when it came to such creations, were no more enlightened in the '30s than they have been in succeeding decades. They rounded on it to a man, or to a woman too, there at least being some acceptance of female emancipation among voters of the '30s in their election preferences for those in power in Glasgow Corporation. Not that it made them any more sophisticated.

Among those to deprecate the book when interviewed by the *Sunday Mail* was Bailie Violet Roberton whose momentous and breathtaking comment was: 'I think the author has rather spoiled his effort by enlisting the assistance of a man from the South!' However, like the other resentful councillors interviewed by the *Sunday Mail*, none of them, unsurprisingly, had actually read the book. They had just 'heard all about it'. And so piqued were they at someone having the audacity to go into print with a story which described what the Gorbals of the day was really like, they immediately slapped a ban on the book from the city's public libraries. Obviously this was not one of their greatest moments in sagacity given that there is no single controversial factor responsible for guaranteeing the success of a book than for someone either to ban it . . . or sue it. And as the library shutters came down, the sales of *No Mean City* went up. And up. And up. Like no other book on the city before, or since. It is reckoned to have sold considerably in excess of half a million copies and after more than 60 years of continuous sale, it is still bought by more than 3,000 people every year.

There's no record of McArthur's views on Long's finished work but he obviously considered that while life for the unemployed baker was somewhat bleak, there was something to be made from this writing game. His first royalties from the publisher had arrived giving him enough to settle down to the task of creating more works, spending many more long nights at his well-used typewriter in the kitchen area of their apartment. The small kitchen was the warmest area because of its coal-fired cooking-range and the added convenience of the house's only table. He tried short-story writing, then some more novels and a couple of plays, but success was to be negligible, for there was nothing of even sufficient merit for another writer to put into shape. *No Mean City* had been a one-off.

Despite all his efforts and dreams and the fact that he genuinely was an accomplished observer of the passing scene, knowing and appreciating the hard end of life in pre-war Gorbals, McArthur sadly lacked the intuition of the writer. All the days he spent studying and taking notes in the nearby McNeil Street Library and the nights spent poring over his typewriter were only to bring the realisation that his dream was more elusive than ever.

A year after *No Mean City* was published and while it was one of the hottest properties in the publishing world, he authored a featured article in the *Daily Record* entitled 'Why I Wrote *No Mean City*'. It was a lengthy piece, at times rambling and repetitive, and obviously created a few problems for the subeditor who handled it. McArthur wrote:

> Having read the various criticisms of the book, I am bound to say from their nature that, in my opinion, none of the critics are really qualified to pass a responsible opinion on such a book. The urge to write it for years consumed my energies. Yet I fought against that

terrible urge till I was forced to realise that, as long as I go on living, I must submit to the natural instinct which I was conscious of from infancy. Many people are bound to be sceptical about that. But the reactions of fellow slum-dwellers to the book have added to my conviction that I, or someone in a similar position, must have written such a book. Working-class people are now becoming slum-conscious. This book ought to add to their number and to their slum-consciousness. I have never been in any working-class 'Labour' party, though I know what it is to labour through the day and through the night so that it must not be understood that I mean class-conscious when I mention slum-conscious. For years I have been convinced that bathless homes without lavatories were not up to the standard for people of the twentieth century. But unemployment gave me time – forced time on me! – to see that demoralisation has many forms. I saw that the old Scottish pride had been carried to such an extent as to become a liability. To conceal poverty may be a good thing in its way but for working-class people to go on living and ignoring their weaker brethren, not caring how low they may have fallen is to me a social crime of the most dangerous kind. I cannot and shall never claim to be a saint, yet I do have within me a desire to see all bathless homes without lavatories abolished. Hence the book *No Mean City*.

McArthur concludes by saying that the book had to be written in order to tell the world just how bad conditions were in Glasgow and his hopes for it 'serving the city well'.

For years after the publication of *No Mean City*, McArthur, an anonymous sort of figure in the universal attire of the day – the cheap, navy pin-striped suit and wire-rimmed specs – was to become a well-known figure around newspaper offices and writers' haunts – mainly pubs – trying to either sell more of his works or find another collaborator to make sense of his ideas. Among the number of scribes who were asked to make something of some drafts by McArthur, were such well-known Glasgow writers as Jack House, Cliff Hanley and Tom Wright. Wright recalled how he was given one of McArthur's manuscripts by a Glasgow publisher of the time, William MacLellan.

'It was about a bakery,' he says, 'but other than that it didn't have a name.' But despite Wright's talents, there was nothing he could make of this McArthur manuscript. It was unworkable. 'The prose wasn't the only problem,' he recalls. 'The absence of any story was what deterred me and, I suppose, the others, from taking on the task. It would have entailed creating a story and writing it with only the setting of the original remaining. And I'll tell you what: if the writer Kingsley, McArthur's collaborator for *No Mean City*, was confronted with the same task then it was he who in all reality was the author of the novel. He was certainly entitled to the biggest share of the royalties which he was to receive. And I know for a fact that other writers who were given some of his work to try and put into shape said the same thing.'

Alec McArthur was just 46 years of age that Thursday night, 4 September 1947, when they found his unconscious body on the banks of the River Clyde, reeking with the overpowering stench of antiseptic, of all things. The first the world was to hear of it was in a 16-line story in the *Daily Record* the following morning saying that a man had been found on the footpath of the Clyde near Rutherglen Bridge at Richmond Park and that the only means of identification had been a food ration book with the name A. McArthur. As he lay there, soaking wet on the path near the river, there was speculation that he had tried to drown himself. His wet condition was due to other factors, however, including his having been sick.

McArthur's life had been riddled with such guesswork and on this occasion the assumption of an attempted drowning had been wrong. What had occurred on that last tragic night of his life, apparently, was that he himself had given a party in the Grosvenor Restaurant in Gordon Street, just opposite the main entrance to Central Station. There was nothing in the Gorbals remotely like the Grosvenor. The restaurant emanated quality and style, from the moment you ascended the sweeping and imposing staircase to the first floor of the classic old building, largely designed by Alexander 'Greek' Thomson. It was said McArthur had thrown a champagne party, which would have meant dinner to boot, and had left from there to go home.

The spot where he was found leads to two points of speculation on his last moments that fateful night. He was discovered just by the Rutherglen Bridge at Richmond Park, a point which is further away from the city than where he was living at the time in McNeil Street. Perhaps he had taken a long way home, meaning a lonely walk through Glasgow Green or through Bridgeton for a final pub crawl, before crossing the bridge. Alternatively, he had taken a direct route home, and then gone out for a walk along the riverside, perhaps the more likely occurrence, since he'd have to have collected his deadly dosage of antiseptic.

There were still signs of life when the police discovered him and he was rushed to hospital, but it was too late. It was there that the strong smell was identified to be that of Lysol, the trademark of a well-known antiseptic and disinfectant, and it appeared he had drunk a bottle of it. There was no suicide note, no obvious reason, all that was found on him was 7½ pence and the ration book.

What made Alec McArthur, the man behind *No Mean City*, end his life so tragically? Was it because of the comment he had made to a journalist once that 'If you find you have to live in poverty, don't live at all'? Had the grinding poverty of his lonely existence in the Gorbals eventually got to him? Most probably, however, it was the fact that he never came to realise his elusive dream of becoming the respected writer. One of the last people to speak with him was an old Gorbals neighbour, Daniel Kelly. He revealed that although McArthur had been staying in McNeil Street for years, he had just sold the old family house in Waddell Street the previous week. Not that this would have brought him any great riches: a good night at the Grosvenor with champagne and friends would easily dispose of that kind of money. What Kelly had to say about his old friend was much more telling, however.

'All he spoke about was his books and the success he might some day achieve as a writer,' he said. 'He was in the McNeil Street library every day spending hours reading and writing his manuscripts. He told me he had written two new plays, but I don't know whether he managed to sell them. He said he intended that week to go to London and see a publisher.'

Had the publisher perhaps put him off? Had he maybe told McArthur that all his new works were unpublishable as they stood and needed considerable rewriting? Had he finally come to the conclusion that he was never to repeat the fantastic success of his great Gorbals novel? Was it out of the frustration he felt that he was never accepted as the writer he had so dearly strived to be? The farewell party! The 7½ pence left in his pocket; the bizarre death by the river-bank; it would all have fitted in so well with that last line of *No Mean City* . . . 'And Gorbals life goes on its way – just as if nobody could help it.'

The successors to those in power in Glasgow's ruling authority have never come to terms with *No Mean City*. In 1991, nearly 60 years after it was published, it was suggested that the city should honour the forgotten author with a plaque or perhaps even a statue. The idea was very promptly and officiously ruled out, one of the senior councillors decreeing: 'This man did neither Glasgow nor the Gorbals any favours . . . and we will certainly not be doing anything to remember him.'

They obviously hadn't been, or did not want to be, aware of some of the events that had taken place in the city the week McArthur died. For some of the incidents which made the headlines could have come straight from the pages of *No Mean City* – like the gang in court arrested for waving razors, scissors and bicycle chains in Springburn Road – the man charged with butting a tram conductor in London Road after the Celtic match; the 18-year-old accused of murdering a 63-year-old spinster in Alexandra Parade; the teenager in court for carrying a razor and pleading he only used it for shaving; the youth shot in Govanhill; and the list goes on.

And as the city heads for the new millennium, its Royal Infirmary is treating more stab victims than any other hospital in Britain. They average three stab casualties a day, December being their busiest month when they treat around 80 wounded by knives, half of them over the Christmas period.

And Glasgow's life goes on its way – just as if nobody could help it.

2

BILLY CONNOLLY

Glasgow has never known another comedian like Billy Connolly. But then, neither has Scotland. Or any other place for that matter. For if ever a showbusiness personality was a one-off, it is this man. He's the man who made the F word respectable (if you're a fan, that is), and he's also the one whom the F word made unrespectable (if you're not). And there are legions on either side of the Billy Connolly fence.

Billy Connolly is not only the most famous entertainer to come out of Glasgow, he's the most successful Scots stage personality since Harry Lauder – remembering that Sean Connery's world is all about films. Billy Connolly and Harry Lauder! The very thought would have Connolly in stitches, though of rage or ridicule, I'm not sure. Perhaps even both, for comics in kilts and och-aye-the-noo jokers were among his first stage targets. Yet that seemingly ludicrous link is no casual jest, because Lauder at the height of his success was the highest-paid entertainer in the world. Every big star in the new place in California they called Hollywood and in the rest of America wanted to meet, and be seen meeting, the funny wee Scot. Will Morris, the man who was his agent in the United States, became so successful through representing him that the showbusiness agency he founded as a result was to become the biggest of its kind in the world.

The Portobello man in the kilt and funny walking sticks who sang about braw, bricht, moonlicht nichts and wee deoch an' doris's, never so much as breathed an oath or cracked a suspect joke in his life. He would constantly chide others in the cast of any production in which he appeared to 'keep it clean'. He would even go backstage in productions in which he wasn't featured, offering comedians that same advice. And when he turned down the greatest-ever hit about the city, 'I Belong to Glasgow', it was simply because he refused to sing any song which was in praise of drink, emphasising that his own song 'A Wee Deoch an' Doris', simply meant a wee drink before you go.

Yet he was to make millions of Scots rue the day he ever set foot on stage, his caricature of the jokey, kilted figure forever spreading the propaganda of the canny and miserly Scot, an irksome falsehood that still plagues the Scots abroad. He wasn't the only one either to play the mean Scot: one of Glasgow's most famous comics – he's dead now, so no name sullying – went to Australia in the late '50s and was paid a small fortune to play the pennypinching, skinflint Scot for a petrol company's TV commercial. And the chances of Scots immigrants proclaiming their munificence dwindled even further.

Glasgow has figured prominently in the history of the traditional Scots comic. Harry Linn, one of the earliest recorded, was not unlike Connolly in a sense, being tall and thin, though with a face that was as joyless as Connolly's is joyful. It was Linn's humour, it is said, that made Queen Victoria utter the legendary comment during one of his comedy routines: 'We are not amused'. It was whispered, however, that she was in fact a secret fan of the Glasgow man and really *was* amused.

Following Linn, there was a whole succession of funny Glasgow men, with the very occasional woman, in the Scots comic tradition, and oldies remember some of the best of them: the famous Tommies . . . Morgan, Yorke, Lorne and his pal George West, Frank and Doris Droy, Sammy Murray, Stanley Baxter and Jimmy Logan in their early days, Jack Anthony, Jack Radcliffe, Dave Willis, Alec Finlay, Lex McLean, Jack Milroy and Rikki Fulton. Each one was a name guaranteed to pack out theatres and music halls and brought great joy to generations of Scottish audiences.

Sadly, it was all to end. Most of the great venues where they played had gone, their audiences watching shows from the Palladium at home. The comedians featured would invariably be sitting on stools and come from everywhere, it seemed, except Glasgow. With the demise of the theatres, so too came the demise of the Scots comics. A tradition had died.

And then there was Connolly. In the old days he would undoubtedly have been a successor to that long list of fine funnymen. He still is, in a sense. He's a comic from Scotland, though anything but a Scots comic.

Glasgow humour is for Glasgow people and any stage performer who wants to make it outside the city, let alone outside the country, has to make radical changes to his act. Very few have been able to make the tough transition from Glasgow to the outside world. Baxter did and became one of the funniest men in the country. Connolly did, too, and has become, albeit controversially – and certainly sensationally – one of the funniest men in the world.

Connolly and controversy are bedmates. But then how else can you make fun out of farts, buffoonery out of bums, laughs out of lavatories, satires out of smells, railleries out of religion and parodies out of penises and pukes? The old-timers would have run a mile from material like that, Lauder birling in his grave doubtlessly quipping that this was the kind of humour that started at the sewer, and went all the way downwards. Nevertheless, when Connolly hit the comedy scene, he was more new hurricane than new wave. The El Niño of la comedia had arrived. The world knows all about that now, of course. But we in Glasgow knew about it first! We knew him first. We heard and laughed at him first. We were the first to buy his albums and treat them like collectors' items. And, anyway, he meant more to us than anyone else because he was one of us. Only we can say we knew his 'faither'. Others probably won't understand that. But we in Glasgow know what it means when they tell you that they knew your faither.

Seeing Billy Connolly for the first time is one of those experiences that leaves its mark, almost in the fashion of that much hackneyed one about where you were on the night of that event in Dallas. It's just like that, especially so if the Connolly you saw for the first time was the one back in the early '70s when he looked like and sounded like someone who had escaped from a Bud Neill cartoon. You could easily have imagined this zany new character riding the prairies beyond Calton Creek along with Lobey Dosser on a two-legged horse that looked like El Fidelmo, chasing people like Rank Bajin and Chief Toffy Teeth. The guy was an event, all right.

He was an advent offering new horizons and new adventures in humour, the likes of which you had probably never experienced before. Then again, perhaps you didn't want to experience it again. But most did come back for more, and more . . . every show an immediate sellout.

Because of his innumerable TV interview and chat show appearances both here and in the United States, we seem to know more about the Billy Connolly story than any other comedian before him: besides being a guest on *This Is Your Life* and appearing with superfan Michael Parkinson so often they started to look like a double act, he's been a regular on the multi-million, top-rating US nightlies, *The David Letterman Show* and its rival runner-up, *The Jay Leno Show*. All we ever knew about the old Glasgow comics was that they had a nag of a wife, a harridan of a mother-in-law, supported that football team you either love or hate and went home drunk on a Saturday night. And that was all fictional, made up for smiles between their routines and one-liners. Other than that, all you ever heard were the whispers that they drank too much and kept their wallets shut, which were fairly consistent and accurate observations about more than one of them.

When Connolly includes background material in his comedy, however, it might seem stranger than fiction, but much of it is true. There really did exist an aunt, babysitters and psychopathic schoolteachers who whacked him. But woven as it is among his wondrous storytelling, he has you splitting your sides with every whack, whack, whack.

Connolly is the classic example of that rather rare, almost unique specimen, the indigenous Glasgow comic. Not the kind that goes on stage – the kind that most of us know, perhaps at the workplace, or the playplace – the true and intuitional wit, of which the Glasgow brand is a rare and brilliant specialty. I've had the privilege of knowing a few of them, some as funny as Connolly and one of them memorably even funnier. His nickname, incidentally, was the Colonel and he was something of a legend among the West of Scotland cycle racing fraternity in the early post-war years.

Like the Colonel and Connolly, these funnymen rarely cracked or remembered jokes per se. They would never ask if you heard the one about the fat lady and the skinny man or the Protestant, Catholic and Jew in the railway carriage together, or the other whimsies with words that passed for witticisms and who endorsed the reality that all you needed in order to be a comedian was a sound memory; and to be a really good one, keep a big fat book of jokes. That wasn't the way with the instinctive funnymen. They were born with the heart of the jester and endowed with that uncanny skill of injecting humour into every event of life they came across. Through their eyes, every day had a humorous side to it. They had a gift of the gab which was sheer genius, turning each and every episode of daily routine into a hotchpotch of hilarity. The news which filled that day's newspapers, the good, the bad, the indifferent, could all be spun into magical tales. They could see the farce in funerals, the drollery in death; they could make burlesque out of the bureaucrat; satirise the supercilious; make gags of the grandiose. If you have experienced the Glasgow workplace, it's more than likely you'll have met at least one character like that. And the only difference between them and

Connolly is that he's the only one to have made it in showbusiness.

The backdrop of Connolly's life is the commonplace story of millions of Glasgow weans. The early days are so archetypal they sound fictional but they're not. Life began up a close, the close being that of 65 Dover Street in Anderston which is now, like so much of the Glasgow we knew, demolished. It wasn't the kind of place where you were likely to see anyone take the fireplace ashes to the midden in an attache case, like they said they did in Kelvinside. His mother was Mary, daughter of Angus MacLean from Coll and his wife Jessie, and his father was William, a wartime RAF man and son of an Irish immigrant. The first born was a daughter named Florence, who was educated at the famous and much respected Notre Dame school and went on to become a teacher.

His mother was just 18 when William Jr arrived on a cold Tuesday morning in November, three years into the Second World War.

The marriage didn't work and two years after the war ended, she left home. The young William, now Billy, was like countless other Glasgow children, farmed out to be cared for by an aunt, in his case a couple of aunts – one Mona, served in the WRNS (the women's branch of the Royal Navy), the other Margaret, a career nurse. And so the story goes about a mile or so further west to another suburb and another tenement, this time in White Street in Partick. His father had been a Catholic so his first school was St Peter's Primary, in Chancellor Street, after which he attended St Gerard's in Govan.

From Partick, Billy (by then 11 years old) moved to Drumchapel, one of those suburban blessings bestowed on us by Glasgow Corporation and called a housing scheme, perhaps more accurately labelled by Billy himself as 'a graveyard with fairy lights'. Life for the emerging teenager from the Drum was to continue as though it were ordained by a scriptwriter. School was over at 15, the first wages coming from a message boy's job at John Smith's bookshop in St Vincent Street, and after that as a van boy with Bilsland's bakeries. Thereafter, it continued its conventional and predictable way like so many other young Glasgow boys with basic education, the slip roads all leading to that career motorway of generations, still in existence in the early '50s – the apprenticeship. His was to be the five-year welder tradesman's course at Stephen's Linthouse shipyard.

In the varied universities of life, few were as comprehensive and as tough and rigorous as the Glasgow tradesman's workplace, such as the big engineering firms, ironworks and varied other industries which had given the city the label of being the Workshop of the British Empire. Among these, the shipyard workers held themselves as something of an élite, which in many ways they were, or had been, having built most of the finest ships in the world.

But by the '50s, all of that was confined to history. When you boasted to the world that the ships they made there were 'Clyde built', the world answered back, 'so what?' And rightly so, for other places were not only building them bigger and better, but faster and cheaper. Yards like Stephen's, meanwhile, carried on with old traditions and practices, one of which was taking five years to train young lads to become accomplished welders.

The ingénue was to learn much about life at Stephen's, an experience that flavoured many of his early stage routines. As well as the banter at work, hilarious lunchtimes (which could be more pantomime than lunch-break) were spent with the varied characters who made up the shipyard workforce. Connolly himself still doubles up with laughter when he relates how funny some of these Glasgow workmen could be, men with that genius and innate comic gift who loved nothing better than seeing the smiles on their workmates' faces. Jimmy Lucas and Bobby Dalgleish were two that are often mentioned. The latter was pursued by the *This Is Your Life* research team as a surprise guest when in 1980 Connolly was the show's star (or victim, whichever way you look at television's great bunfight of the vanities). But the particular Dalgleish they produced happened to be the wrong one, although the viewers were never to know, since Connolly acted out the part as though they had got the right one.

Had he been interested in a theatrical career in the days of the old music hall Scots comedian, Connolly would by now have been serving his apprenticeship in buffoonery, learning the various routines, collecting his own joke book. Instead he stuck to the typecast script of the Glasgow tradesman apprentice – hard graft during the week and weekends off. The latter involved the customary dancing and bevvying, deviating occasionally from the usual theme by indulging in more exciting pursuits like motorbiking with a group called The Men (full marks for originality) and parachuting, courtesy of weekend soldiering in the local Territorial Army unit of the Parachute Regiment.

The apprentice became a fully qualified journeyman welder and found himself earning his first major cash on a contract to an offshore oil-rig in Nigeria. For some time he had been nursing the ambition to play a musical instrument of some kind and being flush enough on his return from Africa, he bought himself a banjo. In the complex pattern of life, it was this small investment which was to be the first thread of the intricate web, one weave leading to another, and yet another, which was to form the fabric of a career in showbusiness. But at that moment, such an eventuality was the furthest thing from his mind.

Connolly and his new banjo were to be natural born partners, the instrument, the music and his leftist political leanings leading him to folk. He appreciated the folkies. Like him, they were different. They didn't conform, although like so many nonconformists they had their own conformities. It would have been unimaginable, for instance, to be a folkie in what was de rigueur of the day: a Billy Eckstine collared Fletcher shirt, a Fusco DA haircut and a Jackson drape suit. Nevertheless, they could be irreverently individualistic and appreciated character, and at the kind of places they frequented – the Atlantic Folk Club in Clydebank, the Marland and Scotia Bars – there were cheers for groups who were to come and go, like the Skillet-Lickers, the Acme Brush Company and the Humblebums, and special shouts for the banjoist who featured in all three: the long thin guy with the raspy voice and Rasputin face.

This one was different, they were thinking. He was making a reputation on his own and showing a preference for musical creations instead of being one of the usual wild rovers in woolly-pullies who sang about Johnnie Lad, Lonesome Boatmen, and jolly men who Roved the World Over. And, into the bargain, he could recount belly-achingly funny stories while tuning up.

Even Connolly himself knew he was different the night he forgot the words to one of his numbers and improvised with more of his funny stories. The laughs he got from that were the impetus he needed: if there was a life to be had from being up on a stage entertaining people, then it was from the kick of getting all those laughs. You really were something when people got laughs out of you like that. And Billy Connolly, professional funnyman, was born that night.

It wasn't easy at first, but then it never is. There were the usual hard times at the coal face of showbiz, picking and shovelling his way towards the hopeful seam of success. Show promoters wanted to rubber stamp him the way they did with other entertainers, but none seemed to have an appropriate brand mark for him and it's much easier to sell an entertainment commodity when it's got a label. They had labels for comedians and others for the category known as folk artistes, but they had none for entertainers with the classification of folkie-comic, which made bookings difficult. They were to forget all about their stamps, however, when they noted the attention this showbiz one-off was creating, particularly in the mountain of albums he was selling and packed shows he was getting in hometown Glasgow.

In a city still shaking off the effects of World War II, Glasgow was badly in need of a good old-fashioned laugh, the kind that made your sides sore, the kind that the stalwarts in the past had given their old folks. One by one the comedy giants of old died off in the '50s and '60s. And then there was just one, which perhaps goes a long way in accounting for the fact that Lex McLean was left on his own to carry the mantle of the great Glasgow comic.

They called him Sexy-Lexie, sexy in his case merely meaning suggestive, his routines based on tediously predictable sketches in which he either chased or was chased by a stage wife with raucous roars round a room-and-kitchen backdrop at the Pavilion. The great tradition would probably have died with McLean had it not been for the arrival of the sensationally new, revolutionary comic they called Billy Connolly.

The people of Glasgow could never imagine that a song with the lyrics 'Three Men from Carntyne and a bottle of wine, and five Woodbines, and a big black greyhound dug called Bob, from up our close, alang our street and a lassie called Senga . . . went to join the Parish', could be so hilarious. And reading it just as it's printed on the page you might very well wonder what's so funny about it. But you would know instinctively if you came from Glasgow and knew the way Connolly sang it.

The stories he told had everyone in stitches: the one about a man called Tam The Bam teaching him about anti-social diseases by watching men going into the Black Street Clinic, or about people called Yehudi McEwan and Engelbert McKenzie or the one named Constantine living in Govan, and the fellah who was The Jobbie Wheecha. Even a routine about the Crucifixion has Jesus Christ Himself and the Apostles starring in the Last Supper at their Sarry Heid pub. People laughed at it like they had never laughed before and then went over it the following morning, word for word, with folk in the workplace who were unlucky enough not to have seen this new stage phenomenon who looked like something out of the Rolling Stones. Glaswegians simply had never known anything like it. Comic revolutionary! This guy was the Che Guevara of traditional humour.

They could hardly produce the *Billy Connolly Solo Concert* album fast enough to keep up with sales. It soared up the charts, first going silver, then gold, then becoming the biggest selling album since *Sgt Pepper*. Successive albums were to outsell established legends like Slade, The Who, and Tony Hancock. Connolly had Glasgow at his feet along with the rest of Scotland, apart from Banff that is (they weren't ready for him).

Connolly was on board the roller-coaster of success, destined to become the first genuine comedian of the rock age. But then a funny thing happened to Connolly, on his way to the forum called fame, that fabled fame of showbusiness where they not only live forever, but learn how to fly . . . He was to learn the hard way that the Press isn't a tap you can turn on or off. Like everyone else on the way up, he had loved all the stories and the photographs that had helped spread the word about himself. That, after all, is what the business is all about when you're new and near the bottom of the ladder . . . spread the word about yourself and never let them forget your name. And there's no better way of doing that than by being regularly in the papers. But when the tap is full on, it can come as a great shock to them that there is no turning it off when other sorts of stories emerge.

Connolly was to get the first real taste of this when he split up with his wife Iris, a partnership of 16 years, and again with the resulting child custody hearing, the divorce, the new girlfriend . . . and the discovery of the mother who had deserted him all those years ago. If it happened to Connolly then it was news and like it or lump it.

Such personal incidents in the case of Connolly, are not the most pleasant or memorable events in one's life. When they occur to the majority of people, it's news only to the family. But not when your're in the public eye. When good things happen to you, there's a story in the paper, and when misfortune comes along it not only goes in the paper, but on the TV and radio too. Stars in any kind of business are public property and the public require to be told everything about them, good or bad. The media, then, becomes the unshakable bridge between them.

Connolly had fallen foul of what might be termed the Sinatra-Crosby syndrome. These two equally successful showbusiness legends were to take opposite routes when it came to handling the media. Sinatra thought he, too, could manipulate the media tap and was to make life more than difficult for himself when he discovered he couldn't, resulting in all the well-documented antics which were to plague much of his showbiz life. Bing Crosby, on the other hand, made it easy for himself by being the open book. At the height of his career, I once asked a writer on my staff to try for an interview with him when he was playing golf at St Andrews. Without any prior contact with press agents or assistants, the writer located Bing as he was having drinks with some friends at the bar of a hotel in the town. He walked straight up to the group, introduced himself and politely requested an interview. The reply, in equally mannered terms, was that if he cared to wait half an hour, of course he would talk. He waited and earned himself a full-page interview, featured the following day in the *Daily Record*.

Connolly treats the Press, particularly the Scottish tabloids, like hecklers, and if you have been to some of his concerts you'll know what he thinks of them. Like other comedians, he can take advantage of remarks from the audience for more laughs, but his retaliation to the voice that dares to speak up is more lethal than laughable. When he retorts 'Away an' bile yer heid', there's a special abrasion of earnestness in the delivery that leaves nobody in any doubt of his sincerity. It is the same with some of his classic put-downs such as 'With a voice like yours, I'd teach my bum to sing', or 'You should get an agent, pal . . . save ye handling yersel' in the dark'. Hecklers don't persist much after that kind of retort and the tone of its delivery. He would be more than delighted, of course, if only the media would do likewise and shut up. But that's not the way the game is played, and there's certainly no chance, no matter how much he thinks they should, of them ever going away to bile their heids.

Most professional media people believe that Connolly's attitude is either a bad case of paranoia or else one gigantic misunderstanding, where he considers newspapers are only interested in sniffing out the stink of sensation and scandal, rather than the sweet smell of his success. They also point out that perhaps he hasn't quite appreciated the difference between the gushes and goshes of *This Is Your Life* on the TV and the biffs and the bangs of 'This Is Your Life' in the tabloids: where one is fulsome the other is frank, where one pats you on the back, the other gives it to you straight from the shoulder.

Editors I know earnestly maintain he has never been the subject of a vendetta by them, concerted or otherwise, and that any anti-Connolly material has been mainly created by himself. He has been known, for instance, to take the odd swipe at his old home town or, indeed, takes swipes of another kind, particularly at photographers. On one occasion, he famously aimed his venom at the reporter Hugh Farmer who copped a couple of whacks resulting in Connolly facing a civil action and paying £400 in damages. Any move to damage the bridge between the Press and the public only ever leads to a soggy mess. But then one might have thought he would have known that by now, particularly after the occasion in Glasgow when, after a verbal altercation at a Press conference, he reluctantly agreed to meet some reporters only to get the invitation tossed right back at him with a repetition of the message he had given them minutes before. And the bite back came with exactly the same profanity he had earlier proffered them.

John Millar, the much respected showbusiness writer and TV interviewer, says he challenges Connolly to visit the *Daily Record/Sunday Mail* cuttings library at any time and see for himself just what has been printed in the papers which he says he despises so much. 'The pile of clippings in his favour is like an Everest; those against, a little Nevis. But somehow he just doesn't believe it.'

And having myself examined an armful of folders containing the relevant clippings from both these papers, I can confirm that Millar's observation is indeed accurate.

In fact, both these papers have lavished good publicity upon him. They've serialised books about him, published his own Christmas story, and for two and a half years in the mid-'70s, the *Mail* ran a strip cartoon which he did in conjunction with the artist Malky McCormick, the finest cartoonist in the country since the late and very great Bud Neill.

Connolly and his home city of Glasgow has been another area of contention over the years. The city and its people were often the butt of his early repertoire and it's hardly surprising. Anyone who knows and truly appreciates Glasgow, will admit that few places are more capable of subjecting themselves to ridicule. Take our drunks, for example: where else on earth could you see so many, so miraculously inebriated?

Connolly lets all of us see ourselves as others see us. Apart from those onstage deliveries, however, there have also been a variety of other comments and remarks about the city, either in interviews or in books, which didn't get quite the same reception as the ones in his act. Remarks such as 'The great thing about Glasgow is that if there's a nuclear attack it will look exactly the same afterwards', or 'I was asked abroad why Glasgow never had a riot. But they did. It was on Friday evening and nobody noticed the difference', or 'If all Agatha Christie books were laid end to end, it would still be raining in Glasgow', or 'I don't damage Glasgow. It does a good enough job on itself', or 'I'm no longer interested in exciting Springburn. I've grown up a wee bit beyond constantly having to prove myself.' And then there was the time when there had been criticism of one of his plays and he huffed about being finished with us and wasn't coming back. All of which has obviously been too much for the rulers in George Square, who at times seem to behave with all the subtlety and sophistication of that well-known Calton Creek character, Rid Skwerr. They've been somewhat disgruntled with Connolly and his comments, with expressions such as 'gross betrayal', 'disrepute', and 'bad image' never far from their lips. The likelihood of their honouring Glasgow's most well-known star in showbusiness, as Edinburgh did for Sean Connery, seems considerably less than very remote. Alas, the city has a long tradition of being miserly with its honours. There once was a time when, to its shame, the city even rejected considerable public demand for acclaiming the legendary boxer Benny Lynch with a civic reception when he brought home to the city it's first ever world boxing title. And they just laughed at the mere suggestion of some kind of recognition to writer Alec McArthur, author of *No Mean City*.

Meanwhile, city conflict and media war or no, the Connolly bandwagon rolled on. The Glasgow comic broadened his routine and proved he could be a Scottish comic, then a British one, and then proceed to take on the rest of the English-speaking world. He has more than once referred in interviews to the fact that even as a little boy he knew he would be a star of sorts one day. He confirmed this to me on the first occasion I had lunch with him back in the early '70s. He was just beginning to make his mark at the time, becoming more and more well known but only in a Scottish context, and mainly in a Glasgow one. I asked him where he thought he was heading in showbusiness, as I had difficulty in conceiving that his particular style of humour – the Crucifixion, Tam the Bam, A Partick Lullabye, Harry Campbell and the Heavies, and that kind of stuff, would have much of an audience outside Glasgow, conceding that the rest of Scotland *might* come to terms with it. Even Banff. The reply was to be no loose bravado, not even the usual showbiz ego, and came in the quiet, assured tones of a man who genuinely believed in himself. 'I'll make it,' he said. 'I know I've got it to take on the world and that's where I'm headed.'

It wasn't the reply I had expected, for I thought that he, too, knew the traditional limitations of the comic who traded in the humour best known and appreciated in their own city. The world stage has never been the place for the Glasgow comic, with the rarest exceptions, that is.

What I didn't appreciate then was that the rare vein of humour he was tapping into could be developed, and other seams explored. And we all know the rest. Develop and explore he did. He has gone right up to the very rim of the volcano of bad taste. And the volcano he chose was Krakatoa. Dangerous territory, but so far he's avoided incineration.

In a world where pushing back the frontiers of comedy seems to require men behaving even worse than badly and where it's difficult to have fun and laughter unless they're in frocks and lipstick, Connolly is healthy evidence that testosterone can still beat transvestism. The man who doesn't give an F, has given the F to the world. In San Francisco, the F count was eleven in the first minute and a half of his show, and in New York someone even went to the length of logging the times he used the word and clocked a total of 127. He has made a cult of the unmentionable, and has taken the tabs off the taboo.

Ticket sales soar in Canada, the US and New Zealand and, in Australia, he's a household name, becoming the biggest draw of all time at the Sydney Opera House where his sell-out appearances reversed the policy of the Opera House company which had previously maintained that such acts would 'lower the tone of the place'. And obviously Sydneysiders quite agree that eleven Fs every minute and a half don't affect the tone at all.

The use of the F, of course, is a sticking point to many who are, or were, fans. They'll point out that in his early days, such language was rationed carefully, and when he did let fly with a well-timed F or two, it sledgehammered home with devastating effect his funniest lines. Now, it seems, the Fs come so gratuitously they grate, so often, they offend. He would no doubt answer that offence and outrage are an essential part of the Connolly game and that we're F-in' stuck with his F-in' F-in'. His old film buddy, Michael Caine, once sagaciously observed, by way of pardoning the peccadilloes of the footballer Gazza, that he reminded him of Marilyn Monroe . . . 'Not the greatest actress but a star, so you didn't mind if she was late.' Maybe he would say the same about Connolly, and that being the kind of star he is, you don't mind the Fs.

Whatever the views on his language, the sultan of swearing has reached that rare and hallowed status of the funnyman who only needs to say 'Pass the mustard', and the audience goes into convulsions. Legends like Bob Hope could do it. Jack Benny too, only in his case he would merely have said 'mustard!' and they'd be falling in the aisles. With Connolly, of course, it would be 'Pass the F-in mustard.' But the reasoning is the same . . . it's him, he's the legend, and he makes us laugh the way he tells it – even though it's just passing that F-in' mustard.

From concerts and record albums he has moved on to TV plays and American TV sitcoms, TV tours of Scotland and Australia. They talk of him in terms of Oscar potential. He's a guest in all the top shows. There have been films with Richard Burton, Michael Caine, and Judi Dench and there's talk of more major movie roles. He has lived in splendid houses such as one in Bray, Berkshire, where the neighbours included the Wogans, the Parkinsons and the Rolf Harris's, and he has lived in a Victorian mansion near Windsor which he called Grunt Futtock Hall. For the last seven years he has lived in Los Angeles where his wife Pamela has graduated with a PhD and is a practising pychologist.

When he was asked in one of his more recent interviews with Parkinson about his living arrangements, the answer was that while he loved living in California and that his house was in Los Angeles, it wasn't where his home was. The question wasn't pursued, but in the more recent of his Scottish tours, he concluded performances with a Van Morrison tune which he readapted and sang to the accompaniment of the most stirring pipe band music.

It's a moving Gaelic number, the emotion of it heightened by that unique ardour of the bagpipes to lyrics like 'Oh won't you stay . . . stay a while with your own ones' and 'I'm going back . . . back to my own ones'. Heard by the good Scot abroad, it would either jerk the tears or send them packing for home, perhaps both. It was sung with much fervour and great feeling, and listening to his rendition of it made it all the more obvious that no matter where his house is, the Connolly heart still beats strong on the hameland.

In confirmation of that, the news was out early in 1998 that he had put his Windsor mansion on the market and bought a 19th-century baronial retreat called Candacraig House, complete with turreted staircases, a dining-room that can seat 24, a bedroom smothered in enough tartan to kit out the Argyll and Sutherland Highlanders, 12 acres and a trout loch, set in the heart of beautiful Strathdon, Aberdeenshire, just a short drive away from Balmoral. The man who can lay claim to being the world's most famous living Glaswegian might not yet be as well known as Connery in America yet, ironically, in political terms he could be the one that gets the knighthood first. Could he equal Lauder's record? With the way the story has gone so far, well, who knows.

3

THE GREAT STORM

It hit the city with a biblical fury. There had been nothing like it before, not, at least, since they had started keeping records. And those who were there and experienced it pray that nothing like that dreadful hurricane of 1968 ever happens again.

Glasgow is well used to its storms and its winter gales. That's why the building laws insist that houses constructed here are built to more stringent standards than south of the border. But no building legislation could ever have conceived the scale and the strength of the storm that was to hit the city with such unprecedented force in the early hours of Monday, 15 January 1968.

More than 20 people in Central Scotland, nine of them in Glasgow, were killed on that horrific night. More than a dozen workmen in Glasgow were to die in the succeeding months as they valiantly clambered over the precarious crests and ridges of city buildings in an effort to repair some of the devastation caused by tumbled chimney-heads, scattered slates and tiles, and roofing timbers that had vanished in the howling winds of the night. A quarter of a million homes were damaged, 70,000 of them in Glasgow, where more than 300 houses were completely wrecked and 1,700 people were left homeless. It was one of the biggest natural disasters to strike Scotland, yet it was to reveal a woeful lack of interest, not least compassion, from a Government which not that many months before had so demonstrably shown its deep concern with offers of immediate relief when a giant tanker had foundered off the south coast of England, threatening the wildlife in surrounding seas.

It had been a fairly normal winter towards the end of 1967, but with the new year there was a deterioration in the weather, thermometers and barometers taking plunges. But it was January, after all, and the freezing temperatures and cold winds were to be expected for that time of year. There had been some bad snowstorms, the south-west of the country being particularly affected, especially around the Ballantrae area. Then, in the second week of the new year of 1968, there was a bitter snap – the kind usually associated with bright moons, starry skies, and little or no wind – yet this new weather front had been associated with blustery conditions, the wind chill factor making it seem colder than that which was registered by the thermometer.

Bitter or not, there was still a festive air about the season and it didn't seem to affect the crowds who flocked to town to see some of the winter shows. Among the entertainments were the likes of the seemingly eternal duo, the Alexander Brothers, together with Billy Rusk at the Metropole, the Frankie Vaughan Show at the Alhambra, (Vaughan fresh from his peacemaker role in Easterhouse where he had persuaded local gangs to give up their weapons, or at least say they had given them up) and Rikki Fulton with Lonnie Donegan at the King's. There was considerably less choice on the TV in those days, and most who stayed at home would be watching the same black and white TV shows, such as the big favourites like *Z Cars*, *Dixon of Dock Green*, and *Crossroads*, although the news of the day was that the kids were to miss out on Sooty, since the BBC had just announced it was axing the popular programme.

Although it's in comparatively recent times, that winter of 1968 seems, in many respects, to be another world away. Harold Wilson was in charge, although if your political rosette wasn't his colour you'd probably find the unions being in charge a more accurate assessment. Millions of low-paid workers were demanding more money and were prepared to strike for it. The average wage was around £20 a week, although many earned considerably less, and who could have blamed the agitators for even then that wasn't really a decent take-home pay.

At least prices were in some way commensurate with the paucity of salaries. 'Going abroad', as they said, was coming into fashion and ordinary people were returning with tans that no Scottish or English seaside could provide. They were telling everyone about the fabulous time they had had in places with strange-sounding names like Torremolinos and Benidorm, the Costa something and the Costa something else and, Franco or not, it was viva Espana. They were off to sunny Spain in future, where the new drink they called Bacardi was just fantastic and flowed in abundance for next to nothing.

People had begun shopping for and buying holidays from catalogues – just as they did with mail order goods – and their glossy brochures were telling them that in the winter of 1967/68, there would be some fabulous bargains for their summer breaks, such as £31.50 for an 11-day holiday to Majorca, £27.50 for the same duration to the Costa Brava, and a more upmarket Global were offering 15 days to Benidorm for £53. All prices included air travel, accommodation and food. If motoring was more your choice of holiday, then the new Imp, made in Scotland, no less, at the Rootes car factory in Linwood, was on sale at £567. Holidays apart, and if you happened to be interested, the biggest liquor advertisement of the day was that for Eldorado wine (old tawny or rich white) at 70p a bottle.

Due to the hard frost which had persisted most of the week, there were doubts about playing some of the football games on that Saturday, 13 January. It had been so severe that racing had been cancelled and the big football clubs were taking measures to protect their grounds. Celtic had postponed their game against Morton, hoping to arrange it some time in the following week, but Rangers were able to play with the help of thick straw blanketing they had laid on the pitch during the week, and the soccer writers were saying that the new teaming of Willie Johnston and Alex Ferguson would be something to watch out for and be the likeliest significant threat to opponents Hearts.

Rangers fans were to receive excellent news with the sports results in the Sunday papers. That prediction about Johnston and Ferguson, the man to become the legendary Manchester United manager, had become a reality, the former scoring twice, his partner once to beat their Edinburgh rivals.

The biggest news of the weekend, however, was the fact that the French were even more stuck for money than we were, and were threatening to withdraw their share for the great new project being planned between them and Britain . . . the building of a proposed Channel tunnel. But then many were saying it would never materialise anyway and, if it did, who in their right mind would use it!

Other than that, Sunday had been a fairly dreary, cold mid-winter's day. The brief details of the weather forecast had indicated the possibility of a slightly warmer Monday, the prediction being that

hackneyed old standby which seems as much reflex as it does repetitive
. . . 'Cloudy with rain at times'.

It was to be a mercy that city and suburban streets cleared earlier in
the late '60s than they do today, with pubs closing by 10 p.m. and the
last of the regular service buses trundling to the peripheries an hour later
(the vehicles were all motor buses now that the last of the trolley ones
had been withdrawn eight months previously). If these same late-night
crowds had still been around a few hours later, or had the incoming
weather front moved in earlier, who knows what the death and injury
toll might have been. But there was little sign of what was in store for
the homegoers, apart from the increasingly blustery wind and a few
spats of rain. In short, just another lousy winter's night.

By midnight, however, conditions had deteriorated dramatically, the
wind intensity fierce enough to be rattling windows, knocking over the
odd rubbish bin, whipping up papers and waste into mini-whirlies and
inspiring a spurt into the step of those scurrying home to be in out of the
wind. But nobody could completely escape this storm that was being
generated with an almighty power in the savage and incredibly wild
Atlantic.

Weather scientists at the meteorological station at Prestwick, co-
ordinating with their headquarters at Bracknell in Berkshire, were hard at
work as usual preparing the hourly charts which is part of their 24- hour
daily routine of studying and forecasting what's coming our way. From
these readings, gathered from information passed on to them by ships and
aircraft, they noted around midday on Friday, 12 January, a small wave-
type depression forming on a cold front about 1,200 miles due west of
that scattering of mid-ocean islands, the nine tiny volcanic outcrops of the
Portuguese empire they call the Azores (reputedly part of the sunken
continent of Atlantis). This placed the depression at a point precisely
equidistant between the Azorean capital Ponta Delgada and New York.

It was to be the very first sign of the embryonic hurricane as it
emerged from gestation. As with all such developments, they charted its
course as it moved in a north-easterly direction, the depression
deepening and the storm intensifying. But still there was nothing to be
concerned about as such depressions come and go: they're Mother
Nature's very own game of Russian Roulette, most of them causing no
harm and blowing themselves out at sea. But there's always the chance
that the revolver hammer will click on a live shot and hit land instead.
Could it be this one?

By midday on Saturday, 13 January, the growing depression had
reached a position in the Central Atlantic, still continuing on its north-

easterly direction and twenty-four hours later the centre of the storm was now about 400 miles west of Ireland, having deepened even further to a value of around 966 millibars, and a glance at your barometer will show you just how dramatically low that reading is.

At 6 p.m. that Sunday night, the trackers noted the centre had progressed to a point 200 miles west-south-west of Tiree, the course changing slightly to a more northerly direction, taking it by midnight to just west of Benbecula, the barometric pressure falling even further to 958 millibars and the associated trough of low pressure extending southwards to the west coast of Ireland. If it had kept moving on this new course, it would have slammed into the sparsely populated Uists, then blasted its way up the North Minch towards the Pentland Firth and nothing more would have been heard about it. Therefore there was no need for any severe weather warnings about an impending storm, and the earlier forecast for Central Scotland of 'Cloudy with rain at times' still appeared to be accurate.

The more intense these severe weather fronts are, however, the more unpredictable they tend to be in their movements, and having already changed course, this one was to do so once again, this time veering sharply eastwards. The barometric reading was now down to 955 millibars.

The effect of the continued deepening of the storm's centre and its new eastward course was to result in the establishment of an exceptionally strong pressure gradient. The resulting wind speed measured at an incredible 140 mph at a height of 2,000 ft, but even more alarming was that its new course now appeared fixed at due east. Its destination . . . Central Scotland.

The West of Scotland, north of the Mull of Galloway, lies fully exposed to the vagaries of the North Atlantic, since it does not have the protection of the land mass of Ireland, all of which lies south of a line between Culzean Castle and the southern end of the Kintyre peninsula. Looking at a map showing Glasgow in relation to the Atlantic, it can be seen how the estuary of the Clyde lies like an open funnel with very little land between it and the open ocean. Draw a line from the gaping mouth of that funnel, the estuary that is, and all that remains are two fingers of land, the broader one of Cowal, the other, that slim and low-lying part of Knapdale along the Crinan Canal. Thereafter, all that remains is the flat, northern tip of Jura. From there on it is sheer and forbidding ocean, 2,500 miles of uninterrupted Atlantic till the nearest landfall which is somewhere between the lonely Newfoundland outposts, or outports as they are known there, of Hebron and Hopedale. And if the epicentre of any violent storm happens to be in that part of the vast ocean and taking an easterly course as the one approaching Scotland was, then it will be channelled into the open mouth of that Clyde estuary funnel with the Kilpatricks to the north and the high Renfrewshire hills to the south, all the time intensifying the concentration of its ferocity as it blasts into whatever structures and obstacles lie in its path. And those nearest structures that early morning in January were the houses and other buildings of Scotland's largest city.

Although the storm had reached gale force levels shortly after midnight, it was as yet nowhere near its zenith which came at last at precisely 2.53 a.m. when the gauges at Glasgow Airport moved to the highest levels they had ever recorded.

According to the Beaufort Scale, the international standard for measuring wind velocities, a gale becomes a hurricane at 78 mph. At Abbotsinch in the early hours of that morning the straining wind gauges were at a new peak reading of 103 mph. It was now officially a hurricane and they labelled it Hurricane Low Q.

Thundering on at a speed as great as our fastest express trains, it swept up the lowest point of the river, testing out every construction lying in its way. It was in the days before work had begun on the major upgrading of the city's old housing stock, largely neglected by war and wanton landlords more interested in what they could take out rather than put into their properties. Thousands of vulnerable roofs, chimneys, and rain-soaked, frost-wracked, age-weakened stone walls were to be no match for the fury of this wind phenomenon.

As it hurtled along its destructive course, police, fire brigade and ambulance information rooms became abuzz with their biggest peacetime disaster. Only the old hands among serving officers, with memories of those dreadful nights back in the German air-raids of the '40s, had ever known anything like this. The others had been trained for such eventualities, but never visualised anything like this.

The majority of emergency 999 calls requested rescue workers and ambulances, each being logged at the police information nerve centre. The calls were received in order of the direction of the storm as it swept devastatingly through the city from west to east, the winds seeking out and wrecking whatever was unable to match its ferocity, like some unseen monster on a rampage of death and devastation. The first of the serious calls brought news of a tenement chimney-head which had crashed in West Partick, leaving a woman dead. Thereafter there was a deluge of calls, each adding, precisely and tersely, to the growing story of the drama of that night.

Another chimney-head collapsed in Partick, four reported dead; from Govan, reports of stairways, chimneys and roofs disintegrating in several buildings, over 50 families evacuated; falling masonry in Anderston, little girl of five killed, others injured; giant building crane in Blythswood Square blown over, number of mangled cars beneath it, drivers and passengers could be trapped, casualties unknown; roof blown from a tenement in Maryhill, man seriously injured; another Maryhill call, this time a young boy seriously injured in a roof cave-in; Crossmyloof, row of garages wrecked and cars damaged; Govanhill, woman pensioner killed by falling masonry; Springburn, two dead in tenement gable-end collapse, three floors of houses left to the full force of the hurricane, families urgently need evacuating; emergency centre Shettleston Public Hall in Wellshot Street opened to take in families from endangered houses; Corporation officials alerted to provide other emergency housing; dredger sunk in the Clyde with at least three crew reported dead.

These were just some of the hundreds of requests for help that were received throughout the early hours of that morning. More messages were coming in from adjoining brigades and services, as extensive damage was being reported in Rutherglen, the Clyde Valley, Loch Lomondside, Falkirk, Fife, and many other areas throughout Central Scotland.

Those experienced ones who said there had never been anything like this before were right. Nothing like Hurricane Low Q had ever hit Glasgow before.

There were stories, too, of great fortune and misfortune. A family in Glenboig, Lanarkshire, had kept their savings in a wall cabinet in their prefab home, in order to buy new furnishings. The hurricane ripped the roof off the prefab, burst open the cabinet, and the last they saw of their savings were the notes being scattered in the wind . . .

On hearing a strange noise, a lawyer in Glasgow opened the door of his suburban home and was stung several times by bees which had escaped from a hive blown over and destroyed in the gale . . . A young married couple, the wife heavily pregnant, were in their bed on the third floor of a Govan tenement when their building collapsed. They ended up on the ground floor, still in bed, but had the presence of mind to pull the mattress on top of them to prevent injuries as they awaited rescue . . . Thomas Fraser, another expectant father, rushed his wife to hospital at 1 a.m. from their house in Eglinton St, Gorbals. When he returned a few hours later he discovered their bed under tons of rubble from a tumbled chimney-stack which would undoubtedly have killed the pair of

them had it not been for those well-timed contractions . . . The high-rise
Red Road flats in Balornock began swaying so badly that eighty families
abandoned their houses and spent the night on the ground. One family
stayed behind on the 30th floor and described the movement of the
building as a nightmare. But the flats, Europe's tallest public housing,
survived unscathed . . . Fruiterer Sam McAleese looked out to see his
new delivery van being blown away to the foot of a steep slope. When
he looked out of the window once more, he saw his week-old Vauxhall
estate car disappear under tons of rubble from a collapsed gable . . . The
SSPCA animal home at Milton, near Dumbarton, was inundated with
dogs, cats, tortoises and goldfish from houses hurriedly evacuated by
fleeing families, but they had no remedy for the thousands of homeless
racing pigeons from hundreds of smashed lofts . . . The Boyle family in
Sighthill watched, helpless, as the ceiling of their home disappeared, the
hurricane then sucking out every item of clothing from wardrobes,
drawers and the clothes pulley . . . An expensive new dream house on
the Clyde, finished two weeks previously, was blown to smithereens . . .
At Ibrox Park, the heavy straw bales used on the pitch for frost
protection ended up in piles inside the enclosure, and the pitch was
covered instead with hundreds of iron sheets ripped from a stand roof.

Glasgow awakened that Monday morning to sights that hadn't been
witnessed since the war. Apart from the hundreds of houses that had
been destroyed, and thousands badly damaged, the city and suburbs had
the appearance of a war zone. Hundreds of thousands of slates and
heavy roof tiles which had withstood scores of violent winter storms had
been whipped from tenement roofs and littered streets everywhere.
Countless cars were either flattened or badly damaged by the flying
debris of the storm. Miles of fences had either disappeared or were
flattened. There was rubbish scattered everywhere, the tempest having
knocked over every bin and garbage can in its wake.

Hundreds of caravans and mobile homes had either been blown over
or blown apart. Some had virtually disappeared, those on Loch
Lomondside being particularly affected. Two cabin cruisers which had
been beached on the shore near Luss vanished without trace at the
height of the storm. Garden huts and homeowners' garages, especially
ones with up-and-over doors, as well as glass hothouses, disintegrated in
the almightiest wind the city had ever known. In the Clyde Valley
tomato growers, first estimate of smashed glass alone was £1,000,000.
One market gardener there reported that six of his seven glass-houses
had virtually vanished 'and I have no hope of raising the cash to rebuild
and replant', he said.

Immediate efforts were made to restore some normality back into city life as the first attempts to assess the total damage got under way. The initial estimates put remedial work into many millions. Damage to house roofs alone would take at least a year to repair. In the meantime, thousands of temporary coverings in various colours had to be draped over acres of roof to keep out the rain, giving Glasgow a whole new look, especially from the air. Air crews would have been forgiven for saying 'welcome to Tarpaulin City' when flying in; the devastation viewed from aircraft gave the most graphic picture of just how badly the city had been ravaged.

Builders merchants, who were inundated with orders for various materials, ran out of supplies very quickly, delaying repair work. Chimney-pots, a big storm casualty, were one of the first items to be exhausted, and many builders resorted to old stock which had been out of fashion for years. Aluminium and zinc ridging became scarce, and in order to get sufficient slates, trucks were making non-stop round trips to quarries in Wales for supplies, one firm alone rushing 200,000 of them north to Glasgow.

Men in dangerous roofing jobs, such as slaters, were working 90 hours a week and within the first few weeks, as they bravely carried out emergency repairs in continuing foul weather, several men were killed and others seriously injured. Such was the risk they were taking, that Glasgow and West of Scotland Slaters' Association were forced to cut the men's working week to 64 hours, ordering them to take Saturday as a complete day off.

The end of the storm may have concluded another chapter in the life of Glasgow, but the story, as the city was to discover to its cost, was just beginning. As in all weather stories, there existed the same set precedence by the BBC in 1968 which continues to exist today, namely that the further away the affected zone is from London and the south-east of England, the less important the story becomes – an observation which, you may be well assured, is entirely free of any nationalist sentiment but based on long experience of the Corporation and its most annoying presumptuous affliction, the Southern attitude. And if ever there was a more classic example of the Southern attitude, it was that hurricane of 1968.

The story, as it was conveyed to them by the southern media, was to make little impact on the government of the day with its Old Labour ruling in which Harold Wilson was Prime Minister and Willie Ross the Scottish Secretary.

The *Sunday Mail*, staunch supporter of Labour and the Government, was the first to put the nation's leaders on the block for what appeared to be abysmal inactivity and utter lack of reaction to the hurricane. It had been discovered by journalists from the newspaper that on the weekend after the storm, instead of every light being ablaze and busy staff attempting to sort out the devastation in Glasgow and other parts of Central Scotland, the Scottish Office in Edinburgh had been closed! Not only was this observed to be the case, but was actually confirmed to the newspaper by a Scottish Office spokesman. Nevertheless, the Government replied to the contrary when challenged, stating that this was not the case and that they really had been at work. Which can only be interpreted as saying 'the lights were out, but somebody was in!'.

Within the first week, initial estimates of the damage were put at £10,000,000, a staggering sum in the '60s (the equivalent in the late '90s would be £50,200,000). Later, when more accurate estimates were made, this figure was tripled. Yet just ten months beforehand, when the huge *Torrey Canyon* oil tanker ran aground off Land's End – undoubtedly one of the major environmental calamities of the day, but offering no real threat to property or endangerment to lives – it only took the Government four days to declare the south-west coast of England a disaster area. Perhaps it was all some gigantic sideshow to take the heat off the prospect of devaluing the pound, but Downing Street hadn't shown so much concern since Dunkirk. They labelled the disaster the 'greatest peacetime threat to Britain' and the Army, Navy and RAF were drafted in to help. Senior members of the Cabinet made urgent journeys, looking appropriately shocked and saddened at the unholy mess the oil slick was making and, at the same time, assuring anyone who might be around and listening that no effort would be spared to make quick amends. Local authorities were offered 75 per cent grants and paid £1,600,000 for remedial work.

Such was the importance the Prime Minister put on the disaster, that he specifically went out of his way to make sure the Press got hold of the message that he and his Government were really on the ball. This was spin-doctoring, generations before the expression had ever been invented. Notes of a telephone conversation between Wilson and Denis Healey, at the time Secretary of State for Defence, read: 'There has been good Press so far and it's important to hold this position. It's important that the Press should say that the Government has been doing the right thing before the oil reaches any beaches.' The public were never to know about that conversation, for the comments were filed among secret Cabinet papers, the details remaining confidential for the next 30 years.

While we all love our seagulls and gannets and adore the coastline, whether they be our own or from any other part of the kingdom, the truth of this shipping disaster was that it was purely these things which were at risk. Yet eight days after Hurricane Low Q had so devastatingly struck Scotland, the Government had said and, worse still, had done absolutely nothing.

In America. France and other places, the President would have been on the first plane. Alas, in London, no responsible Minister had been appointed to take charge of the relief operation while the Scottish Office HQ at St Andrew's House, Edinburgh, continued to work normal hours whether the lights were on or off. The Queen did despatch a message of sympathy, but no mention of the storm was made in Parliament until an all-party group of ten MPs signed a demand for a debate.

Outspoken as always on such matters. Teddy Taylor, the then Tory MP for Cathcart, was to exclaim that the only reference to the extent of the disaster had been made when the Scottish Secretary announced that the first estimate of the damage caused was about £16,000,000, and that the Government would be releasing an immediate £500,000 to help repair work. 'No one in Whitehall has got across the sense of urgency that a disaster of this nature demands. That's why we want an emergency debate,' he said.

Belatedly, and largely due to the hostile reaction of the *Sunday Mail* and other newspapers, the first overture of help eventually came from the Government. But the offer did more to infuriate than alleviate, for after having it rammed home to them that Glasgow and Central Scotland had suffered countless millions of pounds worth of damage, as well as great loss of life, all that was initially on offer was a tawdry half a million pounds. The miserliness had commentators and opposition parties apoplectic, particularly when Lord Provost John Johnston revealed to a fractious Corporation that the repair money donated by the Government was purely an interest-free loan.

Later, in a bid to appease growing bitterness in Central Scotland at the Government's pathetic reaction to the crisis, Scottish Secretary Willie Ross was to give the assurance, albeit the typical politician's verbal one, that no local authority would have to bear any undue rate burden as a result of the storm, although it may well involve Exchequer assistance running into millions of pounds.

Heartwarming news, until the analysts got to work and dissected the Government's financial pledges. It didn't take much going over to detect the first sour notes, namely that there would be no help for home owners, except for the interest-free loans. And when would repairs be effected? Ah, now, that was a really awkward question to ask!

Unlike the *Torrey Canyon*, there was to be little military assistance: the tarpaulins draping countless house roofs came from a consignment of 13,000 drawn from Government stores in England and were transported to Scotland by the Army and RAF; some Territorial soldiers helped to remove furniture from damaged houses. Having come to grips with the horrific extent of the damage, builders were now confessing that such was its scale, that it would take them at least another year before they would be even nearly completed. This was then confirmed when town clerk James F. Falconer addressed an angry public meeting arranged by the Corporation to discuss repair work. Despite the hecklers, he got his message across to the meeting. When the Lord Provost got up, however, tempers flared and it was all he could do to be heard. A woman shouted to him that dysentery had broken out in the property in which she lived due to the damaged state of the building and the primitive conditions to which they had been reduced because of the hurricane. She put her plight and that of her neighbours to the Lord Provost in a very Glasgow fashion . . . succinct and appropriate. 'We're not talking about wee birds like in the *Torrey Canyon*,' she yelled. 'We're talking about wee babies.'

'Why was there no national disaster declared in Glasgow?' another man bawled to the wildest applause of the night. It did little to pacify the audience when the Lord Provost replied that the declaration of a national disaster would have made little difference. Was he merely trying to restore order to the rowdy meeting, or did he really mean that the Government was simply ineffective when it came to matters like this?

Whatever he meant, whatever way he put it, it was to do little to assuage the hurricane-ravaged city, by now seething with righteous anger and bitter recrimination. It might be argued that the Government reacted with reasonable promptness by providing £500,000 to help with immediate storm repairs. In so doing, it gave the impression that this had been an emergency measure and, being aware that the damage amounted to many, many millions, that there would be heaps more to come. But then, governments and promises have always been the best of bedfellows. Property owners were to get no grants for their storm-damaged properties, except for the interest-free loans, and this resulted in thousands having to dip into vital savings or going into debt. Neither did those with better memories for detail forget that a tanker accident in southern waters had coaxed more than three times the amount Glasgow received for its thousands of damaged homes.

Perhaps all the huffing and puffing and political mouth music from the Government of the day regarding their generosity and response can be seen more clearly in the context of a debate in Parliament almost a year after Hurricane Low Q smashed into Glasgow. It was in the early hours of Wednesday morning, 25 November 1968, a time when the House of Commons chamber is virtually deserted, when all senior Government officials have either gone home or are elsewhere, with only the *Hansard* writers and interested journalists taking notes. It was 12.56 a.m. when Tom McMillan, the stalwart Labour Member who represented Glasgow Central, got up to speak. Little wonder there were few Government ministers around. The story McMillan had to tell was not pleasant listening for those in power.

'Two or three weeks ago,' he began, 'a constituent came to my home and pleaded with me to go and see the conditions under which he and his family had to live. I suggested that the first thing to do was to get in touch with the Storm Damage Centre to see whether we could get the machinery going to help him immediately. On contacting the centre, I was informed that there was no one available to be sent to the house.'

For the next 14 minutes McMillan went on to relate the horrific conditions of his constituent's house as well as give some details of the post-storm scenario in Glasgow ten months after the hurricane. The following is a summary of his address.

'I welcome this opportunity to bring to the notice of the House the dreadful conditions in which hundreds of my constituents are living. If I do less than that, I feel I shall be failing in my duty . . . I feel that the best way to do this is to give a typical example of the hundreds of cases which have come to my notice since the storm . . . I found in my constituent's house what can be found in hundreds of houses in Glasgow now when it rains. Rain was coming into every part of the house, and no food could be cooked on the cooker because of the danger of using it . . . In one house in my constituency, a girl was taken to hospital with rheumatic fever and another also had a fever complicated by a heart condition. The fever was due to the storm damage. They had no roof and the Corporation would not house them . . . Since the storm, 30 people have died, 11 by falling from roofs. I see the workmen on cold windy days trying to bring comfort to their fellow citizens . . . The workmen have told me that they get a bonus of ls 6d (7½ new pence) an hour for roof work, but that if for any reason, even through illness, they take a day off, they lose a whole week's bonus. I assure the ministers that my constituents – there are still 3,500 houses under repair in the area – would be only too delighted if all possible steps were taken to tackle this problem now.'

As one headline writer at the time put it . . . 'Surely no one can shrug off a hurricane'. Sadly, when it came to the disastrous Hurricane Low Q, that's precisely what the Government did.

Almost 20 years later, on Friday, 16 October 1987, a similar hurricane struck the South of England and parts of Wales causing severe damage and a similar loss of life as Hurricane Low Q. Three days later, Environment Secretary Nicholas Ridley announced in Parliament that the Government would meet 75 per cent of local authorities' extra costs in dealing with storm and flood damage in the affected areas.

4

THE STORY OF OSCAR SLATER

When you think of famous miscarriages of justice, you invariably turn to a number of much publicised English cases that were the subject of innumerable TV programmes, discussions and debates, appeals and inquiries. The most outstanding of these, of course, were those relating to the groups of Irish people convicted for bombings in Birmingham and Guildford. While it may be fair to make the observation that such errors are rare in the Scottish legal system, they are, in fact, not unknown. There have been numerous occasions when innocent people have been wrongly accused and, worse still, wrongly convicted. But one case stands out among them all: the High Court trial of Oscar Slater, accused of the brutal murder of an elderly woman in Glasgow.

The trial of Oscar Slater is probably the most celebrated case of its kind and one which still evokes debate and controversy. It has been rated as one of the most flagrant miscarriages of justice ever known, not only in Scottish, but in British legal history. For decades after his trial, allegations emerged that Slater was not merely an innocent victim of a slipshod police and court system, but that he was deliberately used to cover up the deeds of influential figures in Glasgow society.

It's a common and loose American term to speak of someone being stitched up by the authorities. If the accusations behind this case are true, and in all probability they are, then few people have ever been stitched up more than this man, Oscar Slater. His case was not only to reveal considerable weaknesses in the legal system of Scotland at the time, but was to cast a most unsavoury light on the prejudices and intolerances which existed in our society not all that many years ago. For what is most certainly true is that this man was widely considered to be guilty for reasons other than any connection they alleged he had with the crime or the crime scene.

There was little, if anything, in Oscar Slater's make-up that could make him in any way favourable to Glasgow society at the turn of the century. If ever anyone fitted the conception of someone who might be wanted for the brutal murder of an old woman, it was the type of person Oscar Slater represented. In a society which at the time was anything but cosmopolitan, he was everything that was outwith the norm of the social order. The type of person who by his looks and his behaviour should be, and would be, treated with scepticism. A breed of humanity whose different culture meant he was someone to be thought of only with mistrust, maybe even to be feared; the sort of stranger whose looks aroused suspicion; the kind of man who inspired wariness and apprehension, whose mode of conduct reeked of the unpalatable; the very last person you would expect to shake your hand in the fashion which meant accepted respectability. He was, in short, the ideal subject to have in the dock when you wished a jury to say what was wanted of them – namely that he was guilty.

Oscar Slater was all of these things which was why, in May 1909, they found him culpable of the particularly savage murder of a wealthy, elderly spinster from the West End in Glasgow called Marion Gilchrist. It was also why Oscar Slater was to spend the next 18 years in prison before being sensationally released and then, seven months later, have his conviction quashed.

Oscar Slater, born Oscar Joseph Leschnizer (sometimes Leschzner or Leschziner), was a German Jew, the son of a Jewish baker and born in a small town in East Germany. He did not follow in his father's humdrum footsteps and became instead a footloose sort of character in a period when relatively few people travelled. He was what we would call today a man of the world. He worked first of all as a bank clerk in Hamburg, but was to learn other ways of earning a living, the kind of ways which to many would hardly meet the requirements of the estimable let alone the heights of the respectable.

He was not a man who would make his way in life by conventional routes – what wisdom he possessed was centred on his wits and how to live by them. This he was to do with an obvious modicum of success in various roles, such as being employed in numerous capacities in gaming clubs, working with bookmakers, being a bookmaker himself, dealing in jewellery and mixing with all those in that animated cast which make up the street trade . . . the hustlers, bustlers, fixers, doers, eager beavers, procurers, the ones who knew all the ladies and the ones who knew all those who weren't ladies – there was no shortage of stories about Oscar, a real-life Threepenny Opera character, but no Mack the Knife.

When the prospect loomed of Oscar being called up for the army, his sharp wits had an answer for that too. Like get out of town, for instance – fast . . . and far. That was to take him to Britain, then on to the United States. He was to work in and get to know New York as well as he knew London. He also worked in Brussels and knew it as well as he knew Edinburgh, Hamburg or Glasgow. Sometimes they knew him as Mr George, other times as Mr Anderson, Mr Sands or Mr Schmidt, then as a Mr Otto Sando. An alias here, an alias there. They even knew him by the name he had come to adopt, that of Oscar Slater, a title he chose because, he said, English-speaking people couldn't say Leschnizer, never mind spell it.

Whatever they called him, they were always to know him as one of those fringe people who drifted from this to that. Some would know him as the one who would sidle up to them to inquire if they might be interested in a nice little piece of jewellery which had come his way. 'For you, my boy, a very special price.' You know the scene! Others would know him as the regular with the studious look as he pondered his chances at the Black Jack or one of the other tables at the gaming clubs he frequented. Or else he would be the smiling and familiar face behind a sloping cue in a billiard hall, or even the one that would catch your eye for being the snappy dresser in the smart new suit and bowler around the trendier bars of Sauchiehall Street or the West End. He had been in Glasgow and done all these things in 1901 and again in 1905. Now, in 1908, Oscar Slater was back in town.

He arrived around the beginning of autumn, coming up from London where he had been living for a few months since returning from New York. He had gone to the States because, as he would tell acquaintances, the prospects for a sharp man like him were good there. They certainly were good for Oscar Slater, whose experience quickly got him top management posts in a couple of Manhattan clubs. The jobs must have paid well, or were perhaps supplemented by his other activities, like gambling, dealing in jewellery, or perhaps the more shady elements of Oscar Slater's life that were never fully known. Whatever he was up to, it had meant being on the move regularly. Such an itinerant lifestyle, however, opened the door to much guesswork as to the reasons behind it – one reason put forward was that there had been a marriage and every time a pursuing wife was about to catch up for money demands, he was one step ahead and on the move again. But perhaps Oscar was one step ahead for reasons other than a chasing wife.

Despite the sums he spent on travelling and the burden and cost of moving houses as he did, the ways of Oscar Slater, whatever precisely they were, afforded him a better than average lifestyle. There was a suite at the Central Hotel, a rather sumptuous establishment and the biggest and best of its kind at the time, until he could arrange more permanent accommodation. There was his French live-in partner Antoine and her German maid, whispered to be at one with her mistress as a lady of the night . . . It was rumoured too that Oscar, the lad, could arrange a very nice lady for you, and the police in Edinburgh knew only too well that it was more than a rumour and that he had been part of that trade's very prosperous scene in the capital. When he did arrange more permanent living quarters, it was to be in that most handsome of fringe West End buildings, the red, sandstone St George's Mansions, which elegantly command the Woodlands and St George's Road junction with splendid views of the moorland hills of Renfrewshire, although the view is more dominated nowadays by the throbbing M8 motorway. Not that certain callers to the house would have been interested in the view from the window in any case.

As he had done before, Oscar, the uptown man, once again moved around those certain parts and places of the city he knew best of all, those certain bars, the clubs, the pawnshops. Being a denizen of the *demi-monde*, he came under the scrutiny of local plain-clothes policemen whose duties, among other things, were to observe the unfamiliar, the unusual, the strange and the stranger. And Oscar Slater wasn't the kind of person they were likely to miss. For a start, he wasn't Scottish. There was nothing of the ruddy, fresh complexion of the local about this man who had a sallow, almost Latin appearance instead. His nose in profile gave him an almost Roman look, although from the front it appeared as if it was more long and with a twist, perhaps the result of a break, a good thumping perhaps. He had, after all, been 'done' for such a thing, his petty criminal record including illegal gambling and fighting in the street.

Then there was also his accent and his mannerisms, neither of them remotely native. Slater would barge in rather than wait in a queue. He could be distant and abrupt, aloof perhaps, in that heartland Continental way which jars with the Glaswegian and made him as noticeable to them as his clipped German accent. His dress, too, was Continental, always fastidiously well groomed, the shoes polished, the moustache as regularly trimmed as his bowler steamed and brushed. Oscar looked every inch of what he was . . . the foreigner.

Settled into the flat at St George's Mansions, Slater quickly re-established his old Glasgow routines. He lived in that part of the city which exhibited the liveliest of Edwardian scenes, crowded, carless streets with men in silk top-hats and canes, elegant ladies in long dresses, their pinched waists emphasising proud and thrusting bosoms, flocking to local music halls, penny geggie shows, theatres, bars and restaurants. He loved that vibrant kind of scenario and set about touring his old regular pubs, the billiard halls, the gambling clubs, resuming old friendships, a contact here, another there, the tipsters, the barber, and the pawnbroker where he pledged a lady's brooch receiving various sums for it totalling £60. Despite the lengthy lease on the flat, however, within weeks he would be telling some of these same acquaintances that he would soon be going to the States again. There were prospects of a job, he said, this time in San Francisco. At the same time he would hustle for money, trying to raise even more on the brooch he had pawned by offering the ticket for sale, but he got no takers – enough had been pledged on it already. The job deal in California appears to have been confirmed for mid-December 1908, and Slater made hurried arrangements to leave Glasgow, booking a passage on a ship sailing on Boxing Day.

The furtive and devious ways of Oscar were, it seemed, entwined in everything he did. While in fact he really *was* heading for San Francisco and had told several acquaintances of this, he told others a different story, one being that he and his partner were heading for Monte Carlo. At the same time he was also in the process of contravening the letting conditions of his flat by arranging for it to be sublet to friends along with furniture he was buying on hire purchase. That was Oscar, and on Christmas Day 1908, he and his partner Antoine left by train for Liverpool to catch their ship for the States.

Not far from the flat at the St George's Mansions is West Princes Street, a few minutes walk along bustling St George's Road. It's balti and bedsitland now, but in 1908 that part of Woodlands was what they termed 'a good address'. An early Victorian development and very Georgian in scale, the handsome tenements have been described as having a 'restrained dignity'. The same could be said of many of the occupiers just after the turn of the century, most of their well-maintained houses being roomy enough to accommodate live-in staff.

Marion Gilchrist would have been one of those very typical, restrained and dignified residents. She was a very wealthy spinster of 83 years of age, and her house in a two-storey tenement was just a few yards along West Princes Street from St George's Road. Whether because of her wealth or the jewellery she kept in the house, she had developed during that autumn of 1908 a great fear, bordering on paranoia, of being burgled or even murdered. She had become even more alarmed when her pet terrier suddenly died, convinced it had been the result of poisoning. She had triple locks fitted to her main door and had asked neighbours to listen out for any suspicious noises coming from the direction of her flat.

In the early evening of Monday, 21 December, while the young maid, Helen Lambie, was away from the house to do some shopping, her mistress, Marion Gilchrist, was brutally murdered. On hearing unusual sounds from her flat, a neighbour who was aware of the old lady's fears went to inquire. He and the maid, who had just returned from the shops, arrived at Marion's door at the same time. As they entered the hall, a man emerged from the bedroom and quite calmly walked past them out of the house. As soon as he got to the stairs, he bolted like someone possessed. In a matter of seconds, the neighbour and maid discovered the body of Marion Gilchrist. She had been the victim of the most savage attack, her appearance hardly recognisable as a result of the frenzied blows, obviously made with some kind of heavy instrument, which had virtually destroyed the fine look of the old lady's face. The intruder had forced open a box containing her personal papers, a pile of which lay scattered on the floor. Despite the thousands of pounds worth of jewellery which Marion kept in the house, Helen Lambie reckoned that only one item appeared to be missing: a lady's brooch.

Due to the nature of the murder, it received major newspaper coverage. Stories about it and subsequent police inquiries appeared daily until later that week there was a very significant development. The police made a special appeal to property and boarding-house owners to report anyone who had suddenly disappeared from a tenancy. On reading this, a regular from one of the nearby gaming clubs told detectives that a foreigner called Oscar Slater, who had been using the club in recent weeks, had suddenly disappeared. Not only that, but shortly before his disappearance, he was offering a pawn ticket for sale. And that ticket was for . . . a lady's brooch.

That was it, surely. They had their man! But it wasn't long before, alas, they met with disappointment. The brooch, they were quick to discover, had been in pawn since November and was not the one missing from the old lady's house. Nevertheless what about this foreigner with the strange ways called Oscar Slater? What about this man whom several people had referred to as being a real shady character? What about these aliases he used? And they said too that the women with whom he stayed were as dubious as he was. What's more, he didn't appear to have a regular job. He hung about billiard rooms. He gambled. He drank. He was foreign. He was shifty. And, most important of all, he had disappeared. Surely? Of course! It had to be!

'. . . Louie Miller, disappeared dear, after drawing out his cash . . . And MacHeath, spends like a sailor . . . Did our boy do . . . something rash?'

All these factors were given much more consideration than the intriguing reports in the *Daily Record* within days of the murder that old Mrs Gilchrist, who was worth around £40,000 to £80,000 – millionairess terms in 1908 – had recently altered her will. Why, asked the *Record*'s crime writer, had she become so afraid of being burgled and, more sinisterly, why had the intruder that night been so anxious to locate the old lady's personal papers?

These questions, however, were obviously of no great interest to the officers working on the case. They had other things on their mind, like this man Oscar Slater and as soon as it was ascertained that he had left for America. They arranged for men from the New York Police Department to meet the *Lusitania* on which he and Antoine had sailed from Liverpool to cross the Atlantic. At the same time, two senior detectives together with the neighbour, the maid, and a passer-by who claimed to have seen a man running from the old lady's flat at around the time of the murder, prepared to sail to America.

None of the three witnesses taken to New York for identification purposes was specific in naming Slater as the man they had seen that night, although the similarity in the twisted, or strange, nose of the intruder has mentioned. Appearing before a City Commissioner who would decide whether or not there was justification in the Glasgow police application for his extradition, Slater protested his innocence, saying he had never at any time had any connection with the dead woman, that his plans to return to America had been made long before the murder, that he had none of her jewellery, and that the pawned brooch, as had been established, was not hers. And so sure was he of his innocence (to the great surprise of the hearing) that Slater took the decision out of their hands by announcing he would voluntarily return to Glasgow and face whatever accusations were being made against him.

The brutal slaying of Gilchrist had the police and the city incensed. His name and photograph had been in all the papers and such was the feeling against this suspicious-looking foreigner called Oscar Slater, that the detectives escorting him back left the ship before it docked to avoid facing the angry crowd waiting to see the 'murderer' as he landed back in Glasgow. Even at that, he was still assaulted by a member of the crew when being led from the ship at Renfrew. They reviled this Jack the Lad as though he were Jack the Ripper. Despite all his pleas and the lack of evidence, apart from his hurried departure, Oscar Slater's trial at the High Court in Edinburgh lasted just over three weeks after which he was charged with the murder of Marion Gilchrist. Notwithstanding the fact that fingerprint evidence was being widely practised at the time and that a heavy chair and an auger boring tool were the likely weapons, no fingerprint proof was offered. The very question of prints wasn't even mentioned. What the jury did not miss, however, was the character of this man Slater, all of which was laboured in great detail by the Lord Advocate to the point that he even mentioned his appearance . . . 'Who could forget his face?' he asked.

Now there was a question! – a question with a whole variety of undertones. Was it because of that unusual nose, long and with a pronounced bend? Or because he wasn't the fresh-faced local? Was it because the swarthy face had a mouth of a rather sinister nature? Was it because the man looked, and was, Jewish? If that was a factor against him, then perhaps it was on account of his being not only Jewish, but German Jewish to boot. Germany was not the most favoured nation at the time – the Kaiser was rattling his sword and there was talk that there would be a war one day. Little wonder Slater's defence counsel was to tell the jury he could not recall public prejudice being roused with such fury as there had been against the accused. 'This man, in many quarters, has been convicted before he has been tried,' he proclaimed.

Despite the fact that none of the alleged missing jewellery was ever found, the prosecution stressed that burglary had been the reason for the terrible crime and had been carried out by a 'daring, clever, cold-blooded, expert performer'. The evidence the court heard, however, was all circumstantial: there was nothing to directly connect Slater with the old lady, Marion Gilchrist. He had never met her; he had never been to her house. Neither had he met the maid Lambie nor had any connection with any of her friends or acquaintances. He was not revealed to have had any of her jewellery and the items he had with Glasgow pawnbrokers were never owned by the murdered woman.

A variety of witnesses, including plain-clothes police officers, gave evidence of having seen a man loitering in the vicinity of the flat in West Princes Street on a number of occasions. This man, some of them said, had a sallow complexion and a foreign look about him. Yes he *did* resemble the man in the dock, they said. But it wasn't elucidated that if Oscar Slater loitered near his own home at the St George's Mansions, whether at the local billiard hall or around the Carnarvon Bar, he would also have been in the vicinity of Marion Gilchrist's flat, for the two houses were only three minutes away from each other.

Helen Lambie, the maid, significantly changed her view of the man she had seen leaving the flat on the night of the murder. She had originally said that she would not be able to recognise the man again. Then, in New York, she gave evidence that she had not seen the man's face at all and finally at the trial it was to change once more. This time she maintained she *did* have a good look at him and positively identified him.

The second witness taken to New York was also of the opinion that this was the same man. However, the third witness, the neighbour who had met Lambie at the door of the flat, insisted that while the man in the dock resembled the man he had seen that night, he would go no further than that.

The forensic evidence of Marion Gilchrist's injuries was of a most gruesome nature, describing how the frail old lady's face had been virtually smashed, leaving gaping, ragged holes in her cranial bones, while her chest was crushed and her rib cage broken. She had been in a dreadful mess as a result of a prolonged and sustained attack in which between 20 to 40 severe blows had been inflicted on her.

Among the possessions in the many trunks Slater had taken with him to the States, there had been a small household hammer and this was produced as a likely weapon. The forensic scientists, on the other hand, were of the opinion that the murder weapon had been something heavier than this light-weight tool. Besides, if it had been used to kill the old woman it would have been covered with blood, none of which was traced either on the hammer or on Slater's clothing, which it surely would have stained. And was he likely to have carried the actual murder weapon away with him, all the way to America?

A heavy, bloodstained auger tool with pieces of hair still attached to it and discovered the morning after the murder in the back court of Marion Gilchrist's house in West Princes Street had been a more likely weapon, the scientists thought. There was nothing, however, to connect Slater to this weapon.

What seemed the most damning evidence of all, and on which they were to labour, was the strange coincidence of Slater hurriedly leaving Glasgow just four days after the horrific murder of Marion Gilchrist. The defence countered this with the testimony of a barber whom Slater regularly visited. He told the court that Slater mentioned on several occasions prior to the murder that he was going abroad and that on Christmas day, the day he actually did leave, he had been in his shop for a shave and was making no secret of the fact he would be leaving that night – hardly the behaviour of a fleeing murderer. The barber added that as well as regularly shaving him, he also trimmed his moustache and he was able to give its precise measurements. Yet all the major witnesses who gave evidence about the suspect said the man was clean shaven.

It took the jury only one hour and ten minutes to deliberate and return a majority verdict of guilty. The judge, Lord Guthrie, donned the black cap and solemnly informed Slater that he would be hanged at Duke Street prison in just over three weeks' time.

It is a tremendous credit to the Scottish public that when this rather questionable and unconventional man was convicted there was to be a huge outcry at the verdict. They hadn't liked what they read about the trial. It was not the standard they required of Scottish justice and were saying so. Such was the reaction and anger at the verdict that a petition seeking a reduction of the sentence, on the grounds that the conviction was unjustified, quickly gathered some 20,000 signatures.

The Secretary of State for Scotland became involved in the backlash, the petition being sent to him by Slater's solicitor together with vociferous protests at the fashion in which the Lord Advocate had weighed against the character of the accused. Urgent meetings were convened with senior law officials as a result of which on 25 May, just two days before Slater was due to be hanged, his sentence was commuted to one of life imprisonment . . . yet another parallel to the Brechtian classic, the wicked old MacHeath also being rescued from the scaffold at the last minute.

But that was only the beginning of a whole series of events which were to reveal that the trial of Oscar Slater had been far from the simple case it had appeared. There had been much more to it than an eager police force and conservative counsel hell-bent on a conviction course for someone who, to such a reactionary collective, was deemed a most unsavoury and morally objectionable character.

A year after Slater's trial, William Roughead, a respected Edinburgh lawyer and criminologist, edited a published transcript of the hearing. He said he was convinced that there had been a gross miscarriage of justice in the conviction. This was to revive considerable interest in the case and the momentum grew for more to be known, more to be said about the more dubious aspects of the proceedings. Sir Arthur Conan Doyle, none other than the celebrated creator of Sherlock Holmes, was as equally convinced as Roughead and lent his support. He even had a work published on the subject.

A major breakthrough in the search for the truth of what really happened that night to the poor Marion Gilchrist was to emerge nearly three years after Slater's sentence when police lieutenant John Thomson Trench spoke up. Trench had been a detective officer closely connected with the initial inquiries of the murder – he had searched Slater's flat and was there to meet him on his return from the States. He confessed to having severe reservations regarding aspects of police conduct during the inquiries, a rare and most courageous stand for any police officer to take.

Not only did he speak of his doubts, but sensationally revealed that the maid, Helen Lambie, had told the murdered woman's niece the name of the man who had walked from the house on the night of the homicide. As the old woman had been murdered just minutes before, that man must have been implicated. And the name she gave was not that of Oscar Slater. This was not pursued, however. A more senior officer at the time said the man whom the maid claimed she saw had nothing in fact to do with the murder and, as a result, this line of investigation was dropped. Following an internal police inquiry, Trench's reward for being courageous enough to speak out was his dismissal from the police, for conduct 'contrary to public policy and to all police practice'.

The can of worms had been well and truly opened. Through the efforts of Conan Doyle, joined by the celebrated crime novelist Edgar Wallace – whose 173 books include *King Kong* – and other writers, much more than the police and authorities would ever care to admit was gradually emerging from the now sensationally revealing murder of Marion Gilchrist. Lambie herself, having emigrated to America, was to admit once more, and this time to a journalist, that she had recognised the man she saw leaving the house as a person who had frequently visited her mistress. Again, that man was not Oscar Slater. Why had she not revealed this earlier? Because the police had persuaded her she was mistaken, she said.

The worms were spilling out faster than ever. The name that the maid Lambie had revealed was that of a Dr Francis Charteris, a nephew of the elderly Marion Gilchrist and a man with a nose remarkably similar to Slater's. He had been in the house with another nephew called Birrell, who was prone to fits. Dr Charteris, it transpired, was a colleague of one of the forensic scientists who had given evidence at the trial. And his brother Archibald, a distinguished lawyer, was a colleague of none other than the procurator-fiscal responsible for the investigations of Marion Gilchrist's murder. Relatives of the old lady had been senior and respected figures in the Church of Scotland and in the Services. In short, the Charteris brothers were the very epitomy of that breed who consider themselves the establishment figures of Glasgow and who habitually refer to themselves as 'professional gentlemen'.

So why was one of these brothers seen leaving the house within minutes of Marion Gilchrist's murder? There have been many theories over the years. Many of them are speculative, but all have more logic than the presentation to the High Court of Oscar Slater as the accused.

Could there have been any truth in the speculation of the Press just days after her murder that it was because the very wealthy old lady had recently changed her will and that the Charteris family were no longer mentioned in it? Perhaps Francis Charteris was there that night anxious to get hold of this new will to destroy it and, as he searched, the old lady remonstrated with the other nephew who in one of his rages so brutally ended Marion Gilchrist's life. All those who have made studied inquiries into every aspect of the murder, have reached a conclusion along these lines. And so, too, have they concurred that Oscar Slater was blatantly used by the authorities to cover up one of the grossest embarrassments to have faced establishment figures in Glasgow.

Despite the campaigns and the revelations, such was the sway of the authorities, and the untouchability of these Glasgow establishment figures, that nothing was to shame them into action and Oscar Slater remained a prisoner in Peterhead for almost 20 years. His story is one of the saddest testimonies on record of the otherwise respected Scottish legal system. The treasured Scots law in which we so proudly believe had, on this occasion, gone beyond belief itself.

Slater was not released until 1928, when his conviction was quashed by the Scottish Court of Criminal Appeal. He was awarded an ex-gratia payment of £6,000. Eight years later he married again, this time happily, and the couple respectably settled in Ayr where he died in 1948, aged 77.

POSTSCRIPT

In 1997, a plea was made for a posthumous pardon for Detective John Thomson Trench and in September 1998, after a year-long review of the case by the Scottish Office, the appeal was rejected by Scottish Secretary Donald Dewar on the grounds that he had no statutory authority to intervene'. The review did recommend, however, that Trench, who died in disgrace in 1919, should have challenged his dismissal from the police. Coming some eight decades after the event, that advice must be considered as either something of a hallmark in Scottish Office incredulity or a token reminder – albeit a disquieting one – that policemen should never rock the boat. Whatever the case may be, it seems the courageous Trench is forever to be condemned a victim of his own integrity and selflessness.

5

THE LAUNCHING OF
THE *QUEEN MARY*

Glasgow has rarely known the excitement which captivated the city that week in September 1934. People had been speaking about little else for weeks beforehand, except perhaps those who were still raving about the big football game which had taken place earlier in the month between Rangers and the English Cup holders Manchester City. The reason they were still talking, you might have guessed, was because Rangers, playing at Ibrox, had beaten the English champs 1–0. But fans apart, the all-important subject was the *534*.

The number *534* doesn't mean much today, but for the five years preceding that week in 1934, that particular number sequence had been on everyone's lips in Glasgow and the Clyde. Five-three-four meant everything to them. Sometimes it meant good news. At other times, when the number was mentioned on the radio, in the press or on street corners, the word signified something as bad as hearing that a dear friend had taken a turn for the worse, or was even dying. Then, just as suddenly, it would be good news again and there would be smiles on faces as they spoke about the *534*.

For *534* was a ship they were building on the Clyde and on which countless thousands of Glasgow and Clydeside families depended for their living. As might be imagined, the 534 was no ordinary ship: nothing like it had ever been built before, nor at a time when the workers of the city and its environs had needed it more. The ship they were building was known merely by that number because it happened to be the 534th vessel to be built at the famous John Brown's Shipyard on the Clyde and that was the traditional shipbuilders' way of referring to a vessel until her launch and christening. The name she was to be given, however, was to mean a lot more than any number. A name that was to become a legend in ships and shipbuilding. A name which proclaimed to the world that the Clyde could build the biggest . . . and the best. For the 534 was to be named . . . the *Queen Mary*.

Nothing like her had ever been built before. Or since. The *Queen Mary* was to be the world's biggest-ever passenger liner: she was to be the most luxurious; the most talked about; and the best remembered. Although she was to be subsequently outsized – but only fractionally – by her younger sister the *Queen Elizabeth* and France's *Normandie* and out-sped by the *United States*, the *Queen Mary* was the greatest ship ever launched from John Brown's, the greatest shipyard in the world.

Nevertheless, the 534th ship to be launched by John Brown's was to have a difficult and most prolonged gestation before her much delayed birth that September in 1934. Following the Great War which ended in 1918, there had been considerable optimism in the Clyde yards. Four years of death and destruction meant there was much to be replaced and the shipbuilders could look forward to many years of work. Cargo and passenger ships were both needed – so many, in fact, that there probably wouldn't be sufficient yards on the Clyde to cope with the vast orders that were anticipated.

Unlike the years prior to the war, however, when Britain had so dominated world shipbuilding, the new peace was also to bring a new age for the trade and other countries, such as Sweden, Italy, France, Japan and Germany were now competing for orders. The Clyde, however, continued to be the focal point for shipbuilding, one in every five new ships to sail the oceans entering the sea by a Clydeside slipway. At the same time it did not go unnoticed that many other orders which in previous years would have come to Scotland, were now going to the emerging industrial nations. And there were fewer orders coming from the Admiralty, the Royal Navy inheriting a surplus of vessels through the huge fleets it had built up to combat the Germans. As a result, there were slumps in the trade from the mid-'20s and the prediction was that there could be leaner times ahead. But for a while that just seemed to be pessimistic talk, especially when the Cunard Line, famous for its transatlantic trade, said they were considering a new passenger ship . . . one of very sizeable proportions which would replace their ageing *Mauritania*.

John Brown's, because of their previous connections with Cunard, looked like being the favourites for the new order. They had already built some of Cunard's most famous ships, including the *Saxonia*, *Carmania*, *Caronia* and one of the most famous liners of her time, the giant *Lusitania*, which was to meet its tragic fate by being torpedoed without warning by a German submarine off the Irish coast.

Despite challenges from the new shipbuilding nations, now building even bigger and more luxurious ships than ever, it was, as had been predicted, John Brown's who were to get Cunard's new order. The terms were quite simple: it was to be the biggest, the fastest, and most luxurious ship ever built. And that's what the *Queen Mary* was to be.

In the hope that they might win the contract and in order to be ready to start immediately if they did, work had begun in 1929 on a specially lengthened and reinforced construction berth at the John Brown yard. It was on the same berth site used for the building of the *Aquitania*, which in 1913 had been the largest ship built on the Clyde. This berth was specially aligned so that ships launched from it would head stern first into the river towards the mouth of the River Cart, which was extensively dredged, allowing them the widest manoeuvring point in the upper Clyde. The biggest, fastest and most luxurious liner ever built would require more depth and more room than any other ship ever launched in the world's busiest shipbuilding site.

A year later, the contract was confirmed and work began on ship no. 534. As it rose on its launching way from between a phalanx of the tallest derricks, the hull was to become an awesome sight on the Clyde, dominating everything around it. It appeared so huge that many wondered if such a monster could ever sail. But such idle speculation was not what threatened the 534 ever sailing. It was the accountants at the yard and in the banks who were the first to appreciate the genuine fears of this ship ever being put out to sea. For as the growing world depression deepened the more the figures had to be studied. It made for gloomy reading at John Brown's, the yard's overdraft being in excess of the limit set by the bank. Word of the company's plight reached the men and it was rumoured that they really *would* be lucky if they ever saw the mighty vessel on which they laboured sail out from the yard. Shipyards all over the world were lying idle while men were being laid off by the thousands on a variety of yards on the Clyde, at this stage reeling under the impact of one of the worst depressions to hit the economic world.

The recession was to have a catastrophic impact on heavy industry. In 1913, output from Clyde yards had been in excess of 750,000 tonnes. In 1932 it was drastically slashed to a mere 66,000 tonnes, and the following year, 10,000 tonnes or even less. Tens of thousands of workers were made redundant, some yards even being dismantled and their sites put up for sale for alternative use. Then the bank gave Brown's the devastating ultimatum that their growing overdraft could no longer be extended: so on Saturday, 14 December 1931, just a year after they had begun work on 534, it was to come to a drastic halt. Glasgow, Clydebank and all of Clydeside reeled under the devastating news. And tens of thousands of families tightened their belts for lean times ahead.

Ships in the making throb with more activity and vitality than any other time during their lifespan with men yelling, hammering, sawing, drilling, slicing through steel – the furnace-hot blue/white flames of their torches cascading brilliant firework displays – men scaling high ladders and men clambering on skeletal stagings. Men everywhere, like feasting ants on some vast carcase. And in shipyard after shipyard up and down the Clyde, that vital and throbbing pace of life accompanied by its unique, metallic symphony, had existed for as long as could be remembered. Then, as dramatically as though someone had thrown a switch, everything was stilled. That was how it was at John Brown's on that grim, cold Saturday in 1931 when the men had gone home from work, stunned at the news they had been given by their gaffers that their yard would be closed. No one knew for how long. Many of them feared that they had reached the end. The end of the Clyde. Whatever the future held, the gates clanged together. The yard was closed . . . until further notice.

Life on the dole in 1931 was a grim prospect, unemployment pay being 85p a week for a man, 45p for his wife, and 10p for each child. The huge monster labelled 534 lay in her berth half-finished and silent, as if it were some monumental beached whale encased in steel commemorating the disorders of world economics. And it was to remain dormant for the next two years. The only sound emerging from the otherwise strangely silent yard was the soft sough of painters' brushes as they applied coat after coat of the life-supporting preservative which would prevent their hibernating giant from a crumbling death by rust.

It wasn't until 1933, the year when Clyde shipbuilding was at its pre-war nadir, that the Government bowed to the considerable pressure it had been under and provided a special subsidy, sufficient enough for work to be resumed and the great new ship to be completed. It was marvellous news for the river as the workforce at Brown's flooded back to the yard to pick up where they had left off. Glasgow was smiling again and readying itself for what was to be one of the great occasions in the city and the Clyde. There was only a year's work left on the ship before it would be at the completion stage set for launching, now scheduled for September 1934. But long before that date was known, they were preparing for the event of a lifetime.

Everyone in the city, and throughout Scotland, it seemed, was caught up in the growing frenzy as the nation awaited the birth of this awesome giant of the seas. Hotels, boarding-houses and bed and breakfasts in Glasgow and surrounding towns were fully booked within weeks of the men returning to work, and that was a year in advance of the launch. The *Daily Record* conjured up a Limerick contest with the best 200 entries getting 75p seats in a nearby shed to watch the wonder of the launch. Some prize, you might think . . . a 75p seat! But that really was something, in fact, when you consider what the prevailing prices – and wages – were at the time. To begin with wages were around £3 to £4 a week so everything else was commensurate. Take the prestigious Rangers and Manchester City Cup-holders game they were to hold at Ibrox: the dearest stand seats were to be 12½p. And for those toe-to-toeing it on the terracing, the price would be a mere 5p. Many other things we pay for in pounds today, were paid in pennies then.

Dancing was the favourite pastime and admission to the Dennistoun Palais de Danse was 5p for ladies, 7½p for gents. If that was too pricey for you then there was the popular F & F dance hall at Partick Cross, where for only 4½p you could have a great night's dancing, provided you very smartly apologised if you bumped somebody or trampled on toes. Over on the South Side, the Plaza, being the Plaza and further up the ballroom social scale, had a special dance for the launching of the ship. They called it the Grand Cunarder Gala Night and it was the priciest dance in town, tickets costing 20p.

The new 1934 model Morris 8 car, which could do 45 miles to the gallon with a top speed of 55mph, was on sale at £118. Road tax at the time was £6 a year.

Cigarettes were 5p for 20, new houses at Garrowhill were going for £395 – and that wasn't the deposit. It was the full price. Semi-detached houses at Williamwood and Giffnock could be owned for repayments of 85p a week and if you were flush enough to go really up-market, a new bungalow at Bearsden cost £850. And bedroom suites to fill each of its three bedrooms were on sale at £11.

'Doon the Watter' trips were booming that summer for both holidays and weekends. A Saturday afternoon trip to Rothesay or Dunoon was

15p, with a smashing 'high tea' of fresh, tasty haddock (no frozen stuff in 1934!) and chips, peas, buttered bread and scones and limitless cuppas all for 25p. The affluent went 'doon watters' much further afield, however, like cruising on the ritzy *Union Castle* for a sunshine-all-the-way trip to South Africa, everything inclusive for £30. Or, if you had style as well as cash, you could do the same trip but in a first class cabin and guaranteed dinner with the captain . . . for £90.

During that summer of 1934, hardly a day passed without a story of some kind in the Press and radio about 534. It featured regularly in the Pathe Pictorial newsreels at the pictures and was the subject of a variety of programmes on the radio station to which everyone listened, the one the BBC called . . . the Home Service. And, being the kind of subject she was, everything about the giant ship that was rapidly nearing completion on the Clyde was mentioned in terms of the wondrous, the stupendous. But they really didn't have to emphasise it, because everybody knew it was all of these and more.

Not the least part of all that was magnificent and astonishing about her were the statistics. They told a truly amazing story of their own. That over 100,000 people, for instance, mostly from the Glasgow area, had been involved in some way in her construction. That she weighed 73,000 tonnes, was over 1,000ft long and was held together by 10,000,000 rivets. She would carry 5,000 passengers and crew who would have the use of 2,000 portholes and windows to view the passing world. And as if that wasn't enough to take in, there was more: like the fact that 40ft of her would be beneath the water-line and 12 decks above, with two acres of space – that's the area covered by two full-size soccer pitches – for promenade deck seats.

There would be 20 public rooms of various dimensions where you could comfortably pass your day reading or just lounging. The first-class lounge was so massive you were asked to visualise nine double-decker buses and three Royal Scot railway engines. Got the picture? Well, all of these would fit inside that grand and spacious lounge. Another suite was so vast you were asked to test out your imagination once more. This time you were to envision that most historic of ships, the *Santa Maria*, flagship of Christopher Columbus on his first voyage to the New World. Got it in your mind? Well, that legendary vessel could fit inside this other suite.

And still the newspapers, radio and cinema newsreels kept up their onslaught of everything that was to be known about the 534, whether you wanted to know it or not. But such was the fervour of interest it seemed that everyone really did want to know more. And more.

She was to be the fastest thing afloat. She was to be powered by four sets of engines, each 55ft long, whose turbines had a quarter of a million blades fired by huge boilers containing 160,000 tubes.

Her generators would be capable of making enough electricity for a city the size of Dundee. Her gigantic hollow rudder weighed 150 tonnes and had two entry doors and a ladder which ran up the middle of it for servicing purposes. Her two main anchors each weighed 16 tonnes. The 28 steel lifeboats also weighed 16 tonnes, each of which would be capable of carrying 140 people. And more! No ship before had been equipped with such enormous, loud sirens as those which would be attached to the foremast of this queen of the seas' three tall funnels. For the deep bass note of the blast would be audible at 30 miles. That meant that if she blared her presence from these almighty foghorns while sailing down the Clyde somewhere offshore around Prestwick or Ayr, you would get the message up in Glasgow!

Nothing was to be spared for the comfort and luxury of the passengers lucky enough to enjoy this floating palace for the four-and-a-half-day crossing to New York. They could relax in Russian, Turkish, Roman and spa baths. The gymnasium had a boxing ring. There would be 5,000 beds and wardrobes, 30,000 chairs, 50,000 electric bulbs and 1,000 baths. Want to take your car along for the trip? No problem. An on-board parking garage was provided.

The 12 decks meant lots of staircases but there was no need to use these for there were 21 lifts – and the cables that were to haul them were so long they would stretch all the way from Glasgow to Chicago.

Concerned, perhaps, that you might be out of touch with what was happening in the rest of the world while you were enjoying yourself on that much anticipated voyage? Again, there was no need to worry. That had also been catered for, the ship having a bank of printing presses capable of publishing its own daily newspaper featuring news from all over the world. And when the presses weren't busy doing that, there was plenty of other work for them, like printing the 10,000 menus required for the three main meals of the day.

Catering was another area where the statistics soared. Starting with the huge stores for the dining-room supplies, you would find 200,000 items of crockery, 100,000 pieces of cutlery and acres of linen which had been specially ordered from Fife and Ireland. The kitchens would serve 20,000 meals a day and huge larders would stock 15,000 eggs, 9,000 gallons of milk, 500 gallons of cream, 500 cases of fruit, 70 tonnes of potatoes, 40 tonnes of meat and 50 tonnes of cereals and vegetables.

As the date in September approached, everything centred on the launch and in order to ensure that all would go well in this most spectacular event, 7,000 experiments with models had been carried out beforehand. And all of them had slid perfectly into their miniature pond without getting stuck in the mud or, worse still, as was feared, running aground on the opposite bank of their replica river.

Everyone, of course, wanted to see the launch and, not being blessed with the glories of television which takes you there without having to leave your own living-room, as many as possible were planning strategic places to get as close a view as possible of the historic event. Workers at John Brown's were given preference in the viewing stakes: tickets for each employee as well as their families were enclosed in the wage packets of more than 9,000 of them on the Friday before the launch. They were given the rightful privilege of having the nearest seats to the Royal platform party who would perform the naming ceremony. Clydebank schoolchildren and local youth organisations were given a stand all to themselves.

After that it was a case of 'market forces'. And anyone and everyone who had that kind of marketing potential was right in there capitalising on it. Messrs William Beardmore, the famous engineers, were as quick as any to spot the golden bandwagon. They had an empty yard at Dalmuir, near John Brown's, which proved to be an ideal spot to see the whole event. There was room for up to 30,000 to view the proceedings comfortably, and at an entry fee of 5p (plus 7½p to park your car) there was no shortage of takers.

Thousands packed the 5p nightly return cruises from the Broomielaw to Clydebank on board the *King Edward* pleasure steamer. If you joined the ship down river at Govan it was a penny cheaper, another penny less than that if you didn't board till Renfrew. Small passenger planes did a roaring trade with commercial flights lasting only a few minutes from Renfrew Airport doing a couple of circuits round the yard and the ship. The 100 winners of the Glasgow *Evening News* contest each got a free flight.

Such was the passion for the occasion, that Poet Laureate John Masefield ('I must go down to the sea again, to the lonely sea and the sky') was asked to compose a special commemorative poem. Seven verses of poetic salutation dedicated to the greatest creation of shipbuilding was the result. It appeared that the only ones unaffected by launch-fever were the Blythswood Policies, as they were known – owners of the acreages on the opposite bank of the river from the John Brown yard which would have provided by far the best spectator point to see the great new liner slip into the Clyde. But the Policies were having none of it, tartly informing Renfrew Council that on the express instruction of his Lordship, no person would be allowed into the estate on the day of the launch, and that, it was haughtily added, included estate employees. So there!

The media of the day was so enraptured by the occasion that, viewed in terms of the late '90s, it appeared they had been virtually transported. For days before there had been seemingly endless pages of photos of the Royals on their annual holidays at Balmoral as they awaited the Clyde's big occasion. Both King George V and Queen Mary (the latter carrying out the naming ceremony) were to be the top guests for the launch and to heighten the expectancy, there were interminable shots of them here, there and everywhere, including that hardy annual photo of them smothered in tartan at the Braemar Games. Others had them in group shots welcoming some foreign, blue-blood relatives to the Highlands to join them for the fun and games in the heather, offering further opportunities to pose in their tartans and plaids. The old king in a rigout of what can only be described as overwhelming check, the same criss-cross pattern going from socks, to breeks, to jacket and tie, giving him all the appearance of some old-time music hall comedian ready to tell his audience all about the funny things that happened to him on the way to the castle.

The coverage gush was such, in fact, that it even outweighed the publicity given to the horrors of one of the worst ever pit disasters which had occurred at the Gresford Colliery near Wrexham in Northern Wales a few days before the launch. In the first reports of this horrific tragedy, the shock news was that 268 men had either been killed or trapped down the deep mine and that only ten bodies had been recovered. The following day the news was that they had sealed off the shaft where the men had been working, the headlines grimly reading 'The Pit Will Be Their Tomb'. But even such a calamity was not to outdo the word about the Clyde's great ship and the Royal well-wishers who were in town to send her off.

Only the weather failed to co-operate as the skies opened up to a non-stop downpour that Wednesday, 26 September 1934. Everything else went according to plan, however: the 534, was christened by Queen Mary in her own name before a bottle of fine Australian wine was smashed into its bow. At the command, she glided gracefully down her slipway just as precisely as all those 7,000 experimental models had done.

The exaltations for the Royals and for the occasion fevered to a high point of ecstasy in the special editions of the newspapers the following day. What in many ways was one of the greatest occasions that Glasgow and the Clyde had ever experienced provided you weren't one of the shipyard tradesmen liable to be on the dole once that iron monster slipped into the river, was variously described in the headings journalese of the day as 'A Moving Masterpiece in Steel', 'Royal Baptism of 534', 'A Great Ship Finds Her Element', 'Inspiring Scene at Clydebank', and 'The Story of a Perfect Launch'.

Around the world, they were just as enraptured according to one report which had been monitoring reception of the event in various countries, under the heading 'World Listens to Launch of New Liner'. Even the French had complimentary comments and in Australia they had heard a recorded broadcast of the event that midnight. It seems that the radio reception, often precariously tenuous in those days, had been clear and the broadcast was described as being 'a complete success for all the voices, including those of the King and Queen who were distinctly heard'. There were special eulogies too for the Queen and her christening ceremony broadcast. 'She has the ideal microphone voice,' said one enthusiastic report, adding that this had only been the second time in her life that the Queen had actually spoken on radio, but had done so 'in an unhurried ease with her well-modulated voice'.

Five years later, after having become the darling of the transatlantic trade, the *Queen Mary* was to change her role and appearance dramatically, being transformed from sparkling, luxury liner to drab, grey troopship throughout the Second World War. There was never any great fear of her being sunk by enemy action. There was no other ship afloat which could catch her. After the war, she resumed service as the world's most luxurious ocean liner until her retiral in the early 1960s to become a hotel and tourist attraction in California at the port of Long Beach, south of Los Angeles.

6

THEY CAME TO GLASGOW

❧

They've been coming to Glasgow ever since that very first Christian among us founded a settlement by the banks of the stream called the Molendinar, the settlement which became the village which grew into the town that became a great city. The man in question was St Mungo who came out of the east, the nearest east, that is, the area that we think of today as the Lothians. He died when the first millennium was just in its second half and we thought so much of him that he has the most venerated grave site in the city, in the very heart of our ancient Cathedral by the banks of that very stream where it all began.

After the religious settlement, which had become so important that St Columba himself was to pay us a visit, came the men who fished for salmon on the Clyde, and then the travellers, who were journeying from the Highlands to the Lowlands and finding the shallows in the river near the fishermen's village the most convenient place for their ford. Many of them liked the place, however, and stayed. The traders came after them because the village was growing and they, in turn, were followed by the merchants who saw great potential in the wide, generous estuary, and when they had dredged and channelled its river, their ships could sail out from the burgeoning town called Glasgow to all parts of the world.

They came for all sorts of reasons after that: Jews fled from the horrors of the pogroms in a variety of Eastern European countries, many of them deluded by buccaneering shippers who charged them passages to America and then dumped them at Leith before returning across the North Sea again for more susceptible souls.

They came too from Russian-dominated Lithuania as starving, hunted men escaping enforced servitude in the cruel Czar's army, trekking all the way to Hamburg where £1 would get them the passage to Leith and freedom. They were joined by others from Poland and the countries of the Baltic, starved out of their existences by successions of poor harvests and the harshest of regimes. Others came up from Italy, from Barga in the north to Formia in the south, with their wares and services and the hope that they would make more from them than they could in their homeland. They flooded in from our Highlands and Islands, hunted and terrorised by rapacious landowners who preferred sheep to people. Countless thousands were to come from across the seas to the west: the famine-starved from the Gaeltacht were among them, as destitute and desperate as latter-day 'Boat People', their only hope and future for their families was a fivepenny deck passage to the place they called Glasgow.

All of Glasgow's migrants were to make their mark in the city that had offered them a home, they in turn giving us their tailors and jewellers, ice-cream men and cafés, restaurateurs and hairdressers, navvies and public-house keepers . . . and a football team called Celtic. And much of that influence which makes up the fabric of present-day Glasgow was to come from the most recent and furthest travelled of all the city's settlers, the Pakistanis. Few immigrant groupings have made such a visible impression on the city. Imagine a Glasgow today without its Pakistani community! No kebab takeaways, no Indian restaurants – they were all Indians before 1947 and the name stayed with the food – no corner shops for the late-night bread, milk and papers, no cash and carries, no cut-price warehouses.

Although paradise has a vastly different meaning to a Muslim, Pakistanis have become as much a part of Glasgow as a place called Paradise, every bit a slice of the city scene as the Barras, the corner pub, a fish and chip supper, or a hauf 'n' a hauf.

You haven't really made it in Glasgow until they've made jokes about you. Ask any Catholic, Orangeman or Jew about that. Now there are as many funny stories about Pakistanis as there are about anyone else. Which only goes to show that the city's newest community has well and truly made it in all grades.

The first major contact men from the Indian subcontinent had with Glasgow was when the Lascar seamen came as crew members on the hundreds of merchant ships trading between Glasgow and all the ports east of Suez, from Aden to Karachi, Bombay to Colombo and round to Madras, Calcutta and further east to all the markets beyond the Malacca Straits. So many of them came to Glasgow, the Corporation were to provide the Asian seamen with their own special toilets, marked for the use of Lascars only, or *Coolies* as they were generally known. (The name *Coolies* maybe sounds derogatory, but it is simply taken from the Hindu word meaning hireling.) The sensitive would argue, of course, that giving them their own lavatories would have been due to racial prejudices. But that was not the case. The provision of these special toilets was out of consideration for the particular way men from the East conduct such ablutions, the details of which, put at their delicate best, are that they are performed in the fashion of a sort of DIY bidet. And having lived in the East, I can assure you that it's a hygienic feat not easily performed in a Western gent's.

These hard-working seafarers, underpaid and underprivileged hirelings that they were, became a colourful part of the Glasgow scene throughout the history of the steam cargo ships which traded in and out of Glasgow up to the late '60s. They were seen particularly at weekends and especially anywhere along the length of Argyle Street; they were always in groups and, peculiarly, always in single file and empty-handed as they strolled from the docks to the city. They were destined for the Barras and Paddy's Market, confident that what they couldn't get at one, they would get at the other.

On the journey back to the ship again they were always burdened with second-hand goods of all sorts, their favourite buys being sensible items like old Singer sewing machines, bicycles, tools and second-hand clothes, often piling several hats on their heads and laughing off the jokes thrown at them because of it and the distinctive, high-stepping gait of their walk. If there were any last laughs, however, they belonged to the Indians for all those goods were tradeable commodities back home in India and they would likely make more money from them than their miserable wages from the shippers. They knew, too, how to live cheaply and others among them would be carrying home their ships' meals – big bags of cheap food bought from the many barrow traders of the day. Fruit and herrings were the favourites, but they always refused flounders because, as they would tell the stallholders . . . 'the devil walked on them'.

One of them even played a few games for Celtic, using bandages tightly bound round his feet instead of boots, much to the horror of some of the locals. He was a seaman called Abdul Salim and his occupation, as far as could be known, was that of a steward with the

Clan Line shipping company. There are, of course, many apocryphal stories about exotic players who played for Celtic, and for Rangers, in the years that only grandfathers remember, or say and think they remember. But the story of Abdul Salim really is true. Abdul, who was also known as Mohammed Hashean, had a brother who worked as a storekeeper at the Elderslie Docks. On his regular visits to Glasgow he had told his brother how much he missed his favourite sport, being as he was an active player at home in the Calcutta area. Hoping to help out, the brother arranged a trial for him with the then Celtic manager, the legendary William Maley – who had a 52-year association with the club. Salim impressed the Celtic boss who offered him a place in the club's reserves, known at the time as the Alliance team.

And, football boots or no, the bold Abdul played in the early months of the 1936/37 season, featuring in games against Galston and Hamilton Academical: he scored a well-taken penalty in the latter and, according to reports, he thrilled the crowds with the way he could trap and lob the ball towards goal.

Incidentally, it is often said that Rangers too had a Lascar play for them around the same era. Sure enough, there was a player with the Muslim name of Mohammed Latif in their reserves, but this Mohammed was from Egypt, not India, and had been studying at Jordanhill Teacher Training College.

Glasgow at that time, not unlike the rest of Britain, was experiencing one of the more fraught periods in history. The war fever with Germany was growing by the day, although an official declaration was still three years away. The war in Spain was growing fiercer and more bitter with each report, the Fascists now using dive-bombers on civilians as well as the courageous Republican forces, but were yet to perpetrate their murderous atrocity on Guernica. Meanwhile, the recently launched *Queen Mary* was out smashing records on the Atlantic run, covering as much as 752 miles in one day.

On the home front many things were, as we know, as they are today. A visiting American executive in the tourist trade said Sundays in Glasgow had 'a depressing atmosphere', the City Corporation responding that 'Glasgow is the London of Scotland'. And perhaps they were so convinced of that proclamation that it gave them justification that same week to announce another increase in the city rates, now up to 5p in the £1. When the new football season kicked off, crowd attendances totalled 118,000, with the top games getting such figures as 23,000 at Celtic v St Johnstone; 20,000 at Dundee v Rangers; 25,000 at Hibs v Aberdeeen; 10,000 at Partick Thistle v Queen of the South; and

14,000 at Falkirk v Hamilton. At the game between Dalry Thistle and Kilbirnie Ladeside the crowd invaded the pitch and attacked both police and match officials.

Abdul Salim, whom the papers were now calling the 'barefooted Indian', apparently never made it to the first Celtic team, which was probably due to the calibre of the squad they were fielding at the time, consisting of Kennaway, Hogg, Morrison, Geatons, Lyon, Paterson, Delaney, Carruth, McGrory, Crum, and Murphy.

Other brave souls from the Indian Punjab, much of which was to become Pakistan on partition in 1947, also found themselves in Glasgow as far back as the early days of this century. Most of them were probably Lascar seamen who saw the opportunity here to earn more than they were getting as hirelings on our merchant fleet. One, however, was known to have been the valet of a Scottish officer in the Indian army who, on his retirement, had brought the man with him to be his servant here. And when the officer died, the valet had been left to look after himself. Others were said to have come to Scotland under similar circumstances.

There were numerous reports of the cruel treatment handed out to the Lascar seamen who were often flogged and beaten while on the high seas, and if their vessels were delayed in ports, their wages were abruptly stopped. Even when they got to the comparative safety of Glasgow, they didn't become immune to hostility. Because of their use as cheap labour by the shipowners, there was considerable venom shown against them by local merchant seamen whose unions had organised various protests regarding the practice of such sweated labour. The culprits, of course, were the owners but it was much easier to vent their anger on the unfortunate Lascars. There were few problems identifying and singling them out. One particularly savage attack took place in 1919 after a mob, flourishing knives and sticks, followed a group of them to their boarding-house in Broomielaw. Shots from a revolver were fired.

It was the same story a year later when a small group of four such seamen found their way to heartland Lanarkshire to work as coalminers. The native miners soon adopted a similar hostile attitude to the British merchant sailors which cut their venture short: the natives would have none of this sort of sweated labour down their mines. Despite assurances from their bosses, however, that the four Indians were working for exactly the same pay and conditions, they wouldn't listen. Their presence, insisted the miners, meant that something wasn't right and they demanded that the four men go. The mine owners capitulated and the Indians headed back to Glasgow.

Several of the Lascars were known to be living and working in Glasgow towards the end of the First World War, the first of note being a Mohammed Tanda who, it was rumoured, had come here as a crewman on an ore ship from Australia. The ship left the Clyde without him, although it's not certain whether he had jumped or been dumped. In any case, he was apparently undaunted at the prospect and went about the business of living as he might have done at home, as a street trader. He bought batches of cheap ties which he draped over a long pole and stationed himself at the Albert Bridge, a good place to catch the crowds heading for the city to shop. It was there that he became a well-known figure: one of the very first Johnnie Pedlars, complete with pole and penny ties, was in business.

By the mid-'20s there was a small number of them living at various addresses in the city, mainly Anderston and Port Dundas. Three of those early arrivals, all of them called Mohammed, with the family names of Noor, Nattoo, and Din, were among the pioneering, intrepid house-to-house salesmen – men with large cases and stout hearts who would walk the length and breadth of the country to eke out a living. Sadly, one of that early trio, Mohammed Noor, was to meet a most tragic and violent end. Noor, aged 27, had only been in Glasgow for nine months and had found a room near his friends in Water Street, Port Dundas. On Saturday, 16 May 1922, a notorious gang of local thugs went on the rampage, singling out the Indians' houses where it was known they kept their goods for trading. Two of the traders managed to repel the attackers, but it proved to be too much for Noor who, in the mêlée as they ransacked his house, was stabbed to death. It was a sensational murder at the time, and the gang was described as being 'one of the most dangerous group of hoodlums to be known in the city'.

On the Tuesday morning following the murder, eight men and a woman appeared at the Northern Police Court charged with Noor's homicide. That morning's paper described the group's appearance in court in the journalese of the time . . . 'the males accused, none of whom appeared to regard his position seriously, were poorly dressed and for the most part wore mufflers. The woman, who is the wife of one of the male prisoners, wore a faded fawn coat with a light grey fur collar.'

Four months later, after charges against six of them had been dropped, the three ringleaders of the gang appeared before Lord Ormidale at the High Court when the story of that violent evening in May was recounted. Witnesses told how the gang had first of all tried to burst into the houses of the other traders, Din and Nattoo, and how both had fought back valiantly and were able to keep their doors lockfast. It was then that they poured into Mohammed Noor's house, making off with his trading goods and stabbing him with daggers. Noor had kept three large trading suitcases in his house and the contents, the court was told, had included 24 jumpers, 2 ladies' dresses, and 35 gent's artificial silk scarves. Noor was described, in fact, as a silk trader.

The line of questioning and the attitude of the judge at the trial significantly reveals prevailing perspectives of the day. In defence, counsel took the line that the wife of Nattoo, a white woman, had been subjected to beatings by him and that when word of this had got round the local community, they had been incensed. Mrs Nattoo firmly denied the suggestions and when counsel persisted with the claims, she turned in exasperation to the judge to ask if she was compelled to answer such false allegations. She was told unequivocally that she must answer all the questions.

In his address to the jury, Lord Ormidale expressed a bizarre racial inference in making the point that 'it made no difference that the man done to death was an Indian' and they were to give the same consideration to the case 'had he been a native-born Scotsman or Englishman'.

Whatever the point intended, the jury took the point and found the three men guilty. John Keen was sentenced to death, Robert Fletcher got seven years hard labour, and John McCormack nine months' imprisonment. Keen burst into tears at the verdict, exclaiming that there had been no justice. McCormack, the papers revealed, had been one of the most dangerous members of the gang and that 'he was not even honourable to the men whom he led into action – on several occasions he "blew the gaff" in order to save his own skin, and had asked to turn King's evidence for this trial'.

It was later revealed that the gang had subjected the people of Port Dundas to a life of terror and had been responsible for a number of serious assaults with such weapons as knuckledusters, knives, razors and iron crowbars.

Mohammed Noor was buried at Riddrie Cemetery, in a plot secured there and consecrated for Muslims, and he was laid to rest according to their tradition, facing Mecca. It is interesting to note that about 50 of his countrymen attended the funeral, which was, in all probability, the entire population of those from the subcontinent living in the city at the time.

It wasn't until the 1950s, however, that the first real wave of Indians arrived as Commonwealth citizens with few questions asked about their entitlement to be here. Like most of Glasgow's new immigrants, they were destined for the Gorbals, the first home to countless Highlanders,

Irish, Jews, Italians, Poles, Lithuanians and others. And just as the unfortunate Mohammed Noor and fellow pioneers had done, this new wave of migrants made their living from suitcases packed with an enormous variety of goods. They would lug their big cases around the suburbs of Glasgow, to places where they were confident – with their incomparable intuition – they'd have the kind of goods householders wanted to buy.

They chose areas away from bus routes and where there were no stores with the kind of knitwear, garments and appealing knick-knacks they had packed inside their cases – which came not only with service, but with an even more tempting attraction . . . credit.

The first to appear got the cream of the inner suburbs, and as each succeeding wave of countrymen arrived, they would ply their trade in more distant suburbs. They were regularly to be seen in such remote areas as the furthest extremities of the counties of Renfrew, Ayr and Lanark where having such salesmen was a new experience, and a welcome one at that.

Just like the Lascars before them, the Johnnie Pedlars were also to become part of the scene in Glasgow and its surrounding areas. Having dark skin and a big case was almost a badge of respect, having built up a reputation for themselves as honest salesmen with bargain goods. Like the best of any foreign group abroad, they clung together and formed their own little club in a house in Oxford Street, in the heart of the Gorbals. It didn't matter that Allan and Gilmour, the bacon curers, was just nearby, and that the fumes of their smoking process permeated the little club in which these Muslims, to whom bacon was as haram as non-kosher is to Jews. Their humble clubrooms, a room and kitchen tenement house, served many purposes. It was their mosque, a place in which they would strive to be for the nightfall ritual of the isha prayers; their welfare association in which they would provide for any of them who may be sick; their contact point with word from home, for the exchange of news about who was who, what was what, and where they could buy their favourite meats and sweets – difficult commodities to obtain with there being so few of them in the country.

The Johnnie Pedlars of the '50s worked all the hours Allah gave them. There were families at home in Pakistan relying on the money that was sent to them, the rest of which was ploughed back into their small but flourishing businesses. A survey around the time indicated that a figure of 271 pedlars' licences had been issued in Glasgow to individuals known as 'coloured men'.

By 1953 there was a total of around 500 Indians and Pakistanis, mainly the latter, living in a Glasgow of cobbled streets, puffers in the Clyde, Jackson the Tailor, queues for the sensational new 3D films at the Gaumont, a Royal yacht called Britannia being launched on the Clyde, grade one house coal on sale at 28p a one cwt bag, Tommy Morgan with his Big Beenie at the Pavilion, tramcars and electric trolley buses, the new and sensational multi-storey houses at Moss Heights they were calling 'a dream in concrete', and a riot in the scramble to get tickets for the Frankie Laine show at the Empire. None of which meant a thing to this growing band of Johnnie Pedlars.

Irish and other immigrants were to latch on to Glasgow life much quicker than these men from the Punjab, since the Celts had the distinct advantage of having open access to the heart of contact and fellowship among Glaswegians . . . the pub. But for the men from Asia, pubs and alcohol, enticing or not, was also haram, forbidden. In the years to come, they were to have far greater contact with their host countrymen, through the diversification of their activities, but for those first years the men with the cases were distant and remote individuals, generally thought of as being alien and ephemeral who would eventually be here today, gone tomorrow. Few reckoned they were here to stay and that they would become a very vibrant and noticeable presence in the Glasgow scene.

The story of the Pakistanis in Glasgow is in many ways a replica of that of the Italians who settled in the city from the middle of the last century. The first of them came from Ciociaria and later arrivals came from Barga in Tuscany. Many of them were pedlars too, lugging enormous suitcases crammed with hundreds of little plaster statuettes made by craftsmen in and around their home villages. When their suitcases were emptied, they would return again to their homeland and after a season or so there, come back again with another load of their popular statuettes.

But the temptation of better conditions in Glasgow was too good to resist and many of them stayed even when the content of their suitcases had all been sold. In fact there was much more to be made from other pursuits, such as selling ice-cream with their little hand-carts in a good summer that would make more money than they could ever hope to earn at home. And as is the way of the eager and ambitious migrant, their little hand-carts became bigger and bigger – first that then a tricycle, then a horse pulling a cart that was the size of a small shop and then finally a proper shop itself. When we think of Italians now, it's often in terms of a subject very dear to their hearts and of which they are consummate masters, namely food. Of course, the descendants of those first Italians who came to Glasgow are to be found today in every walk of life, as tradesmen, as prominent members of the professions and eloquent participants in the arts. Nevertheless, it is still their names that top the proprietors' lists of many restaurants.

Just like it was for those early Italian itinerants, it was a lonely life for the early Pakistani pedlars, a life that consisted of non-stop work and saving enough either to return home and buy a small business, or send for wives and families and settle in Glasgow. The majority opted for the latter, their target being to save the £100 down payment for a small house in the Gorbals.

It was not the Asian way to pay landlords rent, their philosophy being that rent money was lost money and no matter how small and poor the house they bought, it put them on the ladder of home-ownership and the next house would be an even better one. And again, just like their Italian counterparts with the ice-cream cart which got bigger and bigger, so too did the wherewithal for selling their goods, the suitcase giving way to the humblest of cars and small vans and an even better display of goods.

When they started their business round, the pedlars would buy their goods from wholesalers since the longest-established of the Pakistanis in Glasgow had branched into that form of business. But when they had made enough to buy their little vans, they sought to deal directly with the manufacturers, cutting out another middle man to provide them with better prices for their customers and, more importantly, better profits for themselves. These men derived from some of the world's greatest traders, descendants of the great Moghuls and those who had traded with the caravans of the Silk Route, people whose very lifeblood was trade and trading and when it came to making money in this new-found land of theirs called Scotland, they required very little lessons.

As well as going with their cases, some took stalls for the weekend trading at the Barras. One of these early Barras Pakistanis specialised in selling caps . . . the Glasgow man's bunnet. I asked him why. 'Well, I looked around for a commodity in which to trade and noticed that every single man wore one of these bunnets. Therefore if there was anything they might be likely to need it would be a new one.' His cap stall was to enjoy a booming business and this particular Pakistani went on to be one of the city's biggest merchants, and a millionaire.

The 500 who were here in 1953 had become 2,000 by 1958, 3,000 by 1962, more than 12,000 by the mid-'70s, and more than double that by the late '90s.

More than twenty years ago a survey, as so many surveys do, provided the predictable answers to the question of why they had come to

Glasgow. A small percentage answered that they had come for a better education for their children, more said they had come because relatives were already here, but an overwhelming 81 per cent answered that they had come for a better way of life. Perhaps included in that latter answer was that the better way of life also meant living in a more democratic society – their homeland is hardly a bastion of freedom as we know it.

To see just how much our way of life varies from theirs, I went to that area of Pakistan from where most of our Asian migrants originate. It is in the heart of the Province of Punjab, a translation of which means the land of the five rivers. Many are from the capital, Lahore, while others are from the small towns and villages north of that city as you head towards the disputed region of Kashmir, places such as Faisalabad, Gujranwala, Gujrat, Mirpur, Rawalpindi, Multan, and Sialkot.

As you might imagine, travelling to such places is no Airtours brochure trip. It was like stepping back in time the moment I boarded an Arab airline flight at Heathrow for Damascus, the Syrian capital, where I was to change for another flight to Karachi and once there try for another flight north to Lahore. I still don't know whether it was the passengers or the air crew who weren't used to flying, although at the time I sincerely trusted it was the passengers. Anyway, such was the chaos in finding seats that the stewards gave up and left the passengers to fend for themselves. They were still searching as the jet lumbered it's way towards the runway, the last of them still not seated, let alone belted up, and as the plane took off, passengers were standing in the aisle struggling to keep their balance, grimly hanging on for dear life while the jet reared up for the skies. Welcome to flying in the Third World!

Booking an onward flight in Karachi to Lahore involved joining a heaving, shoving mêlée at a flight desk where a woman carrying a baby tried to push me out of the way. Maybe I shouldn't have resisted, but when I stood my ground she shoved again shouting at me . . . 'Push! You must push. You must learn to push in this country. It is the only way ... push, push, push!' And that was just get to an airline desk. Welcome to Pakistan! Fortunately I had travelled around many of these countries before, remote places in the Far East as well as the Middle East, and shoving and pushing one's way was no surprise, just a reminder of the ways.

The sights and sounds and smells of Lahore and all its little surrounding towns and villages have no equivalent in our modern Scotland. The first impressions of Pakistan can only be described as a rich tapestry of dazzling oriental colours which begin with those unique early morning dawns, their delicate pale mauve merging to a dramatic rose-pink edged with gold as the sun warms the sky; and already at that early hour their world is alive with exotic sounds and the sight of plodding camels hauling heavy carts, prancing horses with their carriages called tongas and Victorias, crowded streets dominated by the have-nots, of veiled women and long-shirted men and members of the hard-working masses who labour in all trades in primitive conditions and for weekly wages that Scots would consider derisory for a day's work. It may sound romantic – more likely trite – to say that it all appears so biblical, or rather koranic, but it's the truth, because much of the life in Pakistan has remained unchanged since the days of Mohammed. But then, on the other hand, with the turn of the head, a brand new BMW or Merc swishes past with its model-like passengers as if in manifestation that amidst all those have-nots, there are also those who have, and have it in abundance. Nowhere do you see such a contrast in lifestyles as you do in the subcontinent.

They don't show you the cripples on those TV programmes with the personality travellers that wander exotic lands. But, to me, the presence of these unfortunate souls is in a way the measure of just how poor and medically backward the particular country you may be in actually is. In the many poor places I've been, I don't recall ever having seen so many noticeably and horrendously handicapped people as in Lahore – heart-wrenching, pathetic creatures so grotesquely maimed and disfigured that they no longer resemble humans. The legless beggar makes his pitiful way at the walled city near the Badshahi Mosque by sitting on a little bogie, not unlike a home-made skateboard, and so that he might be seen, he has it mounted with a three-foot cane stick topped by a piece of orange towelling; the little girl by the Elephant Gate has twisted stumps of unformed legs whose method of traction is to place before her two old door handles screwed to pieces of wood, like a couple of flat irons, then drag the rest of her puny little body a few inches at a time across the ground; the man on the Circular Road is so hideously crippled that his means of perambulation resembles that of a grounded tree monkey, and I imagine that he is probably the most incapacitated person I had ever seen until yet another passes by, his entire body so gruesomely impaired and contorted that in order to move around, he is reduced to that of a quadruped: he lies on his back, his arms and hands behind him acting as one pair of feet, his legs stretched out before him, moving for all the world like a human crab.

There's no such thing as mobility allowance or disability allowance, and there's never likely to be a single-parent allowance. Neither is there any unemployment money, which means that everyone has to find a living . . . at something. If you're not employed, you trade, if you can't trade, you sell, if you can't sell you serve and in the end everyone is busy trying to make ends meet. Sometimes it only amounts to a paratha or a bowl of rice and some fruit for that night's dinner.

With all the competition, making those few daily rupees demands the utmost in human ingenuity. Men, women and children find a myriad of ways to make their day's living, perhaps a classic being the poor old man I watched by a pothole in the pavement near the gates to the Shalimar Gardens. That little pothole had given him an idea. He put some charcoal into it from a little plastic bag he carried, and after the flames from the small fire he lit had subsided and the coals glowed, he produced some raw poppadums and began cooking them. Minutes later he was a poppadum seller, and customers came from far and wide to savour his hot, freshly cooked snacks. Another day, another rupee . . . and another way of making it.

But Pakistan is not all about these unfortunates, although the sight and number of them are a stark defence against complacency. And while we associate those early Johnnie Pedlars as being men from the poorest backgrounds, I was to meet one who had also been to Glasgow with his suitcase, although by no means through necessity. His stay in Glasgow, however, led to much greater things.

Chaudhry Sher Mohammed is the elderly patriarch of one of the most well-known families in Northern Pakistan. He lived and traded in Glasgow for many years and still has sons in business in the city. I went to see him in his hometown of Sialkot, several hours bus journey north from Lahore towards the disputed border with Kashmir, near enough for the shells to come firing over during the periodical tiffs with neighbour India. It was late at night when I eventually located a small hotel in the district and, as had been arranged, I phoned Mr Sher to let him know I had arrived. He said he would send his car for me in the morning.

There were two vehicles in the driveway when I got the call that a car had arrived – a Fiat and a Rolls Royce, complete with uniformed chauffeur.

I made for the Fiat, only to be stopped by the bigger car's chauffeur who came to a slick military attention and saluted. 'It's this car, sir.' And there were more salutes and humble bows from others along the route as they recognised the car. The man with the case had certainly made good.

As we relaxed in a comfortable lounge of his bungalow mansion, Sher Mohammed told me of his Glasgow connection and his days as a

Johnnie Pedlar. He had come to the Gorbals back in the '50s because he wanted to be a trader. His parents had been wealthy enough to afford him a university education and for him to qualify and become a member of the élite Civil Service in the old Indian Government. But trading was what he wanted to do.

'It was my ambition, for I knew the traders and merchants and how much money they could make and that was what I wanted to do.' And so, against the wishes of his parents, he left his secure Government post and linked up with a sports equipment manufacturer who agreed he could be an agent for them in Britain. Sher Mohammed did this by setting up his base in the Gorbals and becoming yet another member of that early community of traders in the '50s. It was to take several months, however, before the first consignment of goods were to arrive and, being no idler, Sher occupied his waiting time by doing the same work as his other countrymen: namely going with the case.

'Although I spoke good English, I thought it the best way to get to know the local language and customs.' He smiled at that. 'I had a little car and took it to a garage but I couldn't understand the man and I had to ask him what language he spoke. He said he was from Aberdeen and I thought that it was maybe him that should be going with the case to learn the language!'

This Johnnie Pedlar went on to be one of the most successful traders in Glasgow and even more so on his return to Pakistan where he became one of the country's biggest sports goods manufacturers.

That Rolls Royce was much more a symbol of his wealth than any Roller or Bentley you might see in this country. When I pointed out just how fine a vehicle it was, he replied proudly, but not boastfully, that there were only two of their kind in the entire country. The other belonged to the President!

Many of those who had been in the door-to-door trade in Glasgow also went on to become wealthy traders and merchants. Although Muslims are forbidden alcohol by their religion, there's no constraint on its followers trading in spirits, and the first of the city's cut-price drink wars were to be instigated by them. This was very much a feature of Glasgow and many towns throughout Lanarkshire of the '60s and early '70s. As soon as the Government dropped the resale price maintenance laws, the Pakistani grocers were the first to seize the golden chance to do even more trading. While the established and conservative native retailers held firm with their prices, the newcomers jumped right in by cutting their mark-up, making up for the drop by buying big, selling big and profiting even bigger. There was nothing new in that for these experienced traders who demonstrated that even more money could be made by cutting prices, a lesson the more cautious and old-line Scottish traders hadn't quite got to grips with. Thanks to these newcomers from far-off places, Christmas and Ne'erday cheer had never been so cheap.

Yaqub Ali, whose A.A. Brothers off-licences are well remembered by the Glaswegians of those hectic cut-price days, was another of the early suitcase pioneers. He came to Glasgow in 1952, being one of the victims of partition in which Muslims had to flee from India, and Hindus from Pakistan, in what was to be the biggest-ever mass movement of people in recorded history and involving between seven and nine million people. Such was the slaughter of the innocents on both sides that more were to die in the first tragic and dreadful six weeks of partition than American servicemen throughout the entire four years of the Second World War.

Ali had just over £4 when he arrived in the Gorbals. Around 30 years later he was heading a highly successful firm with a turnover which put it among the top 50 companies in Scotland, ahead even of such business giants as D.C. Thomson of Dundee and Motherwell Bridge Engineering.

When the suitcases were put away, these new Glaswegians became much better known to the public at large by driving and conducting on the buses. At the time, Glasgow Corporation Transport Department couldn't get enough staff for it's expanding bus fleet and the new immigrants, some recruited specially for the job, came as a godsend, or more appropriately an Allahsend. For the newcomers, there was no better way of getting to know Glasgow and its citizens than by being on the buses, despite the jokes about them that they drove passengers here, there and everywhere except the place it said on the bus destination screen.

Their career on the buses was relatively short-lived, each departing as soon as he had the money for the next rung on their particular ladder to wealth. For some it was the corner shop and for others – due to the Glaswegian demand for the gastronomic delights of the Orient – it was the curry. New flavours and spices aroused and excited local taste sensories as they had never done before. Strange words like vindaloo, burryani, tandoori and tikka were to become so much a part of the language, the joke was that when tourists to the city were asked how they found Glasgow food, their reply was that they thought our kebabs were just wonderful.

The Indian trade boomed as few other new ventures had, outdoing the success of the Italians before them or their Chinese rivals. Like everything else these new migrants did, they achieved it through adaptability. They narrowed down their menu selection, much as the Italians had done with their universal 'Bolognese' sauce, and chose items that were not too remote from Western tastes while at the same time maintaining something still recognisable about their dishes. Many of them even retained that old Glasgow favourite – mince – choicely renaming it on takeaway menus as mince naan, or mince burryani. And they charged £1.50 for extra gravy. Who could blame them for not replicating the kind of food you get in the restaurants of the Punjab? I went to a small side-street restaurant in Lahore's Dil Mohammad Road. The waiter suggested chicken to which I nodded, whereupon he extracted a live one from a cage near my feet and within half an hour it had been halal slaughtered, plucked, tandooried and put on my plate, complete with a sauce that put new demands on the taste buds – and which gave a whole new meaning to the term 'fresh chicken'.

Then there was the hot food stalls nearby where the alluring aroma of their specialities dominates the streets. Crowds gather for their favourite delicacies like goat brains and bull testicles quick-fried on cartwheel hotplates and the oily, yellowed chicken tea which comes from giant urns crammed with dozens of fowl carcases brewing a broth you could waltz on. So do you blame them for adapting their 'Indian' menus?

Glasgow's Pakistanis continue to adjust and accommodate facing up to new challenges with ever-changing trade developments. It was they who gave Glasgow its late-night shopping . . . remember the days when you couldn't get a loaf, a pinta or a paper after five o'clock? Or when a take-away was a fish or pie supper and little else? They changed all that. Remember the days when there wasn't such a thing as a cash and carry warehouse? There is now a virtual city of them in the Clyde end of Tradeston. If something new comes along that we need, they'll be selling it there too . . . cut price of course.

Because the national supermarkets have counter-attacked with late-night and Sunday trading, some even introducing 24-hour shopping, business in the small Pakistani corner stores has been affected. They've never had it so tough and even one of their main suppliers, the Ali brothers' giant Castle food and liquor cash and carry, the biggest of its kind in Europe, is no more. Housed on the site of the former Dixon Blazes Ironworks in the Gorbals, the business has taken on another form and is being developed into a new retail park.

Because of the stringency of the new migration laws, the community of 125,000 Asians now living in Scotland is virtually static, the only new arrivals permitted being a close relative, and even then only with the greatest difficulty. Through their arrival, Islam is now Scotland's second religion and the three-million-pound central mosque in Glasgow, one of six in the city, is the biggest and most expensive place of worship built in the city since the war. They have a variety of their own institutions and welfare organisations which take care of those in misfortune and the elderly, and they have their own grounds in which to bury their dead in Cathcart Cemetery. Most of the community are still self-employed in small shops and catering businesses, but are experiencing new pressures because of changing market forces. In the years ahead, many of these small shopkeepers may also be forced to alter their form of trading.

'But these are challenges we will accept,' says businessman Tufail Shaheen, who received an MBE for his work with the community and one of those early arrivals who traded at the Barras and lived in the Gorbals back in the '50s. He's not pessimistic about the future of his community. 'Many have already moved from the traditional small food shops to newsagents, post offices and small dairies. We can move on to other things. Business is our way of life.'

With the kind of ingenuity that only takes a pothole in the pavement to make a living it is more than likely that this rather remarkable community of Glaswegians will indeed handle any future problems as well as they have in the past.

7

THE GREAT TOMMY MORGAN

Just mention his name to anyone old enough to have seen him and their face will break into a smile instantly. They'll throw their head back in laughter, in fact, and probably recount one of his routines. And always they'll tell you that they don't make them like that any more – which is true, in a sense. For there isn't anyone around today, and hasn't been since he died in the late 1950s, who compares to the late and great Tommy Morgan.

As Scottish showbusiness legends go, there was the inimitable and unforgettable Sir Harry Lauder. At the height of his fame, he was the highest-paid entertainer in the world. Superstars from all over would specially include Scotland in their itinerary just so they could meet him at his Strathaven mansion, where he spent his long retirement years. They revered him like some high priest of the stage.

And, of course, Glasgow has its very own Billy Connolly; multimillionaire, a cult figure in comedy across continents and a legend in his own lifetime, or (as it would so often appear), if he had his own way with tabloid journalists he might also be a legend in his own lynchtime. Maybe not the high priest Lauder was, he is nevertheless the greatest of the iconoclasts and whether you like him or not, he's made a huge dint on the showbiz scene.

For a variety of reasons, a war being one of them and pre-television days being another, Tommy Morgan was never to make it on the world scene. There was never anything of the cult about him. He would have baffled audiences in Melbourne and bewildered them in Miami, but to Glasgow audiences of his day, from the '20s right through to the '50s, there never was and never will be another quite like him. He was the very essence of Glasgow humour, the way Connolly is remembered in his home city before the world discovered him, and he discovered the world.

Like Connolly, Morgan shared that dislike of the precious and disdained the pretentious. He had the same intuitive, almost uncanny, sense of observation of all that was unique about Glasgow and Glasgow people and was able to exploit a variety of situations to create the kind of laughs that Glaswegians appreciate the best. To Glasgow audiences, Morgan was the undiscovered Billy Connolly of his day. A Connolly without the Fs, that is. Today's humour would never have been tolerated in Morgan's day, just as Morgan's humour would be struggling to surface now. He could be rude, but never lewd; he avoided crudity and would never have dreamt of nudity. He could be rough and tough, but never dirty and filthy; amusing, but never abusing. If today's craving of the funnyman is to be obscene and heard, Morgan was just happy to be seen and cheered. He was the crown prince of pantos. The king of comedy . . . the way the Glasgow of the past liked it. And yet, the great Tommy Morgan was hardly known outside Scotland, or even places where Glasgow humour did not prevail. Belfast, perhaps; Brighton, never. Comedy divides like that.

It was a vastly different kind of world, in terms of showbusiness, into which Tommy Morgan was born just two years before the beginning of this century. Theatres in Glasgow were comparatively new and the main form of entertainment still derived from you, your family and friends – you provided your own comedy, rather than have it provided for you. In the more grand and spacious apartments of the West End, many would have their regular evening parties, carpet dances or soirées of one kind or another, at which those who attended would be expected to contribute to the night's entertainment in some way. Perhaps they'd sing a song or give a rendition on the ubiquitous piano or organ; alternatively, they'd thrill the party with a little bit of amateur magic or mystify them with a few card tricks. And so it went on down the social scale, parties and evenings on a horses-for-courses basis.

Smoking concerts, amateur theatrical productions and charity concerts were in vogue and offered great opportunities for young showbusiness hopefuls, the new and the untried. Many areas of the city staged talent contests in competition against each other. It was to be from these that the first of the Scotch comics, as they were known, were to emerge. In the 1880s, a number of restaurants, saloons and theatres opened up in the city, like the Grand in Cowcaddens, the Royalty, later to become the Lyric and home of comic opera and musical comedy, the Royal Princess which was to become the abode of Glasgow pantomime, the Queen's, the Scotia Music Hall, later the Metropole, the Gaiety Music Hall, later to be the Empire. Some inner suburban halls also opened, which were the first of the music halls and wonderful professional outlets for a new breed of professional entertainer, the funny man.

Tommy Morgan was just a young lad of 14, having left school when music hall was at its peak in the city. He would regularly study the entertainments columns in his dad's *Evening Times* which gave details of all the shows that would be playing in the city, 'up the toun', as he would have put it. What magic there was, it seemed, in just looking over all the various advertisements with the names of the performers, many of them household names, and descriptions of how good they were, or at least how good the advertisements said they were, as well as pithy mentions on what their act was about. They made great reading for the young Morgan.

They make even greater reading all these – sophisticated! – years later. They are caught in the passage of time, somehow, and manifestly proclaim the other world in which they were written. Even the choice of some of those yesteryear performers' stage names were in themselves, it appears, part of the entertainment. Which of the funnymen would Tommy Morgan have seen, heard or even known as the young, hopeful lad read his dad's nightly paper?

Here's a selection of what was showing one of those weeks when Tommy first became interested in the business, although it might well have been just an average night's entertainment in the city at the time. There were highlights such as the Princess's Theatre panto, which was apparently nameless except for the title 'Harry McKelvie's Panto', starring Peter Wilkins, Maud Mortimer and Peter Birmingham 'and a chorus and ballet of 60'. The price of admission started from 3p. What absolutely glorious names . . . Maud Mortimer! Peter Birmingham!

The Metropole featured 'The Secret Service Spy', which was subtitled, doubtless to stir imaginations, 'The Morals of a Mill Girl'. Topping the bill at the Empire was the legendary George Robey, perennially labelled 'the Prime Minister of Mirth', supported by another with the choicest of names – Daisy Dormer – whom they hailed as being 'an artiste to her finger tips'. Further down the bill was the Tourbillon Troupe, 'extremely clever lady cyclists' followed by Hugh J. Emmet, 'a ventriloquial entertainer'. What a show that must have been! A Prime Minister of laughs, birds on bikes, a ventriloquist who would get heckled if he overworked his lips and a lady called Daisy Dormer!

The famous Albert Whelan was performing at the Pavilion, but the ad was most curt about him, merely saying he was 'at the piano with songs and stories'. In the same show was Fred Barnes, who got a double acclamation, one being 'the Glasgow favourite', and the other 'the famous light comedy star'. Rounding off the cast were 'George Madegan's dogs' – performing pets which jumped, barked, leap-frogged, see-sawed, walked on two legs, played dead and leapt through flaming hoops to George's commands. Such acts were regular features in variety shows.

The Alhambra's show was called 'Go Ahead', and featured 'expert Highland dancers', 'rhythmic impressionists', 'sensational aerialists' and 'a real acrobatic treat'.

And so it went on, with similar shows at the Grand, Coliseum, Palace, Lyceum, Savoy, Pickard's Panopticon, the Partick Star Palace and the Empress, which as well as variety was also showing a movie called *Detective Finn* with gallery seats at 1p.

Tommy Morgan was a great fan of those early shows and their comedians and would have loved nothing better than to be one of them, but there was a more pressing need for his services at the time. It was called the Great War.

Born in an old Bridgeton tenement when Queen Victoria was still on the throne, he left school at 14 to begin work in a local chocolate factory. He was just 16, a tall, gangly youth, when he presented himself to an Army recruiting officer, successfully persuading him he was actually 18. A few weeks later the young Morgan was in the trenches of Flanders amidst all the hell of World War I.

His father, a plater in the shipyards, and fearful of the consequences of his son's innocent bravado, sent copies of his birth certificate to a succession of commanding officers in a bid to get him home, but Tommy kept changing regiments and they never did find out the lie about his age.

Ironically, it was to be as a soldier that the young Tommy Morgan was to get his first taste of the showbusiness for which he hankered. After being on the staff as an orderly of Commander-in-Chief, Field Marshal Douglas Haig, he had got himself into an Army concert party as stooge to one of the comedians, a man by the name of Alf Vivian, who was well known on the London stage. He also got to know others in these popular Army concerts, performers with long-forgotten names of yesteryear but who, in their day, could pack out the biggest theatres. These were stars such as Eric Blore, Leslie Henson, and G.H. Elliot who billed himself as the 'Chocolate Coloured Coon', a title that in today's world would not only induce apoplexy in the panjandrums of political correctness, but would send the Race Relations Board running with a writ. Morgan enjoyed their company, but more importantly he had become addicted to the thrill of being able to make people laugh. This was the life, he thought, and he vowed there would be no more chocolate factories or shipyards for him when the war was over. But that was a plan that was easier to contemplate than put into practice and for a time after demobilisation the necessity called living forced him back to the shipyard to earn his keep. He worked alongside his uncle, also a plater, for a while but was always on the lookout for any amateur shows in which he could get a part.

The amateur concert parties which had been all the rage when he was a schoolboy were still much in vogue and eventually he was to get an invitation to join a five-man show called 'The Rockets'. They sang, danced and cracked jokes and their show in Govan, where tolerance was not always an audience byword for the ingénué performer, was a huge success. So much so, they were booked up for another a fortnight later. But this time only two of them turned up: Morgan and one of the others named Tommy Yorke, the singer in the show. Two turning up for a show in which where there should have been five was risky but these two Tommies were game and they were so well received with promises of further bookings that both decided to give up their work and make a go of it in the new career of professional entertainer.

One of the many showbusiness agents on the go at the time said he would fix them up with a booking. It didn't sound the best to them, but they had learned one of the first rules in showbusiness which was that you really did have to crawl before you were up and running. Which is why they gladly accepted that first date – to a picture house in Kirkintilloch. It was in the days when movie theatres featured some stage entertainment as well as films for evening shows, this particular one featuring two films and three live acts, Morgan and Yorke 'starring' as top of the bill. They were an instant hit in Kirky, not that being a star in that little village of the time meant big-time, but it meant an awful lot to Morgan and Yorke, especially the bit about being 'top-of-the-bill'. Neither did it make them rich, the wage for the show being a mere £2. And that was between them. But armed with their top-of-the-bill posters as references, other agents were persuaded to get them further dates and for the next ten years they worked together round the scores of music halls in the west of Scotland, every wee town from Largs to Lanark, Girvan to Greenock having its own theatre, some of them with more than one.

Scotland had never been an easy venue for the comedian. It was most certainly no joke being on stage in the '20s and '30s as a funnyman. If you didn't give them the bellylaughs they were looking for, you had to watch out. They wanted their money's worth out there on the bleachers. Relentless hecklers plagued them most nights and on Fridays and Saturdays it was Wild West time. Tommy would often tell the story of the night he made his first appearance at the old Panopticon music hall in Argyle Street. Going into the theatre, he overheard the doorman commenting to a customer, 'See you've got your supplies, Wullie!' The supplies, as it turned out, were a bag of bashed fruit and veg. Others had the same. Morgan recalled, 'I hudnae said two words on stage before somebody in the audience shouted, "Hey, big bawface". Then a rotten tomato hit me smack between the eyes.'

'Big Bawface' Morgan and his partner were to survive a variety of such horror nights as they toured the music hall circuit, gaining more experience and gathering more supporters. Their wages improved too, going from a £2 shared fee to as high as £10 in revues.

Morgan, the star of the act, had many fans by this time who were nicknaming him 'Clairty'. That word was a regular expression of Morgan's and had become something of a catchword with him. His astute delivery and immaculate timing were enough to bring the house down. Contrary to what you might expect, it didn't stem from the old Glasgow word clarty, meaning dirty. It was an abbreviation in the absolute of a favourite saying of his own mother's . . . 'I declare tae goodness', which she would express in all simplicity as 'Clairty'.

Such was the competition on the stage at the time that it was to take Morgan and his friend Tommy Yorke those ten years on the hard grind around the revues, music halls, picture shows, and backwoods theatres before the big break of which every performer in showbusiness dreams. Morgan had already worked in a small-time capacity at the Princess pantomime in Glasgow, just one of many similar acts who came and went during the panto season. But he had made his mark and was to be invited to an even bigger panto which in turn led him to score the plum job as chief comic at the Metropole for the panto season. In today's world of multi-million TV audiences with Saturday night spectaculars and the like, being top funnyman at the Metropole in Glasgow might not seem much. But in the '30s that was big-time. Starring at the Metropole meant you had a city at your feet. 'Clare to goodness. that really was the case.'

Perhaps Morgan's best-loved character was when he changed into drag for his hilarious role as Big Beenie. There was nothing of the Danny La Rue sophistication about this drag act and most certainly nothing of the transvestitism to plague latter-day television screens. Big Beenie was nothing short of glorious. A cross between a cartoon character from Bud Neill and something from the funny pages of the *Sunday Post*. You know the sort of Glasgow woman . . . shaped like a Post Office pillar box with a turban scarf over her head. And a rasping voice like a news-vendor at Central Station. Big Beenie was a truly impressive character.

Everything about Tommy was big, and loud, and gallus, and Glesga. Therefore everything about Big Beenie was even bigger, louder, more gallus and 'merr' Glesga. She was blonde. Hugely blonde. Her fashion was always the latest. But none of it ever suited her. And when it came to the Second World War, Big Beenie went even more man-daft than ever before. And the kind of man Big Beenie wanted was an American GI. Her adventures in the regular Pavilion shows were the stuff of soap opera addiction and had become such a huge part of his act that Morgan was fearful of ever dropping her. 'I would be inundated with protests if I did,' he once said. And true enough, he would have been.

Clairty and his Big Beenie went on to become the most successful-ever funny acts. He did a record 19 successive summer seasons in his own show at the Pavilion, an unmatched achievement at the time anywhere on the British stage. Summer and autumn at the Pavilion, winter and spring in the pantomime at the Metropole, occasional starring visits to pantos at the Empire and Alhambra. Over a period of about 30 years, there was always somewhere in Glasgow you could see Tommy Morgan live on stage. There were also regular trips to Belfast, Ulster folk appreciating Glasgow humour as though it were their own.

Tommy Morgan's humour was centred on the things that meant the most to Glasgow audiences therefore obviously including the subject of football which was always a part of his regular routine. And there was never any hiding the team he supported. Compared to today's understanding of humour with TV audiences having been fed over the years with the best of world talent broadening their spectrum and taking it to realms never dreamt of back in the 1950s and early 1960s, Morgan's comedy had a disarming simplicity, full of the innocence of another age. It was an age when pantomime characters had such guileless names as Sir Anderston Cross and Daisy Darnley, Tam the Postman and Fairy Harmony, Simon Slyfox and, surprise, surprise, a Fairy Spice. It makes you wonder whether there was Clairty clairvoyance!

It's difficult to appreciate that routines such as the following had them literally rolling in the aisles and talking about it in workplaces and homes for days afterwards. But they did.

Morgan plays Andy Andrews, a poor Scot, and Tommy Yorke plays Duncan Lochinvar, a wealthy Scot, in the Princess pantomime 'Hi Diddle Diddle' of 1924.

Yorke: 'Ah weel, ma steamer got wrecked up on the shore. But who cares? I've cash to buy a dozen mair. Now s'pose I was to be generous and gie you £1,000. Whit wad ye dae?'

Morgan: 'Count it!'

Yorke: 'S'posing 1 was to gie you it all in gold?'

Morgan: 'I'd bite it.'

Yorke: 'Well, if I gi'ed you Treasury notes what would you do then?'

Morgan: 'Sterilise them.'

* * * *

Another typical routine at the Metropole has the pair of them on a visit to a place very well known to everyone in the city: Ibrox.

Morgan: 'Oh what a lovely seat this is.'

Yorke: 'Do you think I'm going to see behind this pole?'

Morgan: 'That's no' a pole. It's a Norwegian.'

Morgan: 'You know, before the teams come out they get a' excited. They lose their rag. They're lucky; ah huvnae a rag tae lose. [Then he gets somewhat impatient] Who do they think they are, keeping us waiting? If Rangers came out now I wouldnae gie them a clap. [The mood suddenly switches again] Oh, look, they're they come! The boys! What a team! Tiger Shaw. Jerry Dawson and Wullie Waddell the wee darlin' o' them a'.'

* * * *

Yorke: 'Celtic will win the cup.'

Morgan: 'Ah know the cup they'll win. The hic-cup. Work the Celtic!'

* * * *

Morgan: 'I've been away shooting lions in Greenland.'
Yorke: 'But there are nae lions in Greenland.'
Morgan: 'Ah know. I shot them a'.'

* * * *

Morgan: 'Am just back ma holidays frae Italy.'
Yorke: 'Did you touch Florence?'
Morgan: 'Naw. Her mother was there at the time.'

* * * *

The delivery was in the coarsest Glasgow speech, *to'al glo'al* as you might say, but the panache with which it was conveyed captivated and convulsed audiences. Sometimes the humour could be rougher and rawer than what was then the norm, but it was always strictly kept within the boundaries of the working code of the era – there was nothing perverse, nothing profane. Nor would he ever go for a cheap laugh out of any kind of physical disability: he was horrified when a man with a bad squint complained to him one night after the show about one of his jokes. It had been about a man who couldn't get a girlfriend because he was cross-eyed and decided to jump into the Clyde out of frustration. But because of his eye affliction, he jumped the wrong way from the parapet of the Jamaica Bridge and landed back on the pavement, exclaiming: 'Jist ma luck. The Clyde's frozen over in June!' Morgan made his profound apologies to the man and never told the joke again. They don't make them like Tommy Morgan any more.

Tommy was not to be blessed with ripe old age. He suffered considerable illness in his last few years, and spent most of his time at his luxury apartment in the Kelvin Court mansions. One of his last outings was a token walk-on appearance at the Royal Variety Performance at the Alhambra just a few months before he died in 1958 and at which he got the kind of reception Glasgow gives only to those they love best. And Glasgow loved no one better than Tommy Morgan.

Such was the passion Glasgow's favourite comedian had for his profession and such was the happiness it brought him in dispensing the great humour with which he was so amply endowed, that his dying wish was forever to be a part of the Pavilion Theatre. And to comply with his instructions, and in the presence of a few friends and some fellow professionals, Tommy Morgan's ashes were scattered from the roof of the theatre.

8

TEARS FOR OUR TRAMS

❧❦❧

They clanged. They trundled. They screeched on corners. They shuddered fearfully on crossings. They rattled, they rocked and they rolled. They lurched and swayed frightfully at speed. They tortoised it agonisingly slowly when it wasn't time yet to be at the bundy clock. The dare-devil could board them on the move. The hare-brained would slither off them at high speed. The gallus would leap on them as they gained speed with all the élan of Raeburn's Reverend Robert Walker skating on Duddingston Loch. They jammed in long lines if one broke down. They froze you in winter. They gusted chill draughts in summer. They were as cheap as they were efficient. They blew no smoke, gushed no effluent, spilled no oil. And everyone loved them.

It was the love affair of the century . . . Glasgow and its tramcars. If you spoke about 'caurs' before the 1960s it wasn't motor cars being referred to. It was tramcars. No variety show would dare hit the stage without a tramcar joke, nor a comedian forget a mention of them in his routine. And the most memorable drawing of famous Glasgow cartoonist Bill Tait has a packed tram's formidable conductress refusing to let a passenger on board with that most memorable of female clippies' commands, the irreplaceable one that goes . . . 'Cumoange'aff'.

Glasgow's tramcars were the most people-friendly of all transport. Love them? Glasgow adored them, as it demonstrated that sad day in

1962 when it finally said goodbye to its beloved trams with a parade of the various models: from the horse-drawn trams to the single-deckers they called Room and Kitchen Cars, and from the double-decker Standard Car to the sleek and streamlined Coronation Car, the Rolls Royce of the fleet. Almost a quarter of a million turned out to bid their farewell that early autumn day in 1962, the biggest crowd the city had seen since the Second World War Victory Day celebrations. Only this time they weren't celebrating. They were attending the funeral of a dear friend which was why so many were reduced to tears. They were showing just what Glasgow thought about its trams.

The harnessing of electricity at the end of the Victorian era brought three great benefits to Glasgow – telephones, electric light and electric trams. It was the trams that many considered the greatest blessing. The city was growing spectacularly, thousands being forced to live in suburbs at a distance from factories and offices, shops and theatres. In all weathers, roads to places like Govan and Rutherglen were crowded every day with commuters walking to and from work and other activities. As always, the wealthy were all right, having their own horse-drawn carriages with attendants, which was an even bigger status symbol in those days than words like Merc, Jag or Beamer are today.

Around the 1820s and 1830s, however, the first form of public transport began appearing with the use of horse-drawn coaches for hire, followed by the first omnibus, again horse-drawn. The first regular routes of these were started up in 1834, plying to and from the various harbours on the Clyde and the city's canals, such as Broomielaw to Port Dundas or Port Eglinton. Both of these were thriving and bustling canal ports, surrounded by the various industries served by long, shallow-draught canal boats. The omnibuses were a big success and competition for customers was brisk between the owners who introduced various new models to the booming routes, such as 'noddies', with four wheels, and minibuses with two wheels. Competition between the drivers was even more than brisk and many of them were stopped by police for reckless speeding. As a result, the city council had to draw up regulations in order to curb their behaviour and set some basic standards – they were to give Glasgow its first highway code.

Two of the most successful of these pioneer transport tycoons were Robert Frame and Andrew Menzies. Frame's first service was between Bridgeton and Anderston and male passengers had to use the open-top deck where they were exposed to all the whimsies of the elements.

Females had the dubious pleasure of the vehicle's lower-deck 'saloon', a cramped and stuffy cabin which bore a greater resemblance to a cattle truck with its floor littered with old, dank straw giving the vehicles a unique smell of their own. Despite all that, these first omnibuses were a speedier and easier form of travel than the universal way of getting about at the time, which was walking.

With further competition from another striving entrepreneur called Duncan Macgregor, who like Menzies had the livery of his vehicles finished in his clan tartan, the earlier cabs and omnibuses were replaced by more robust and better maintained models. They even did away with the stinking old straw. Timetables, too, were sharpened up and you could get a Menzies horse-bus from Glasgow Cross going right along Argyle Street to Anderston every 2½ minutes. (Time how long you wait for the bus the next time you use this route!) Actually, you could go a lot further with Menzies as the enterprising transport pioneer began running holiday coaches from Glasgow to Glen Coe, and another from Balloch to Oban.

Still out to improve his services and expand his business, Menzies was one of the early advocates of tramlines to be laid in the city, which would create an even more efficient service for the public – and would also, no doubt, make life much easier for his hard-wrought horses, still the only means of power in the late 1800s. But laying tramlines meant new laws and Westminster not only had to debate but approve legislation on the subject, and that didn't happen until the usual Parliamentary procedures – and delays – had been completed in August 1870. The Tramways Act gave the right to local city and burgh councils to create and possess their own tramlines, but not to actually run the tramcar system on them, at least not for the first 21 years.

Despite its reluctance at the start, Glasgow Town Council, as it was known at the time, eventually approved of the revolutionary new form of transport, and the city took on a temporary bombsite appearance as one of the biggest schemes of roadworks began. Teams of navvies aided by huge steam crane machines began ripping up New City Road. Cambridge Street, Sauchiehall Street, Renfield Street and Jamaica Bridge to Eglinton Toll in order to lay down tramway rails. There was no problem in finding someone to run the new service: Andrew Menzies and his company were again to the fore and winning the contract to operate the first service, from St George's Cross to Eglinton Toll. which began on 19 August 1872. Other routes came quickly into service, and included Cambridge Street to Royal Crescent; Bridgeton Cross to Candleriggs; Bridge St to Paisley Road Toll; Whiteinch to Bridgeton Cross; St Vincent St to Dennistoun and Eglinton Toll to Crosshill.

The new horse-drawn trams were a huge success and instantly

popular with the public, many of whom were to show an immediate profit in the saving it meant for them in shoe leather. And effort. The statistics of this early and efficient transport service were more than impressive, reinforcing just how successful the tartan trams were. In 1894 when the City Council, now with its new title of Glasgow Corporation, opted for its right to take over the system from Menzies, his company figures showed they were carrying some 54 million passengers a year and that they owned and stabled 3,500 horses. It was such a well-organised service they boasted that there was always a tramcar in sight when you went for one. And know what? There usually was too.

Acquiring the tramway service, to be titled the Glasgow Corporation Tramways, made the city the first authority in Britain to own and operate its own public transport system. Their service began on 1 July 1894, and was to carry on and improve on the success of the founding company. It won even more popularity from the travelling public by drastically reducing fares, some by as much as half. The average fare was around 1p, but you could travel up to a mile for an old ha'penny, and the maximum fare for the 14 miles from Uddingston to Paisley was only the equivalent of today's 3½p.

The new lower fares meant even more people using the horse trams. and in their first year Glasgow Corporation Tramways carried more than 57 million passengers over a total distance in excess of 5 million miles making even more profit for the Tramways – much of which was prudently ploughed into more lines and a more efficient service. And that made the statistics even more impressive. By 1900 they revealed the staggering fact that they were carrying a fifth of the total number of passengers being carried on all of the tramways of England and Wales.

The turning of the century was to mark the beginning of the end for the horse as the ubiquitous source of power. Mechanisation was in, equinisation was out and transport bosses were looking around at some of the new methods which were either being experimented with or had been adapted and were proving popular for powering trams. There was a wide variety of new traction forms, such as steam, continuous cable channelled underground between the rails and adding a third electric rail. Progressive passenger-transporters in America – where else? – were ahead of the field and seemed sold on the overhead electric traction method, that is, the tramcar receiving its power from overhead supply lines linked to the tram by rooftop trolleys. There were about 200 such systems working with great efficiency in the United States by 1889. Eight years later, Glasgow experimented with a simple single route system from the city centre to Springburn. Part of the route included taking the trams up the steep slope of West Nile Street, an appropriate test for the new electric system, steep enough to require trace horses to assist single-horse, loaded carts up the hill to Buchanan Street railway goods station. The electric trolley tram passed its test with flying honours and Glasgow Corporation Tramways were hooked on the new method of traction.

Mechanisation was well and truly 'in' and the city embarked on an ambitious programme of re-equipping the system to cope with electric propulsion. About 40 miles of tramline had already been laid and if only these could have been used, changing over to the new electric system would have been no problem. But transport life is not that simple, and once more city streets were ripped up by yet another army of labourers who relaid over 40 miles of double heavy-duty tracks strong enough to support the weighty new electric cars.

The new rails were accompanied by a forest of tall, steel poles to support a vast web of electric wires which would feed their current to the trams. Complete electrification of the system was to take four years but the mammoth operation proved to be well worth all the costly and daring expense, all the tough and exacting effort. Okay, so the Americans may have been more than 200 systems ahead of Glasgow by the time it got round to its electric upgrading, but it was worth the wait. By 1902, the horse trams were phased out and the city was blessed with the biggest and best tramcar system of its kind in the UK. Not only that, there was nothing to compare with it anywhere in the world.

Drivers and conductors for the new service were issued with dark green uniforms, not unlike the colour still worn today by the crews of the city bus company which, by various routes, is a descendant of that very first transport service. The Tramways operated a smart and efficient facility which made travel in Glasgow simple and easy, not to mention economical. More often than not, there was a tram in sight when you went for one and until they adopted a number system, you could even tell from a mile off which tram was yours because the panels of the upper decks were painted with an identifying route colour code: red for Milngavie, blue for Maryhill to Shawlands via Gorbals, white for the University to Dumbreck and yellow for Paisley Road Toll.

From 40 miles of double track, Glasgow Corporation Tramways grew and grew until there was eventually an astonishing total of 135 miles of rail line. Neighbouring towns' services such as Paisley, Kilbarchan, Coatbridge and Airdrie were acquired and there was even the suggestion of extending the line from the furthest Lanarkshire terminal on to

Bathgate, with the possibility of linking up with lines reaching out from Edinburgh. Although that was never to happen, public transport in Glasgow worked on a grand scale and while the journey from Glasgow to Edinburgh was never possible, you could go all the way by tram from Newmains to the shores of Loch Lomond at Balloch. And for about the equivalent of today's 3p, you could rail it comfortably – albeit with a few sways, bumps, bounces and lurches – all the way by tram from Milngavie to Renfrew Ferry, from Airdrie to Paisley, Cambuslang to Anniesland, Springburn to Burnside, Bishopbriggs to Rouken Glen or Dalmuir West to Auchenshuggle. Aye, despite all the music hall jokes, there really is a place called Auchenshuggle and it was a well-known tram terminus. (If you're looking for it, it's just north of Dalbeth Cemetery and Crematorium, between London Road and Tollcross Road.) By the beginning of the First World War, some 300 million passengers a year were using the trams, making a handsome profit for the Corporation.

Ever progressive, and bidding to encourage even more travel, the American idea of end-of-the-line attractions was adopted, an example being the establishment of a 'pleasure park' at Rouken Glen where there was a tram terminus. Trams made the park one of the city's favourites, a status it still maintains to this day.

Envious of Glasgow's superb transport system, other Scottish towns were founding their own, and eventually there were 25 different systems with more than 1,400 trams ranging from Aberdeen to Ayr, Kilmarnock to Kirkcaldy. There was nothing, however, to match the efficiency of the Glasgow service, nor the dedication of its staff, not only to company but country. When the First World War broke out, an incredible 1,110 tramway employees, in one astonishing 16-hour period, voluntarily enlisted in the 15th Battalion, Highland Light Infantry, which from then on was known as the Tramways Battalion.

Losing so many so quickly to the armed forces meant a quick turnaround on the all-male crewing policy and Glasgow Tramways scored yet another first in March 1915, by employing women conductors, the trams of the day carrying poster advertisements announcing that 3,000 females were wanted for the job of fare-taking. A lot of attitudes changed overnight regarding women and how competent they were in the workforce. The women who founded one of Glasgow's very own institutions – the clippie – had made their mark. Smartly dressed crews had always been a feature of the Tramways Department and those first girls they hired were to be no exception, crisply turned out in neat military-style green tunics, collar and tie, and long Black Watch tartan skirts (ankle-length was *de rigueur* in 1915). That same neat turnout of the women crews became a permanent feature for the remaining years of the service. Mind you, some of the things they did in the latter years of the trams with their hats, the knots in their ties and the extra long straps they added to their cash bags – all in the name of fashion – didn't half put uniformity to the test. But then, the way-out has always been a feature of the Glasgow mode. And just like Bill Tait's cartoon, they really could, and would, give you the order 'Cumoange'aff'. The hilarity was endless: what greater laugh could there be than the Bud Neill classic of the conductress hanging on to her platform's support-pole singing . . . 'I dream o' Jeannie wi' the light-brown herr . . . wan inside an' two up the sterr.' The city took on another shade of grey when, like the tramcars on which they worked, the clippie vanished from the local scene.

Despite Glasgow public's affection for them, the life of the electric tramcar was to be comparatively short-lived. A mere 50 years after being introduced, they talked of scrapping them. More and more motor buses had found their way into the transportation market, with a pioneer route having begun as early as 1914. There was to be an imperceptible increase in their popularity, mainly because of their flexibility: trams were confined to main roads, while buses took customers nearer their homes, particularly as the suburbs began to grow. In 1924, Glasgow Corporation instituted their own bus service and a year later there was an early foretaste of what was to come with the first surrendering of a regular tram route to the new motor buses.

Other world cities had also begun curtailing or abandoning the tramcar for the more compatible motor bus. Dundee and Edinburgh discarded theirs in 1956, Aberdeen two years later. Glasgow slowly followed suit, buses replacing more and more tram routes and establishing new services of their own. More and more miles of rail were hauled up along with the cobbles which surfaced most of the city's main roads. One by one all the well-known routes which, over the years, millions of Glaswegians had relied upon so much, disappeared. Route numbers that had become a by-word as the means of getting from home to town, to work, to cinemas, to theatres, vanished from the Glasgow scene. Some of the numbers still ring a nostalgic chord with pre-1962 commuters . . . among them, some of the more popular ones like the No 2 Polmadie to Provanmill, the No 5 Clarkston to Kelvinside via Botanic Gardens, No 6 Riddrie to Scotstoun, No 8 Millerston to Rouken Glen, No 9 Auchenshuggle to Dalmuir West, No 10 Rutherglen to Kelvinside, No 13 Mt Florida to Milngavie, No 15 Airdrie to Anderston Cross, No

19 Netherlee to Springburn, No 27 Renfrew Cross to Springburn, No 30 Cambuslang to Blairdardie and No 32 Elderslie to Provanmill.

On Tuesday, 4 September 1962, Glasgow's tramcars made that last memorable public parade. The love affair with the trams had come to an end.

9

PLAGUE IN THE GORBALS

❦

It was the most shocking item of news, perhaps the worst the city had heard in centuries to which Glasgow awoke that mild summer's morning on the first year of this century. Nothing, certainly, has had such a devastating impact since. Every man, woman and child in the city felt immediately threatened when the stark reality of the shocking, grim details dawned on them. The life of every citizen in the city was in peril. The fear of it was worse than a war – at least precautions could be taken for wars, but none could be taken for this. Who knew how many would die, how many would be seriously ill. Going on previous experience it could be countless thousands.

The fearful news that broke that day in late August 1900, was that there had been an outbreak of the plague in the city. The Bubonic Plague! And the citizens of Glasgow prayed . . . Almighty God, save us. The very name, the mere thought of it, induced cold sweats, which was hardly surprising if you knew anything about the bubonic plague. The pandemic in London of 1660, the one they called the Great Plague, claimed more than 68,000 lives, no doubt more had it not been for the cleansing of the Great Fire which was to follow it. The Black Death had been the scourge of the Middle Ages and had killed countless thousands in cities across Europe. They had known all about it in Scotland too in those times, when it had been a regular and terrifying visitor. There had been innumerable deaths from epidemics occurring in Leith, Peebles, Paisley, Falkirk, Stirling, Lanark, Perth and Galashiels. It had been so severe in Edinburgh in 1646 that Parliament adjourned for a month, resuming its meetings in Perth to be out of harm's way; Ayr and Stirling were almost desolated by outbreaks; in Brechin, over 600 had died in a few months; in Dunfermline, they ordered the town gates to be closed and locked; in Burntisland the ferries across the Forth were halted to prevent its spread.

It was the most loathsome and deadly disease which brought with it all the horrors of its vile nature, the gruesome sores, the agonising sickness.

Such was its impact throughout Europe that it was to bring about sweeping changes in numerous aspects of society. Many feared that the word of God was now taking place, that the end of the world was nigh, while others believed that it heralded the Second Coming. As a result, there was great religious fervour. Roman Catholics were particularly terrified because of the suddenness of death following infection, fearing they would die without first being able to confess their sins and thus suffer the consequences of lengthy purgatory. The usual victims of fear and ignorance, such as Jews, gypsies, homosexuals, the handicapped and varied transients found themselves the brunt of more disfavour than ever before because ignorance was such that they were being blamed for the spread of disease. Italy prohibited the importation of cloth because it was said it could carry the germs of the malady. To prevent the return of the worst known illness, towns and cities across Europe were to take on new and certainly more pleasant aspects. The cleansing of streets was instituted, a factor which had never been considered a requisite of health, let alone environmental appearance, in the past. City authorities set about creating a system of organised waste collections from households. More meat was to be eaten and diets altered because it was said that the healthy body would be more immune to contracting the disease. Now the spine-chilling news was that, after centuries of freedom from the scourge, it had returned. And of all places, right in the very heart of tenement Glasgow.

Few knew at the time just how awful a disease it really was: apart from only rare exceptions, such as expatriates who had worked in Africa and the Far East, no one had any first-hand knowledge of it. The bubonic plague had long since been confined to the history books and modern civilisation had come to terms with its causes and rid itself of the sources of this horrific affliction. Which was why health experts across the world were stunned when the sensational news reached them.

How could it be, they asked, that the bubonic plague had hit a progressive country of Western Europe? And as others asked the questions, Scotland's biggest and most modern city prepared itself for the worst.

Conditions in Glasgow as the city entered the twentieth century – days experienced by the grandparents of many still living today – were vastly different from what we know now as we near the millennium. By far the biggest difference in today's Glasgow is in living standards. Although by 1900 it was already a bustling, thriving metropolis, it was blighted by slum housing which was among the worst in Europe. Only the housing in Naples, they said, was in a comparable state of dilapidation and squalor. The tenement homes of most of Glasgow's working-class lacked the most basic necessities. Few had hot water, even fewer their own toilets, and less had their own baths. Food waste and other rubbish, often including bedpan contents, lay together in open bins in back courts adjacent to what little play areas there were for young children. Before their weekly collection, the bins would have overflowed into a noisome, stinking pile, scavenged by street dogs, cats, rats and other vermin. Not surprisingly, diseases which have long since been virtually wiped out, were rife. Tuberculosis, for instance, accounted for about 15 per cent of all city deaths. There was typhus, diphtheria, smallpox, scarlet fever and cerebro-spinal fever, sleepy sickness and lobar pneumonia, septicaemia and many others. Some would come in epidemics and kill hundreds like the smallpox epidemic of 1901 which affected 2,250, claiming 276 lives. There was another one in 1920, where 113 died out of 542 affected cases. The average death toll in cholera epidemics was around 2,000, a curse which was not eliminated till its final appearance in 1926.

Despite the thousands of slum homes, Glasgow by 1900 had the reputation of being one of the most progressive cities in the world, a pioneer and centre of the industrial revolution, and hailed as the Second City of the Empire. It was also to be one of the last places in the civilised world to be struck by the vilest disease known to mankind.

It was a different story, of course, back in the Middle Ages. When the pestilence made one of its regular visits to Glasgow, they would lock the city's gates at night for fear that any diseased intruder would enter our streets. All those with dogs and cats were warned that if they couldn't keep them locked up then they were 'to hang thame'. Its spread was so dreaded in one of those earlier century outbreaks that the campus of Glasgow University was locked up and thousands fled en masse and settled in Irvine, Ayrshire, till the epidemic passed. What they lacked in courage, perhaps, they obviously didn't lack in sagacity.

In 1900, just as they are today, these were all but stories of the long past. The plague was something of another age. Perhaps you had read about it in history lessons at school. Maybe the teacher had related gruesome chapters about the night carts going round the streets picking up the dead. But it could never happen nowadays, though – not in the modern Glasgow of 1900. All of this only served to compound the shock news that this most morbid of afflictions, one which everyone thought had been eliminated forever, had not only returned, but was right here with them in Glasgow.

The outbreak had been slowly and unknowingly spreading for between two and three weeks before it was confirmed that the cause of a mysterious rash of deaths from fever was in fact the abominable bubonic plague. By then, however, it had been transmitted to several families and health officials were at their wits' end trying to trace not only the source, but the reasons for its alarming spread. The first suspicion that it might be an extremely serious disease, perhaps even bubonic plague, had been when two young victims were examined by two local medical men from the South Side.

Dr C.E. Robertson and Dr Colvin had conferred over the symptoms from which their patients had suffered and subsequently died. In a report to the authorities, Dr Robertson stated: 'We were satisfied that they were cases demanding the attention of the Sanitary Authorities, and I agreed with Dr Colvin that, having both seen them independently, we should both notify them as cases of enteric fever, with a mark of interrogation after it to imply that the diagnosis was not definite, but as they were evidently of an infectious nature, should be removed at once.'

Enteric fever was the medical men's description of typhoid, an acutely infectious disease characterised by rose-coloured spots on victims' bodies, intestinal bleeding, abdominal pain and high fever. But as the doctor pointed out, there was a question mark on their diagnosis. A very big question mark. For the two men had suspicions that they were dealing with something even worse than the awful agony and outcome of typhoid. Upon their recommendation, the children were 'removed at once' – to hospital.

They were admitted to Belvidere Hospital, which specialised in infectious diseases and fevers, that same day, Saturday, 25 August, and were immediately examined by Dr John Brownlee, the Physician-Superintendent. In consultation with two other senior physicians the suspicions of the two doctors were confirmed. It was the plague. The bubonic plague.

None of the medical people concerned had any direct experience of such a pestilence, no other notifications of it being known anywhere in Britain since the 1600s. As samples from the victims were taken for tests at the university, urgent meetings were convened between senior physicians, health and sanitary officials. Files of recent sufferers of similar fevers which had not, until then, been identified as the plague, were hurriedly produced. Teams went to work studying the disease – how it occurred, how it was transmitted, how it could be cured, how it could be treated, and how it could be prevented.

'The two most important items on our agenda,' one of the first meetings were told, 'is that we must, with all the haste in the world, locate both the originating source and the reasons for the spread. Unless we do this, not in weeks or days, but within hours, we will have one of the most appalling tragedies Glasgow has ever seen. If this outbreak is to get out of hand, who knows what we face.' That grim warning was taken to heart . . . well, at least by health authorities.

Ancient medical books were studied. Every reference to it from every medical university and school was asked for and gone over in minute detail. Experts who had knowledge of it when working abroad were contacted. And every conclusion reached about what they were faced with had them truly and deeply shocked. For despite all the other horrid diseases which were known and prevalent at the time, there was nothing any of them had ever experienced which was as gruesome as this.

Their hurried studies into the plague were to tell them that the disease was caused by the bacterium known as *Pasteurella pestis*, an internal parasite of rodents, particularly the rat. The bacterium was spread from rat to rat and rat to human by the rat flea. Every single detail of the illness's source, gestation and spread was to fill them with disgust. For instance, when the bacterium establishes itself in the stomach of the flea, it multiplies rapidly until the stomach is completely filled with a solid mass of it. The flea then becomes ravenously hungry, so hungry that in default of its preferential host, the rat, it attacks any animal within reach, usually man. They suck human blood so insatiably that their gullet becomes distended to its utmost limit whereupon they then regurgitate some of the blood, by now infected with the bacilli. Its transfer to humans is usually caused by the germ being deposited on the victim's skin, then inoculated into the circulation through the puncture wound made by the flea as the individual scratches to relieve the bite's irritation. One rat alone could carry scores of fleas, each capable of transmitting the disease. Little wonder it had once been known as the Filth Disease. Little wonder they felt alarmed at what lay ahead of them. Descriptions of the ailments and suffering that were brought about by this hideous disease were every bit as revolting as its source.

The name bubonic comes from *buboes*, the characteristic large swellings of the groin and armpits, which quickly follow infection. These buboes are unusually huge, ulcerous distensions filled with an odious pus and accompanied by skin mottling, fever and delirium which quickly culminates in an agonising death. Such is this agony, it had been known for sufferers in previous centuries to leap from windows, run into rivers, hurl themselves into ponds and run naked through streets until they dropped. If, indeed, there was anything merciful about the plague then it was the fact that it's progress could often be so swift that a person who contracted it could go from perfectly good health to extreme prostration followed by death in a matter of hours.

As samples from the victims were taken for tests at the University, urgent meetings were convened between senior physicians, health and sanitary officials. Files of recent sufferers of similar fevers, but not identified as plague, were hurriedly produced.

The medical sleuths went to work. Their initial study was of all the cases of serious fever which had occurred in the previous month. It didn't take them long to trace the fact that there had been a flurry of apparently unrelated deaths from such a disorder, all in streets in and around the Gorbals. The first of these had been when a Mrs Bogie and her granddaughter had taken suddenly ill on the evening of Friday, 3 August. The Bogie family lived at 71 Rose Street, later renamed Florence Street, in a ground-floor single-apartment house, the kind known in Glasgow as a 'single-end'. Four of them lived in one room, Mrs Bogie and her husband, their daughter, and their daughter's two-month-old baby.

This was by no means overcrowding in the poorer Glasgow tenements of 1900. Countless single-ends were home to many more occupants than that. Often there could be as many as eight to ten in one room in which they cooked, dined, slept, washed, played and relaxed. And made love. All cocooned in that unholiest of household fugs of the day, it was a cloying, choking ragout of stale aromas . . . of tobacco smoke, the fry pan's overworked lard and unwashed bodies, an odour almost beyond the comprehension of today's olfactory senses. Immediately outside the house it was seldom better, as a pervading stench emanated from the rotting garbage piles in back courts combined with tenement entrances that were used as urinals and communal stairhead lavatories which were frequently out of order.

The infant in the Bogie house was to succumb to the fever the following Tuesday, the grandmother two days later. As the precise nature of their illness had not been established, the causes of their deaths were put down as 'zymotic enteritis' and 'acute gastro-enteritis'.

It wasn't long before the files gathered by officials revealed that within days, others in the same neighbourhood as the Bogie's, and some of them related families, had also taken seriously ill, some of them fatally, as a result of contracting a similar type of fever. These had been recorded mainly as acute pneumonia or enteric fever. Among those affected were four members of the Molloy family in nearby Thistle Street. Then it showed up in Oxford Lane. After that, Mathieson Street, followed by other local addresses including South Coburg Street, South Wellington Street, Cook Street, Thistle Street once more, as well as further cases in Rose Street and Well Street. It was like a wildfire, out of control. But why . . . why . . . why? What was the link?

The first assumption was simply that there appeared to be something suspiciously unusual about the cases, particularly regarding the rapidity of the infection, and the Sanitary Authorities were therefore notified immediately. Health and sanitary officials flooded into the area, questioning every available source who may have had some connection, no matter how loose, with the Bogie family.

They studied ancient records of centuries before, when Glasgow was first burgeoning as a trading centre, and around the time when the professors and students from the university had fled to Ayrshire for safety, noting that as well as locking the city gates at night to keep out those who may be bringing in disease, they had also banned the customary wakes which followed the deaths of plague victims.

Simultaneously, sanitary detectives also noted the first outbreaks following Mrs Bogie's death had been among families of those who had been at the two wakes held at her house in Rose Street, one for the grandchild, the other for herself. And when there had been wakes for these new victims, further outbreaks had occurred among some of those who had attended them. The chain reaction had been pinpointed. Most – but crucially not all – of those who contracted the plague had done so by attending the wake of a victim.

Waking, or watching with the dead in the hours before the burial, was commonplace in Glasgow in the days before funeral parlours. The body, in an open coffin, would lie in the principal room of the house (often the only room of the house) for a day and night prior to the funeral and would be visited by friends and relatives as a mark of respect. Often as not, because a drink would be offered to attending mourners, the dead person would be visited by more people than it was ever suspected he knew. And sometimes even more often than that there would be a lot more than one sob-gargle of a drink for the taking, and the sorrowful occasion would quickly change from a funeral to fête, dirge and desolation becoming cheers and celebrations. As the night wore on, the merrier they became and other factors would be introduced to the proceedings, like playing party games as they 'grieved'. Numerous children would run in and out of the room from the street outside and join the carousing adults in the innocent, fun-like games they played, like hiding the thimble! And where better for that than some discreet hiding place among the corpse's clothing! Then somebody would say, 'Gie's a song'.

That old Irish ballad 'Finnigan's Wake' perhaps tells it all:

> *His friends assembled at his wake,*
> *Missus Finnigan called for the lunch,*
> *First they laid in tea and cake,*
> *Then pipes and tobacky and whisky-punch.*
> *What, Fol-de-dooh-dah, dance to your partner,*
> *Welt the floor, yer trothers shake,*
> *Isn't it the truth I've told ye?*
> *Lots of fun, at Finnigan's wake?*

Gorbals' wakes of the time were among some of the liveliest parties in town. Pipes, tobacky, whisky-punch, dancing to their partners and lots of fun, to be sure. Sometimes as many as 100 would be crowded into one little room of a single-end . . . together with the body. And, of course, the booze. In fact, in the report drawn up by the Medical Officer of Glasgow following the outbreak, it was mentioned that more than 100 had attended one of the Gorbals plague-victims' wakes where, it was noted, there had been considerable 'indulgence'. That particular report, couched in the usual stuffy terms, continued . . .

Waking is primarily an act of reverence and of sympathy. But 'wakes' as we know them are an abuse of this custom. They are lacking absolutely in reverence and only a distorted conception of friendship could construe them into expressions of sympathy. Hospitality is, perhaps, natural in the circumstances, but its excess becomes debauchery, and when, to this, indulgence in games is added, the last remnant of reasonableness in the custom has gone.

Senior medical officers were unanimous in their opinion that the conducting of wakes following such deaths had been a 'powerful factor in the spreading of the disease'. Because of this, Glasgow Corporation was forced to issue a public notice on the question, although it was subject to the creaking machinery of local government, haste not being one of the wheels, and was not to be issued until 12 September by which time many more wakes had been conducted with similar fatal consequences. The Corporation's decree read:

> The Lord Provost and Magistrates have had under consideration the prominent part which has been played by the holding of wakes over the dead in the recent visit of Plague and would strongly urge upon the public the necessity and the duty of discontinuing the custom. These ceremonies, while meant to be acts of friendly remembrance, are fraught with danger to the health of all who take part in them and thus to the well-being of the community at large. They would also remind the public that it is illegal to hold a wake over the body of a person who has died of any infectious disease.

Health officials were quicker off the mark, officers touring the bereaved and discouraging wakes as well as instituting an impressive clean-up operation to prevent further spread of the plague. Houses where there had been an outbreak were disinfected, their walls and furniture sprayed with formalin, lobbies and staircases washed with chlorinated lime solution. The houses of those having any kind of contact with plague victims were ordered the same treatment. Every house in a building in which there had been a reported case had to be disinfected and cleansed by the Sanitary Department, its lobbies, staircases and common passages similarly treated. Back courts had to be washed and hosed down with chloride of lime whitewash, their ashpits and garbage bins limewashed, cleansed and emptied thrice-weekly. The district surrounding any outbreak was to be defined as a special cleansing area, receiving similar sanitary procedures. Extra ratcatchers were to be employed, and inspectors and police ordered to check on overcrowding and cleanliness.

A scrupulous check was made on 'ticketed' housing, that is houses of not more than three apartments which, under a Glasgow Police Act, had official metal tickets attached to main doors, stipulating the number of persons the house may legally accommodate. On one of these first checks, they discovered that a family of five had taken in four boarders in their one-roomed dwelling. It was a measure of the scale of the city's dire housing problem and was most certainly not an isolated case. There were many worse examples of flouting the ticket rules, a common practice being to deface the allotted numbers on the tickets, which were made of tin. To combat this, they began issuing new tamper-proof models in die-cast metal.

There was considerable alarm among the officials when the plague made a sudden leap from the Gorbals, this time to Govan. Despite their efforts, no link was traced to any of the Gorbals victims. It hadn't been a wake on this occasion. Nevertheless, the same cleansing work was carried out and no further cases were reported from Govan. A woman in another part of Glasgow, nowhere near any of the outbreak loci, was found with the fever, but the source was quickly traced back to her husband, a medical worker who had transmitted the infection in his clothing. Justification for the Italians who had banned its import all those centuries before.

While they had sourced the wakes as being responsible for the spread of the disease, it was not as easy as tracking down the origins of that first case in the Bogie household. Hugh Bogie, the man of the house, had been a dock labourer and at first it was thought he could have brought the disease from an infected rat on one of the ships which packed Glasgow's numerous docksides, many of them coming in from Africa and the Far East where such fevers were still rife. But when they investigated further, they discovered that Bogie had only worked on vessels in the coasting trade, ships which never left British waters. His wife, however, had been a fish hawker and it was the custom of many hawkers at the time to keep supplies of their various goods at home, usually in the dunny at the rear of the building to which ground-floor tenants, such as the Bogies, would have access. That too could have been a source.

Thanks to the swift and highly efficient efforts of the various Glasgow health and medical agencies at the time the fearful prospect of this outbreak of the plague becoming the customary and anticipated epidemic was not to be. Mercifully, it was to vanish almost as suddenly as it had appeared. By the last week in September of that year there had been a total of 36 confirmed cases of bubonic plague in the city, 16 of them resulting in death. Seven years later there was to be yet another mysterious outbreak in Glasgow, but this time there were only two cases, one of which died. And in 1911 there was one further case, that of a visiting Lascar seaman and his was to be the last reported case of the dread disease in the city.

In honour of the valiant nursing staff who had so bravely cared for the victims of the 1900 plague outbreak at Belvidere Hospital, Glasgow

Corporation made the presentation of a gold medal. One of the victims had been one of these young Belvidere nurses who had been on duty in the wards which had tended some of the sufferers at the hospital. Fearful as it was, these courageous nurses faced other dangerous fevers which took much bigger tolls than the bubonic plague of 1900. An epidemic of relapsing fever which lasted for three years resulted in a huge death toll: they were to experience more than 2,000 deaths from the 19,000 typhus and scarlet fever admissions.

A large headstone at Sandymount Cemetery erected by the city commemorates the brave nurse who died in the plague outbreak as well as her many colleagues at Belvidere who paid the ultimate sacrifice for their calling.

10

THE WORK-IN

The real song of the Clyde was the most beautiful and most unusual of symphonies. There was the rat-tat-tat-tat of riveters banging, the thump-thump-thump of powerful steam hammers, the screech of woodworkers' lathes, power-saws and drills, the softer and more rhythmic melody of joiners' handsaws, the beats and pulses of caulkers and shipwrights, platers and riggers and labourers as they banged and clanged, whacked and walloped at sheets of shaped steel. All of them were conducted by some seemingly great unseen leader whose baton was a steam whistle which would begin or end or interrupt each movement of the wondrous musical score with the loudest sound of them all, a strident and shrill shriek which every performer recognised as being that of their own. Further up or down the river, another conductor's whistle would scream its message, followed by yet another and another, each controlling its own very individual industrial orchestra.

The sound of such music meant everything to tens of thousands of Glasgow and Clydeside families for this cacophony was the melody of their livelihood as the menfolk of the river went about their famous business of building ships. Every beat, bang, blast, stroke, rap, knock, scream was to them the most dulcet of sounds, a warranty that another week would mean another wage.

It was the greatest industry Glasgow ever had. For years, no one else had the reputation for building the magnificent vessels that emerged from the shipyards which were household names in the city . . . Barclay, Curle and A. & J. Inglis, Stephen's and Connell's, Fairfields and John Brown's, Yarrow's and Harland and Wolff's. The yards had huge workforces: at one point up to 10,000 alone were working at John Brown's. If someone in your house wasn't employed in them, then a relative more than likely was, and almost certainly a neighbour or two.

Every third ship constructed in Britain had that proud stamp on it . . . *Clyde built*. In achievement and impact, the industry itself was rather stupendous, most certainly spectacular. And just as it lived its ending as a major player in Scottish industry was to be marked with a gesture that was every bit as impressive as one of those historic launchings of a world-famous ship. The venue for the event was the workplace which had become the Upper Clyde Shipbuilders. And it was called The Work-in. It was to be one of the most outstanding and inspiring displays of worker-solidarity and popular support seen in the country since the days of the Chartists, those brave and determined reformers of more than a century before. It was to be one of the greatest dramas performed before the public with one of the most significant protest marches held this century. It brimmed over with the hallmarks of occasion that merited all the glories of victory. There were, of course, triumphs in the legendary Work-in – but they were to be short-lived. For the coffin nails of the Clyde as a great bastion of shipbuilding had all been in place long before that workforce staged their magnificent industrial Dunkirk.

Ask any expert on what happened to shipbuilding on the Clyde and you'll get as many different answers as asking a count of economists about the financial status of the country. Among the hackneyed explanations are that it was the men; it was the management; it was the managers; it was the owners; it was the unions. You get the same assortment of reasons if you ask when, exactly, it all started to go wrong. There are those in the know who'll tell you that the first warning signs came as long ago as before the First World War, others pinpoint the '30s as being the start of the real rot, or the '60s as being the time of genuine anxiety, while some even record optimism right up to the '80s. But there's no disputing the fact that after the 1939–45 post-war flush, it was all downhill for the once-great industry.

Once into the '60s the only news that seemed to emerge from the shipyards was another dispute, another demand, another warning, another strike. It was no joke if you worked there, but it certainly seemed like one huge burlesque if you didn't. Strikes were so commonplace it was as though every yard had a Peter Sellers's Mr Kite in charge of each union branch. And on re-reading some of the events of those days, there were even more comical characters around than the unbending Mr Kite.

To understand the strikes, the disputes, the problems over demarcation and the Work-in itself is to understand the nature of the industry as it pertained to the Clyde. For our very own river was the birthplace of modern shipbuilding. The number of industrial geniuses and entrepreneurs of the craft as well as the great craftsmen who emerged from in and around the river was not less than astounding. It didn't matter to them that ships little bigger than lifeboats couldn't proceed further upriver than Bowling due to the silted-up condition of the river, or that nothing sizeable could sail over the 1,000-ft seam of rock just eight feet below the waterline at Elderslie: these early pioneers were industry's trailblazing movers and shakers, so when they had a river along which ships couldn't sail, they set about making one that could, the silt and the unpassable rock both being removed so that you could navigate all the way up to Rutherglen. The ships that were to be Clyde-built came from a river that was man-built.

The first ships, of course, were made of wood, but Glasgow wasn't an easy place for obtaining supplies. So they thought about alternatives. Iron seemed a good option, and in 1831 the foundry of John Neilson and Company, halfway up the Garscube Road and a good mile or more from the water, got the contract to make the first iron ship. Neilson's foundry was more used to constructing other things, like locomotive engines and factory machines and a vessel was a new challenge for them, but these people were innovators, another member of the family having a few years before invented the hot-blast furnace. And so the first iron ship, the very first sailing machine, was constructed in a factory, something that wasn't to be done again till nearly a century later when indoor construction came into vogue.

They named that first iron ship the *Fairy Queen*, bearing in mind it was in the days when fairies and queens were rather delightful creatures. And, propped firmly upright between huge wooden wedges, a team of heavy Clydesdales hauled this pioneering *Fairy Queen* down Garscube Road and along the Cowcaddens to pass through much of the city. It was cheered on by huge crowds proudly watching their own little bit of industrial history as it made its way to the launching site at Broomielaw.

It was an auspicious beginning for these wonderful men and their sailing machines. Now that they had so successfully gone from wood to iron, their lively and forward-thinking minds took them on to new and greater challenges. From iron they went on to steel, from twin paddles to the single propeller; the single propeller then became a twin, which was followed by a triple, and eventually a multiple; and the early reciprocating engine became a turbine one. There was just no stopping their inventiveness, a whole variety of new and improved forms of steam engines being made in Clydeside, the expertise of the brilliant engineers who created them attracting as many new orders for Clyde-built ships as the actual vessels themselves.

The first steamship to sail on open waters was to come from the Clyde and within ten years of her launch there were 48 under construction in Clyde yards. It was a Clyde-built ship which was the first steam vessel to ply the Thames . . . the first to cross the straits at Dover . . . the first to sail on the Greenock to Belfast run. Such had been the expansion by 1906, and such had been the prestige of what was happening on the river, that the English-based boiler and marine engineering shops of Yarrow and Company on the Thames moved to the Clyde, by now so dominant it was responsible for a third of all British shipyard production. So great was its reputation that even the Germans were lining up with orders.

About six years later, the Clyde had another incomer, this time from Northern Ireland. In 1912, around the time when the most legendary of the many great ships built by the yard was making its maiden voyage across the Atlantic following its launch the year before, Harland and Wolff of Belfast purchased three adjacent Govan sites, with the idea of building an integrated steel fabrication and engineering ship factory, featuring hammerhead cranes, which was to become an industrial showpiece for Glasgow. In the ensuing half century, Harland and Wolff were to become one of the great forces of shipbuilding on the Clyde. And the name of that ship making its maiden voyage was . . . the *Titanic*. Incidentally, it was the arrival of the shipyard company from Ulster which many maintain put the Protestant backbone into Rangers Football Club. The new Glasgow shipyard had a Scottish-Ulster social club and an annual evening to celebrate their arrival in Glasgow, and although they undoubtedly bolstered the true blue element of Rangers, there's ample evidence that this element was already firmly established: the club and its sentiments would have been little different had Harland and Wolff not branched out from Queen's Island, their home base on the Lagan in Belfast.

The grand symphony of the river had reached its crescendo years before, in fact, and along the Clyde in the latter part of the nineteenth century there were over 150 yards in and around the river and estuary in places such as Ayr, Troon, Rothesay, Dumbarton, Bowling, Greenock and Port Glasgow. In Glasgow itself, at various locations including Blackhill, Govan, Meadowside, Whiteinch, Hamiltonhill, Scotstoun, Maryhill, Kelvinhaugh, Lancefield, and Linthouse, including neighbouring Clydebank, Paisley and Rutherglen, there were 55 yards.

The golden age of shipbuilding was to see order after order pouring into the yards, the entire river virtually reverberating with the energy of countless workplaces – keeping in mind that for every yard at work, there would be up to a score of other companies engaged in sub-contract work of various kinds. In 1841, there were nearly 2,000 employed in the industry on the Clyde. In 1921, that figure had increased to almost 100,000 with two or three times that number in back-up industries.

Golden age or not, it was probably during this most prolific time on the Clyde when there was work for everyone that the very first seeds of what eventually led to the legendary Work-in were actually sown. The masters were no slouches when it came to governing the huge armies of men who made them their vast fortunes. Their tens of thousands of employees had to be kept in line and reminded just who were the bosses, the philosophy of the shipbuilders being identical to that of any other Victorian manufacturer: labour is merely a product and a product to be bought as cheaply as possible. If that meant being ruthless, so be it. When times were bad, wages were cut as quickly as possible. When times were good, wages were raised as slowly as possible.

The best of the big sticks the shipbuilding overlords were to produce was the formation of the Clyde Shipbuilders Association. It was for all the world a trade union – of bosses. The Association was to give them enormous power, the most formidable aspect of which was the lockout. If the workers over-agitated on any demand, they were simply locked out of the yards. And with no dole monies or relief of any kind, the lockout simply meant submission or starvation. The former usually won and, if it didn't, the latter, in time, did.

In 1847 the engineers presented the masters with new demands and their collective answer was a lockout. They were to be out for more than seven months before yielding.

As a means of keeping the men in order throughout the country, the lockout, as was so amply demonstrated in 1895, was a brilliant tactic. There had been a general movement for higher wages for engineering workers and the workers and managers on the Clyde had reached an early agreement. But just across the water in Belfast there had been deadlock at the huge Harland and Wolff yard, a main sticking point being the piecemeal rates for riveters. The Ulstermen wanted the same rates as men in other yards but the employers said this would erode their profits and refused. So the riveters went on strike and Harland and Wolff locked their gates – and up to 8,000 men were kept from work.

Fearing their engineers would take the short trip over to Glasgow (you could get cheap fares for around 5p at the time), the Belfast company asked the Clyde shipbuilders to lock out their engineers, a quarter of their workforce, to ensure that none of the Harland and Wolff men signed on. The Association agreed and along the Clyde, all the way from Greenock to Glasgow, thousands of experienced workers, men who had no quarrel with their employers, found themselves out of work. The sympathy strike had been invented . . . by the employers! The engineers weren't slow to catch on, however. They warned that if the masters had the right to lock out their men with whom they had only an indirect cause of quarrel, then the federated engineers would also have a right if they were ever out of work to bring out fellow workers in other areas.

Had only the workers been as united and organised as their bosses, things might have been different. Instead, different unions existed for each of the crafts and disputes with the employers were on a piecemeal basis. The strength of the men was further weakened by the number of semi-skilled assistants to the various craftsmen, those who were helpers and holders-on, or in Clydespeak, hauders-oan, the men who held the near molten rivets in place till the riveters banged and shaped them home. Craftsmen such as the riveters worked in teams and it was they, not the shipyard, who employed the hauders-oan, further complicating and weakening any solidarity among the workforce as an entity.

After forming their Shipbuilders Association, the bosses set the rules which were to govern virtually every aspect of life and work in the yards. The rule book laid down when employees would work, and for how long. Generally the men would work a weekly total of 54 hours, divided into a working week of five and a half days. From Monday to Friday they would start at 6.15 a.m. till 9 a.m. when there would be a stop for breakfast. Labour resumed again at 9.45 a.m. until the piece (lunch) break at 1.15 p.m., for which they were given the same time as breakfast, three-quarters of an hour. Then it was back to work again at 2 p.m. until the finish at 5.30 p.m. Saturday started in the same way, but finished at 12.15 p.m.

Work hours were regulated by the steam whistle, the great unseen conductor which was one of the pillars of the 59 principal rules set by the masters. Scenes from Chaplin's *Modern Times* were not confined to the USA of the 1930s. They were taking place right here on the Clyde many years before that and nothing exemplified it more than the steam whistle. That first unholy and stentorian screech of the day was the command for workers to be through the gates by an even unholier 6.15 in the morning, and remember that not all of the men lived near the yard in which they were employed. Despite Glasgow's superb public transport of the day, there were often long walks at the end of the journey to the yard's main gate.

Many travelled by bike, leaving home just after five o'clock in order to be at work on time. And being on time was sacrosanct. If you were more than seven minutes late, timekeepers, with watches in hand, slammed the tall gates closed and no amount of pleading got you entry after that. And when they were barred, the latecomers had to hang around at the works' entrance until the breakfast-time break at 9 o'clock, usually breathless and sweaty after a long and hurried bike ride, or having run the last part of the journey from the tramcar only to stand in the cold for the next two and three-quarter hours. If there was any overtime to be done that day or later in the week, the delayed and dilatory had first of all to make up their lost two and three quarter hours before qualifying for any extra cash. Life could be remorseless for those whose only possession of any material value was their labour.

It was also part of the daily diktat that each employee was known by a number as well as a name. This number would be on a ticket handed to the employee when they entered the yard for work. The ticket was their proof of having worked that particular day and their guarantee of getting a wage at the end of the week, therefore it was guarded securely during the long day at work. And if it wasn't . . . well, there was a rule for that too. A system of prescribed fines was part of the elaborate code of rules and one of these specified that the loss or defacing of the daily work ticket would incur a fine of tuppence for a new one. The fines encompassed a whole range of codified rules. Typical of these were such misdemeanours as oiling or cleaning a machine while it was in operation, a fine of 2½p, 5p for a further offence; leaving any woodwork machine in motion after use, 12½; leaving staging or ladders in an unsafe position, 5p; possession of alcohol, 10p; being intoxicated, 10p; smoking in the joiners' shop, boat sheds, upholstery shop, sawmill, 12½p, instant dismissal for a further offence; exiting the yard by an unofficial route, 15p; any time worker giving assistance to a piece worker, 12½p; breaking open another worker's tool box, 12½p.

Work for the majority in the shipyards was long, hard, heavy and dangerous and most of it out of doors, no matter how atrocious the weather. The masters set the rules and the rates and offered little else. Work conditions were primitive. There were no locker-rooms and you hung your jacket where you worked, which might be ten flights up on a shaky open staging swinging a hammer with a gale blowing round your ears.

Shipping and shipbuilding was to make wealth of regal proportions for the owners who lived in the most palatial mansions, many owning estates. Others, like the Burrell family, who were shipbuilders and owners, amassed an opulence of riches that bordered on the obscene. The good times had rolled well for them but not for their workers who were never to be liberated from the barrack confines of their soot-blackened tenements. In the early days there had been something of a spirit of collaboration between employees and emloyers, even to the extent that the boilermakers had a song in tribute to the co-operation, the closing lines of which were: 'Labour should co-operate, And to help with all their might, Masters to compete!' Had any worker chanted such words in years to come, they would have been thrown out of the yards. The worker was in an industry whereby the harder he laboured, the faster the ship he was building would be completed . . . and the sooner he would likely be out of a job. And when the good times had gone, as they had between the two world wars, there were no further ships to be built when the one on which they were working was finished. The symphony had come to the end of its first great movement and the most sinister of silences was to descend on the Clyde.

Nowhere did those two dread words 'great depression' mean more than in the shipyards of Britain. At John Brown's in 1920, there had been a huge workforce of about 10,000 and the average wage was £4.10p a week. A year later, the numbers were down to 6,322, wages dropping to £3.67p. By 1922 there were only 3,653 employees and the pay was a mere £2.70p. The workforce was to be continually eroded over the next ten years or so, in 1932 plummeting to only 422. The men of the Clyde and their families never forgot those terrible years of starvation and the kind of deprivation that makes a mockery of the word as it is used in the late '90s. While their wealthy employers never even had to cash in the family silver, the workers had it ingrained into them that their kind of livelihood swung on a very slim thread.

Even when the Second World War came and there was work again – unlimited work – and the Clyde was by then building even more than a third of all Britain's ships, they couldn't shake off the horrors of those fearful years of the Depression. An endemic spirit of fear had been irrevocably engendered in the workforce and morale was so bad in the yards, that the Government's wartime Ministry of Information which controlled the nation's propaganda – our very own Ministry of Truth! –

engaged a firm of business management consultants to make a study of the situation. Why was it, the Government wanted to know, that with most of the nation wholeheartedly participating in the war effort, there appeared to be this malaise on the Clyde with its continual workers' problems and threats of strikes? The Ministry's study team were to produce an engrossing report on conditions, attitudes and behaviour in Clydeside shipyards, although any single caulker or riveter could have told them, word for word, the very same story.

'It is not that Clydeside workers are against the war or for peace,' began their findings. 'They want to win it as much as anyone. It is that Clydeside workers are also having a war of their own and can't forget the enormous battles of the past 30 years or overcome the bitter memory of industrial insecurity in the past ten years and their distrust of the motives of managers and employers.'

The consultancy scrutineers were staggered at the amount of alcohol consumed by the workers. One of the observers was to report that, as an Englishman, it had seemed that a large proportion of the wages found its way 'down the stream of alcohol' and that one of the principal fascinations of their examination had been 'to watch workers steadily absorbing alternative draughts of beer and whisky'. Eureka! They had discovered the hauf 'n' a hauf.

One of the aspects they had been asked to look into was that of slacking. One of the survey managers said that as he couldn't believe the stories he had been hearing about the amount of work-dodging, he had taken a look at the problem himself. His experience, which he refers to as being 'astonishing', was as hilarious as the best scenes from *I'm All Right, Jack*.

'There must have been at least 100 men on board [the ship he was visiting] of whom no more than ten can really have been working. The author came upon a man lying in a bunk reading a newspaper and one group of ten men having a political discussion for 20 minutes. An electrician was leaning through a porthole smoking (which was prohibited) for minutes on end. Whenever a bowler hat [a manager] came round, there was a slight appearance of activity, but most of the men did not pretend to be doing much. It was the unavoidable feeling on board of casual work; there was no question of a determined drive to get the job done and the ship at sea. There was a vague feeling that people here didn't want to finish the job so much as go on working on it and having their chats and smoking while they were at it.'

However startling the management consultants' findings might have been, one of the most noteworthy parts of their report was their observation on the future for the Clyde yards, their comments being, 'There is a strong feeling that after the war, the scrapheap will be higher than ever. In our view this is one of the most important points for action in Glasgow morale.'

Presumably the costly report, like so many of their kind, was read, perhaps noted, filed and forgotten. There never was any action taken about morale on the Clyde. Employer–employee relations continued as they had done for the best part of a century, namely conducted in an atmosphere of distrust and mutual hostility. From the comfort of their mahogany-panelled boardrooms, each with its blazing coal fire, and other home-from-home comforts, the masters' view of the workers was that they were an easily disposable commodity, to whom they need be no more grateful than the shopkeeper who sold them their provisions. Much like the generals who thought in terms of the human fodder they sent over the top of wartime trenches, there were always plenty of replacements.

About the only boost the workforce could get for their morale, it seemed, was from the protection offered them by their trade unions, to whom they clung with universal solidarity. The union was friend and family, and was vital. It's zeal, as the great protector of its members, was boundless. Sadly, it could often be mindless, and sensationally so. Each craft had its specified job to do and woe betide anyone who infiltrated on their patch, regardless of whether he, like them, was a worker and a trade unionist. The strict rule for a century and a half had been one man, one job: it didn't seem to matter that with the Second World War now over, former enemies together with emerging countries were learning this shipbuilding game and that their men were capable of doing four, five or even more jobs. Nor did it seem to matter that these countries were now building ships cheaper, building them faster, building them better. No matter what, the demarcation rules were not for bending.

The practice was a hilarious three-ring circus, albeit as long as you weren't one of the performers. If, say, an electrician wanted to fit a cable to a bulkhead, it would have been a simple enough task, if he had the tools, to do the job on his own, as they were doing in foreign yards. But the demarcation rules made this operation a far more complicated one: first of all the electrician had to inform his foreman what he was about to do and request that he find a driller. The electrical foreman would then speak to the drillers' foreman and ask for one of his tradesmen. When one could be found he would then confer with the electrician and drill the required holes. The electrician would then go back to his foreman and tell him he now needed the drilled holes prepared for his fixtures which would require a caulker, the tradesman who ensured all joints and apertures were made watertight. To get this man the electrician's foreman would then repeat the same procedure, requesting the caulkers' foreman for a man, the electrician having another wait till he then showed up and performed his part in the operation. The entire industry was riddled with such farce. It was a work practice that had been acceptable for generations, but only because other countries hadn't perfected the art of building ships. But when they did . . .

The rot had well and truly set in by the '60s when the Germans, Italians and Japanese, together with a host of other countries, were making their own ships. It was perhaps easier for those who had been former enemies. Their yards had been mainly destroyed and starting from scratch again meant constructing workplaces that were compatible with the modern era in which they were now in.

Enormous hangar-like buildings were built so that workers could labour in more acceptable conditions, not a minute being lost with the weather. In Japan the top jobs in the yards were often held down by young people who had studied in yards overseas and, on graduating, returned home fired with enthusiasm on how modern ships really should be made, how new methods and innovations could speed up the process. Their speciality was in planning, working out in advance every single detail of how their ship would eventuate, from the way it performed, right down to such minutiae as the size and colour of the door knob on a cabin wardrobe. Time scales and costs were worked out with uncanny precision – and adhered to.

'Sweated labour', was the usual response from many in the trade here when the Japanese example was held up to them. And if wages were examined, it was true they were earning less. But they had a scale of benefits that put the Clyde men's conditions to shame, perks such as cheap travel, company medical care, low-cost housing, free meals, and a hot bath at the end of the day's shift.

When the boss of one Clyde yard made a study tour of some German yards he was flabbergasted at their work rate. At one yard on the Elbe which he visited they were sliding new tankers out to sea at a rate of one every three weeks. And not least of the reasons was the fact that the electrician didn't have to see his foreman to ask the other foreman to contact the driller to find his foreman to request the caulker to fix thoses damn holes in that blasted bulkhead.

By the '60s, Britain couldn't compete with the prices or delivery dates being offered by shipbuilders in Europe. Denmark, Sweden, France, Germany, Italy, Holland, Germany and Yugoslavia were all undercutting

British quotations. The proud nation that had been in the forefront of the industrial revolution couldn't come to terms with industrial evolution. Management and workforce played the same old two-way ball game of rules and attitudes that belonged to the nineteenth century. Denny's of Dumbarton had gone out of business. Fairfields of Govan also announced its closure, although in the end, with the aid of two industrialists and the Government, it was saved.

Excuses that many of the foreign yards were being heavily subsidised by their governments weren't good enough. Something had to be done. So we did what we had always done, and still do, when confronted with controversial problems in which the origins and solutions are patently obvious. We formed a committee. It was commissioned by the Government in 1965 under the chairmanship of J.M. Geddes – its remit, to inquire into the state of the shipbuilding industry. As anticipated, there were to be no surprises when the findings, the Geddes Report, was made known in March 1966. There was nothing new in the conclusions; the newspapers had been spelling it out for years. Only this time, it was official. It was official that ships from Japan were bigger and better, and being built more cheaply and more efficiently. It was official that it took, on average, 87 working hours for UK yards to build the equivalent of one ton of steel. It was official that on the Clyde it was taking them 110 hours to do the same job. And it was embarrassingly official that in Japan they were doing the operation in just 29 hours and that they could produce a ship with a third of the effort.

It was like a shipbuilding version of our premier sport when in those vital games in which we are a goal or so ahead, that rogue component in the national character manifests itself and we end up losing. Ask any football fan about that World Cup game against Peru! For years it had been Scotland 1, World 0 in the building of fine ships, but the tide was changing and the world was making a comeback.

Geddes recommended that the remaining Clyde yards be reformed into two groupings, the one at the Glasgow end of the river to be known as the Upper Clyde Shipbuilders, and comprising the shipyards of John Brown of Clydebank, Charles Connell of Scotstoun, Fairfields of Govan, Alex Stephen of Linthouse (closed in 1968) and Yarrows of Scotstoun. It was intended that the new company would carry the debts of the old yards as well as the costs of compensation to the owners. The Labour Government under Harold Wilson approved, and despite it being pointed out that there were too many workers and too many yards to make profitable ships, they bunged the new company £5,500,000 of taxpayers' money to get going and hoped for the best. It wasn't to come.

There was another handout of £3,000,000 in March 1969 and yet another in June of that year, this time £9,300,000.

Meanwhile, the rush to the undertakers continued with pay demands, strikes, late deliveries, outmoded and sometimes faulty ships, the ultimate ignominy being when, amidst all the problems at UCS, the shipping company Cunard rejected delivery of their new superliner, the QE2, from the John Brown yard for various faults. Then, when it eventually did sail to the Canaries on a shakedown cruise with Cunard employees, 250 workers from the Clyde had to go along to complete 80 unfinished cabins and fit out one of the huge state rooms. There were other problems, like doors without handles, showers without water, leaky pipes, and cabins with no air conditioning. And as if that wasn't bad enough, the engines broke down four days out of Southampton and the QE2 humiliatingly limped to the nearest port, Las Palmas. Don't even contemplate what might have happened had the cruise been across the Atlantic instead, and those wonky engines been called upon to dodge a stray iceberg! On board, 80 international journalists, who had all been invited by Cunard to spread the word about their beautiful new ship, were preparing to tell another kind of story . . . that they were on board the biggest lame duck afloat. Once there was a time when you wanted to shout from the rooftops that a vessel was Clyde-built. Now you felt you couldn't even whisper it.

Despite the shame of this and the Government's prop-up millions, shipyard managers continued to squabble with the workers, unions had barneys with other unions (when they weren't having it out with management who bickered with the Government), while the electricians still had to ask their foreman to ask the other foreman! The Laugh-in on the Clyde was happening long before the Work-in.

Tony Benn, the Labour Government's Minister of Technology at the time, appreciated more than anyone the value of UCS to the Labour Party. Its workers were the most loyal supporters of the party, its unions handsome backers. And if they couldn't be protected, then who could? When he visited Glasgow in March 1969, around the time when UCS was being given another dollop of taxpayers' money, he warned that the Government couldn't go on paying out (a few weeks later they stumped up another £9.3 million!) and that there would have to be some 'slimming' of the 13,000 workforce. No mention of redundancies, it should be noted. Just 'slimming'. Benn had also commented on the high level of absenteeism, said at the time to be 'around 14 per cent'.

That, in fact, was a conservative estimate, because the figures at one yard were that 15 per cent of the workers were more than a quarter of an hour late every day and absenteeism averaged 17 per cent . . . in other words, more than one in every six men employed was unavailable for work. In addition, some 8 per cent of all items delivered from outside contractors were rejects and had to be returned or rectified. And some weeks, the reject figure could be as high as 40 per cent. So much for that wartime report on slacking and morale. And so much for Benn's warning that they couldn't keep pouring out money to them for, by the end of that year, UCS were cap in hand again and in December were given a £7,000,000 loan.

The slimming process began and in the months following Benn's visit, 1,500 were trimmed from the payroll with the warning that the same number would be paid off by the following August. Then in March 1970, it was revealed that 3,000 would have to be discharged, twice the earlier estimate, and that 1,000 boilermakers would be among those coming under the axe. The powerful boilermakers' union immediately responded with a unanimous vote from its members that if just one of their number was faced with redundancy, then all of them would strike.

Three months later, despite being ejected from office, some members of the ex-Labour Government were to heave the mightiest sigh of relief. For them, the chaos on the Clyde with its losses, embarrassments and continual conflict was over. The verdict of the June 1970 general election meant that shipbuilding was someone else's problem and they couldn't have wished for anyone better to be landed with the migraine – the Conservatives.

It had already been rumbled by the Tories that if they were returned to power there would be some butchering on the Clyde and, sure enough, within months of their taking over, they were backing their words with swift action. UCS was holding out its hand once more, declaring that it needed £6,000,000 urgently just to stay in business. This time the money was refused and there was the immediate prospect of the company going into liquidation. Confidential papers alleged to have been written by Shipbuilding Minister Nicholas Ridley and leaked to the unions, revealed that UCS would be either liquidated or reconstructed and that the Government holding in the company would be sold off, for a pittance if necessary. One thing would be certain: there would be no further funds going to 'lame ducks', this time the expression referring to the shipyards, not the ship.

In June 1971, having limped from one crisis to another, UCS was about to be killed off, but the announcement by Trade Secretary John Davies had to be delayed. There were other problems – Northern Ireland. Because of widespread rioting, every available Army unit had been despatched there, and now the Government was faced with the prospect of civil unrest in Glasgow when the truth about UCS was to be revealed.

With no available troops to keep order, nothing was said until Thursday, 29 July 1971. On that day it was stated that UCS, minus Yarrows which had already left the group, was to be restructured. Future production would be at the Govan (Fairfields) and Linthouse (Stephen's) divisions, which would be State owned. Known as Govan Shipbuilding, it would be allowed £35,000,000 Government funds during its first five years. The shock part was the withdrawal of support to the remainder of UCS, namely the Clydebank (John Brown's) and Scotstoun (Connell's) divisions of the group which would go into immediate liquidation.

Davies had perhaps overlooked the full significance of his plan, the closure at Clydebank meaning that his Government would be committing the very act which Hitler had failed to carry out during the Second World War when it had been one of the main Scottish targets of his Luftwaffe bombers.

The unions' response was immediate and unanimous: they would fight to a man. But this time it wouldn't be by a conventional strike, which would have been pointless since getting the men out of the yards as soon as possible was precisely what the Government and the liquidator wanted in order to close them down. The shop stewards' action was to be much more dramatic than that. Instead of coming *out*, they would be staying *in*. They would take over the yards and they, not the bosses or the Government, would be in charge, and they would have a Work-in. They would count all who went in, all who went out; say who could enter and who could exit. UCS, they declared, now meant 'Unity Creates Strength'. How John Maclean and some of the old Red Clydesiders would have loved it! And it certainly was Red, all right, because the principal activists coming to light were fully paid-up members of the Communist Party, which was hardly surprising: Clydebank was a major centre of its strength since its foundation in 1920 and Scotland at one count had a quarter of the UK membership, until, of course, the truth was discovered about all the crimes committed on the other side of that Wall.

Communists or no, the reaction to the shop stewards' Work-in decision was nothing less than remarkable. It captivated the country, even the south of England. It was like some kind of revolution in the making. But not one of those terrible bloody affairs – no one even got hurt. This was a benign revolution, one without bullets, bombs or riots;

a revolution where rhetoric, not rifles, ruled. Two very charismatic characters, both of them Clydeside Jimmies, one called Airlie. the other Reid, were seen to be lecturing the comrades that there would be no shenanigans in their Work-in.

It was Reid who laid it on the line with a compelling speech that electrified the huge nationwide audience watching that day's TV news, a speech which is still repeated any time there's a playback on events of the early '70s or of workers' momentous struggles. A handsome figure of a man, almost Burnsian in appearance and certainly poetic in parlance, he addressed a mass meeting of the workers at John Brown's where he was to spell it out in those deliberate, almost theatrically emphatic tones which were to mark him as one of the great and natural orators of the day.

'The liquidator can do what he wants but we are not accepting redundancies and the Connell workers [John Brown's UCS partner yard] or anybody else involved, will be reporting for work as they should have been, that is, a week next Monday [they were on their annual holidays] and, if necessary, will line up in South Street [the main thoroughfare leading to the yards]. We will identify ourselves with them and we will march into this yard because, brothers, I want to make this point. Everybody talks about rights. There is a basic elementary right involved here. That is our right to work. We are not strikers. We are respected people and we will conduct ourselves with the dignity and discipline that we have all the time expressed over the last few weeks . . . And there will be no hooliganism . . . There will be no vandalism . . . There will be no bevvying . . . Because the world is watching us and it is our responsibility to conduct ourselves responsibly and with dignity and maturity.'

Everything and anything that happened in and around the Work-in was headline material. Not since the launch of the *Queen Mary* back in the '30s, or those German bombers which headed west, had the Clyde known such spotlight attention. Which was why Reid emphasised that the workers had to behave responsibly. As he was to explain later it was paramount to their cause. 'It was essential because the Work-in was like a goldfish bowl, the yards constantly full of journalists and television cameras.'

Everyone tried to crush in on the act, of course. Not least, but certainly the least likely, was Glasgow Corporation: within days of the Work-in announcement, the ruling Labour group at the City Chambers announced they were to discuss plans for a city take-over of UCS. 'Municipalisation is the only answer,' said one impassioned councillor. No doubt the Socialist stalwarts of George Square were sincere in their wishes for the UCS workers but as that particular suggestion had all the hallmarks of something from the Ministry of Daft Ideas – Politburo with a blend of Python – little more was heard of it. And Glasgow's beleaguered ratepayers gratefully returned to breathing normally.

Meanwhile, in Westminster, there was to be some more realistic talk. A debate on the situation was set for the following week, the former members of the Labour Government relishing the embarrassing prospect of Prime Minister Ted Heath's Government having to deal with the problem, yet without as much as an assuaging whisper to each other that had it not been for electoral fate the problem would have been theirs. It was one thing for a Tory Government to be taking on this novel kind of workers' insurrection in which Communist trade unionists figured so prominently, but for a Labour Government to have been confronted with such a situation! Perish the thought. Communists, despite the revelations about Stalin, were still respectable in 1971, and in a country as democratic as this they didn't have to be Reds under the bed, although many wished that's where they might have remained.

The Labour benches cheered wildly when Tony Benn, the former Technology Minister, opened the crucial debate for Labour and rounded on the Government. 'The Prime Minister's epitaph will be that he is the man who forgot the people . . . and the people will never forgive him for that.' Even louder cheers! Benn went on to say that the Government's decision would create a Clydeside disaster area. It would be worse even than the areas of highest unemployment in Northern Ireland. He did add, however, that he accepted full responsibility for the Labour Government's policy before, during and after the establishment of UCS.

The Work-in continued to captivate the public who supported it as in no other labour dispute in living memory. All sorts of fund-raising functions were organised, one of the big events being a show at the King's Theatre featuring stars of the day such as Roddy McMillan, Jim Craig and the Islanders, Iain Sutherland conducting the BBC Radio Orchestra and an act which brought the house down, composed of four former shipyard workers who had gone on to other things . . . Johnny Beattie, Glen Daly, and actors Russell Hunter and Archie Duncan. Money poured into the shop stewards' fighting fund which would help pay the wages of the men participating in the occupation of the yards. It came from all quarters – churches, pensioners, even Conservative Women's Associations, the General Workers' Union in Ireland, miners in South Wales, Soviet shipyard workers and, because exchange regulations prevented them donating money, East Germans offered a free three-week holiday to 100 workers, gratefully accepted despite the dubiousness of that particular delight. At one of their regular meetings, a beautiful bouquet of red roses was delivered together with a cheque for £500 (or £1,000 depending on which paper you read), the donor signing himself as simply 'Lennon'. In the local patois, the pronunciation of that name confused someone into thinking the money had come from the ghost of Vladimir Ilyich and not simply John.

In all, more than a quarter of a million pounds was received, a staggering sum in the early '70s, the equivalent in the late '90s of more than £1,300,000. Several protest marches were organised, one of which was on Wednesday, 18 August, and was the biggest-ever demonstration of its kind in the city. It was a brilliant summer's day and the enormous turnout staggered the organisers: more than 100,000 had left work for the day in support (more exuberant reports quoted more than double that figure). They walked from George Square to Glasgow Green: their destination was appropriate because it was Scotland's most historical parkland, the area where huge Chartist demonstrations had taken place in the 1830s and where John Maclean endeavoured to proclaim a Scottish Republic. And now the Work-in was the highlight.

So vast were the crowds, that those at the head of the march – 13 abreast across the road, arms linked in unity – were to arrive at the Green before the tailenders had left the city centre. Leading them were some of the people who had figured prominently in the fight for the Clyde men, the MPs Tony Benn and Willie Ross, Reid and Airlie among the savvy of shop stewards, together with the power brokers of the mightiest unions – names like Vic Feather, Dan McGarvey, Hugh Scanlon and others, the *capi di tutti capi* in this most vital of labour struggles.

They travelled from all over Scotland and from the North of England to be there, to be part of it and show their solidarity in having none of the Tories' industrial devastation on the Clyde. A party of 400 retired boilermakers, due to be spending a day out at Largs, turned their buses round to join the demonstrators. A feast of Nardini knickerbocker glories could be no substitute for this special day. Banners were flying proclaiming 'Save Our Yards', 'No Closures', and 'UCS Forever, Liquidation Never', and the rousing music of the Polkemmet Miners' Band put a stir into their step. It was a real Hollywood spectacular.

Jimmy Reid, having already established himself as one of the most compelling orators, full of passionate beliefs for the worker, but without the spite, bitterness and acrimony of some of his soapbox comrades, was again a top draw man. 'To-day the Clydeside speaks,' he said, his assertive and now familiar delivery having become the hallmark voice of the Work-in. 'To-day Scotland speaks. Not the Scotland of Edward

Heath or Gordon Campbell [the Scottish Secretary] or Sir Alec Douglas-Home. They have never represented Scotland. This eruption will sweep Heath and his colleagues into political oblivion. We are going to fight them to change their policies or we will change the Government.'

The others came up with all the appropriate words for the occasion, Benn saying that in all his political career he had never seen a demonstration like the one in which he was participating that day – he then returned to London and received what he termed as 'a roasting' from his leader, Harold Wilson, who belatedly expressed support for the Work-in, 'provided it stayed within the law'.

Jimmy Airlie said the demonstration had an atmosphere which he had never experienced before . . . 'an expression of the Scottish people, a sense that the decline of Scotland's manufacturing base and its industrial heritage must stop. There was a feeling that the Scottish people were once again on the move to claim what was theirs.' Stirring stuff, even though one might have been left in doubt as to what, exactly, it was the Scottish people had to claim.

During the ensuing weeks, many of the UCS men accepted redundancy terms and left the yards, some doubtlessly persuaded by the temptation of advertisements for platers and welders to work in Australian shipyards, with the enticements of cheap passages, wages at double the current basic rate on the Clyde, less tax and unlimited sunshine. But the unique Work-in held firm, albeit as more of a spectacular gesture of worker solidarity than in actual participants. One head count put the highest number at 390, which had dwindled to 161 by June 1972 – their wages paid from the shop stewards' fighting fund.

'We have told the Government that if they want us out of the yards then let the Prime Minister and Davies come and try to do it. We don't only build boats on the Clyde,' said a defiant Reid. 'We build men.' Which was pure Irn Bru-speak, but then that's something they wouldn't have understood around Westminster.

Early in the crisis, when the shop stewards demanded a meeting with Prime Minister Heath, the request was immediately granted, No 10 informing them that he had scheduled half an hour to listen to their grievances. After speaking for nearly two hours, Reid mentioned that something to quench their thirst would be appreciated, whereupon the contents of an expensive drinks' cabinet was thrown open to them containing some of the finest malt whiskies, much relished by more than Reid among the delegation. But when each was asked his preference, the reply was simply . . . water! Heath was so taken with the men's principles and steadfastness that he whispered the incident to a press aide and it was one of the first questions to be brought up at the Westminster Hall press conference following the meeting.

As the weeks of the Work-in turned into months, the summer into autumn, autumn into winter, winter into spring, the men remained unyielding as promises of buy-outs developed, some of them dissipating while others disappeared as suddenly as they had appeared, such as that whimsical 'municipalisation' proposal of Glasgow Corporation. It was the unions themselves, however, who were to find a solution. Dan McGarvey, president of the powerful boilermakers' union, and Jack Service, general secretary of the Confederation of Shipbuilding and Engineering Unions, had gone to Houston, Texas, to speak to companies there, among them one called Marathon Manufacturing, builders of more than 60 per cent of the world's offshore oil production and drilling rigs. Having a yard at Clydebank seemed a good idea for one of their production centres, being handy for the huge amount of development work taking place in the North Sea, and Wayne Harbin, the Marathon accountant, arranged talks with the British Government for a deal in taking over the John Brown yard where they would build jack-up oil-rigs.

Impressed at the skill and dedication of the craftsmen there, Harbin was shocked at the outdated and neglected state of the yard with its sparse signs of maintenance. It was a prime example of the obsolescence brought about on the Clyde by managerial dynasties, apparently suicidally conservative in all aspects of modern shipbuilding. Undaunted, however, the American persevered in his negotiations with the Government to get some kind of deal, although he was soon to discover that if managements had been suicidally conservative, the workers and their unions could be suicidally bloody-minded. As Harbin went about the long and slow process of bargaining with Ministry civil servants, union supremos McGarvey and Service were tough-talking it out, or as was said at the time 'bullying and threatening', with defiant shop stewards to get them to come into line with the kind of deal they had in mind.

Harbin was to spend frustrating months in his negotiations, finding British attitudes as antiquarian as their shipyards. Although coming to an agreement with the Government in April 1972, over cash aid for the yards, an agreement which the papers reported had the workers cheering victory, there were to be many months ahead of further tedious negotiations to try and bind the deal. There were problems with the management, the unions, the civil servants and the shop stewards and the baffled Texan demanded: 'How come, after two and a half months of us submitting our proposals, you still haven't come to a deal?' Things like that didn't happen in America. They did in Britain where it was one thing buying a shipyard, another trying to buy attitudes.

The Work-in was by now 15 months old and the talks on the details of the Marathon deal had been going on through the spring and summer of 1972. The circumventions, baulkings, and negativeness with which he was confronted in his talks were eventually becoming too much for the man from Marathon. The ethic of his normal workplace, to which he was accustomed, was that problems meant solutions – here it seemed solutions meant problems.

At one point he snapped, turned on the shop stewards and called them 'a bunch of Commies', threatening that it still wasn't too late to call off the deal. That, apparently, was too much for some of the men's sensitivities so he later withdrew the Commie bit, irrespective of any accuracy it may have had, but made sure the quit bit of the threat stayed. He put it in oilman's language: 'When you drill for oil, you expect to find it at 10,000 feet. If it's not there, you don't keep drilling till you get to China. You pull out.'

By this time Marathon had already paid £1,125,000 to the liquidator for the yard, aiming to pull it apart and rebuild it from scratch at a cost of £12,000,000. At the same time, they couldn't avoid the thought that it might be cheaper, and certainly less problematic, if they made their North Sea rigs in established Marathon yards, such as in Tennessee, or even Singapore. But they hung around for a little while longer. After all there was a good deal for them on the table . . . more than £35 million of Government aid and a series of cash incentives, the most lucrative of them being 30 per cent of the wage bill for the first three years of their ownership at Clydebank.

Come the autumn, however, there was still no final settlement, with the shop stewards demanding total victory in their fight and unwilling to concede any form of compromise, particularly one which would entail redundancies. But by now even the men were becoming disenchanted as inter-union rifts widened and shop steward rivalry became more embittered. For all the glorious talk, the splendid solidarity was frittering away in the face of the byzantine ways of British industry in the 1970s. Finally, the *Daily Record*, the staunchest of Labour supporters and who had wholeheartedly backed the workers during the long months of their Work-in, was now firing broadsides across the union men's bows, castigating them on the eve of a final showdown meeting with a sensational special issue on Thursday, 5 October 1972, the page one headline reading 'The Marathon Malarkey', and pleading, 'Brothers, let's have some sanity – Scotland is sick of your brinkmanship. It's time the Clyde settled down to the job of building ships and oil-rigs.'

Whether that blast had any effect or not (and it probably didn't), a deal was reached that weekend. Guarantees had been given by Marathon and the liquidator to absorb 'almost' all of the labour force. 'This is not just a victory for the shipyard workers,' said Jimmy Reid, 'it's a victory for the Scottish community.'

Victory? Well, that was the way it was seen then. But time was to judge differently. Four years later Marathon suspended 1,000 men at the Clydebank yard and by 1977 the workforce was down to a mere 500. Finding their Scottish rig-making experience just marginally profitable, the Americans only stayed for eight years, selling out to another foreign-owned rig construction company, UIE of France. There had been 7,000 employees at UCS alone, just before the Work-in. By the late 1990s the workforce at UIE and the two remaining shipbuilding yards in the Upper Clyde – the Norwegian-owned Kvaerner's and Yarrows – was around 4,400. By the late '90s there were more than four times that number working in the catering trade in the city. McDonald's, Burger King and Brewers Fayre were having as much relevance in the workplace as building ships. Victory?

More than 35,000 vessels were built during the hectic and active lifetime on the Clyde, which was the most prolific shipbuilding river in the world. Many magnificent, forward-thinking and hard-working men contributed to making it one of Scotland's greatest-ever achievements. The debate may continue as to why the shipyards are virtually no more and who was ultimately responsible. Perhaps it may even be considered that a pernicious, self-destructive factor was involved. Victory?

The silent song of the once great symphony on the Clyde has much to say about that.

11

THE GLASGOW OUTRAGE

༄

It was as though a film director had given the command for 'action' in the most exciting scene of some gangsterland movie. You know, the big gunfight that everyone has been waiting for, the showdown for the baddies and the goodies. Well, in this particular scene, the 'baddies' were the men who had come running as if from nowhere, their guns blazing; and the 'goodies' were the brave policemen firing back at them, before falling either dead or wounded. But this dramatic scenario being played out on our streets was no movie. This was for real. Those blazing guns were firing authentic bullets and the men falling to the ground really were dead or badly injured – and it all happened right here in the very centre of Glasgow.

Glasgow, fortunately, escaped the wrath of the IRA terror campaign with its various atrocities against mainland Britain which began in the late '60s. For whatever reason – backlash, perhaps – Scotland's major city has never experienced the wanton horrors unleashed on places like Birmingham, London, Manchester, Warrington and others. But it hasn't always been the case for, in the past, Glasgow has had its fair share of havoc.

Bombing and creating mayhem and terror have been a traditional form of Irish nationalist warfare against mainland Britain for more than a century and Scotland was involved in their early campaigns. A hundred years before the present troubles which began in the late '60s, the forefathers of today's IRA sent men to Glasgow to murder and bomb. It was in the early days of the Fenians, a word more often used today as a derogatory term for Irishmen, supplemented, more often as not, with a choice of obscenity. But to active nationalists, the name that derives from Fiann, an early Irish folk hero, or Fianna, his legendary band of warrior heroes, there is nothing derogatory about Fenians. And it was the Fenian movement of the mid-nineteenth century from which today's Irish Republican Army is the direct descendant.

Around the middle of the last century, a movement known as the Irish Republican Brotherhood had begun simultaneously in Dublin and in New York, more than 200,000 of its founding members, all known as Fenians, having fought in the American Civil War. Their leaders hoped they could form an Irish army strong enough to combat the British on Irish soil. In 1867 there had been an attempted insurrection in Ireland and also a planned raid on the arms arsenal at Chester Castle in England, but British intelligence had been a step ahead. The insurrection was thwarted and the raid at Chester postponed because an informer had leaked their plans.

Not many months later, on 11 September 1867, one of these Irish-American veterans together with another man were arrested in Manchester and identified as activists. A week after their arrest about 30 Fenians ambushed the police van carrying them to prison, shooting a police sergeant dead and freeing the prisoners. That event on the streets of Manchester was to be spectacularly re-enacted with an almost uncanny and tragic similarity 54 years later. But this time it was to be on the streets of Glasgow and was to be one of the most sensational shoot-outs ever witnessed on a British street.

Glasgow was to experience intermittent incidents involving the Fenian movement in the years following the Chester Castle raid and the Manchester police van rescue. In 1883, bombing attempts were made by these forerunners of today's IRA on the Tradeston Gasworks, the Buchanan Street Goods Station and Ruchill Canal Bridge. Two gasometers at Dawsholm were also bombed in 1890. As always when terrorists attack such random targets, it was the innocents who were to suffer. Thirty civilians died at Clerkenwell in London after their houses, adjacent to a prison, were blown up in a botched rescue raid, and there were many casualties, too, in the Glasgow bombings a few years later. The revulsion held for the Fenians was not to deter them and they were back in Glasgow again in 1921.

Their target this time was the telegraph poles at Darnley carrying the main communications link between Glasgow and Ireland. Mercifully there were no casualties in this new venture – but the same was not true of the dramatic event which occurred right in the heart of the city that same year. It was to be one of the most spectacular attacks ever carried out on the mainland by Republicans, then usually referred to as Sinn Feiners. It was just before 12.30 p.m. on a beautiful spring day in 1921 when one of the dark police vans used for transporting prisoners, or a Black Maria as they were known then, slowly drove up High Street from Glasgow Cross towards Drygate, the little street used at the time to enter the old Duke Street Prison. The old prison, now a pleasant housing estate, was bounded by Drygate, Duke Street and John Knox Street, and is one of the oldest and most historic parts of the city: in fact, as it made its way up the steepest part of High Street, known in ancient times as the Bell o' the Brae, the police van was virtually on the site of the legendary battle of that name which occurred near the end of the thirteenth century. At the summit of the hill around that time, an English garrison had been stationed in the Bishop's Castle, strategically sited so that it dominated the established part of Glasgow. It was on the very spot now occupied by the Royal Infirmary. Sir William Wallace had been harrying such outposts throughout the country and the Bishop's Castle was next on his list. Braveheart and his brave men made a direct assault on the castle and the English sent out a formidable force to repel them. Wallace and his men made a tactical retreat down High Street before turning to face their pursuers. Just at that moment other Scottish warriors led by Auchinleck, Wallace's uncle, came up the Drygate, and completed a pincer movement on the English who thereupon turned and fled.

Now, in the twentieth century, transporting prisoners in the sombre Black Marias was a regular part of daily police routine at the time. There was always a morning run after the various court hearings, in several local police courts that were scattered all over the city, such as Maryhill, Partick, Bridgeton, Crosshill as well as the main Central Police Court in St Andrew's Square. Male offenders who had received sentences would be taken directly to Barlinnie Prison, in Riddrie, and women to the Duke Street prison. However, there was also a remand wing for males at Duke Street and it was there that the police van was heading with two men who had appeared in court that morning. And it was one of these passengers that was to make this Black Maria's assignment no ordinary journey.

Just like today, police escorts on such runs are not normally armed, if the detainees are ordinary prisoners, that is. But that day this rather special delivery trip to Duke Street required sidearms to be carried because on board was one man who was no ordinary prisoner. He was a man the authorities warranted would most definitely require an armed escort. He was an IRA man called Frank J. Carty, also known as Somers, who had been recognised in Glasgow as being a wanted man – among the things he was being hunted for by Irish police were jailbreaking and the theft of a revolver. But there was a lot more to Frank J. Carty than that, for just as he was no ordinary prisoner, he proved to be no ordinary IRA man either.

Carty was wanted on two counts of jailbreaking, first in Sligo in 1920, where he had also stolen a revolver, and from Derry Prison, from which he had escaped just three months before his arrest in Glasgow. On the run, he had fled to Glasgow where there was no shortage of safe houses on offer from many fellow countrymen and sympathisers living in the city. Special Branch officers on the lookout for such men had arrested him on Friday, 29 April 1921, and he was making an appearance before the magistrate at the Central Police Court on the following Wednesday morning. There was a simple remand request from the procurator-fiscal, the magistrate granting that he be held in custody at Duke Street until such time as an escort with warrants arrived from Dublin.

Three police officers were allocated for escort duty in the van which would take him the short journey from the court, just by Glasgow Cross, up the Bell o' the Brae, to the Duke Street Prison. Police intelligence further reinforced the need for arms on the receipt of word after Carty's arrest that there could be the likelihood of a rescue attempt organised by friends who had fled with him from Ireland. Men, they were warned, who were experienced in armed struggle and would stop at nothing to free their comrade, hence the requirement of those sidearms carried by the escorting officers.

Redevelopment has considerably altered that part of old Glasgow, where the prison has now been replaced by houses, but at that time part of the narrow Drygate, the section that led up to the prison doors, had an almost gully-like appearance. On one side there were the high prison walls, made of a drab-coloured stone, and on the other side a water-pumping station. Knowing he would be held in the prison there, Carty's friends had made several reconnaissances of the short route, and what they observed at that particular part of the Drygate had brought broad smiles of satisfaction: for that narrow canyon of buildings was a tailor-made ambush site. The police would have no chance against what they had in store for them and their man Carty would be easily freed. That, at least, was the plan.

High Street was crowded with its customary Wednesday midday shoppers as the police van slowly drove up towards the Drygate, passing long lines of heavy horses hauling loaded goods, carts coming and going from the bustling railway goods yard (which for 400 years had been one of the first sites of Glasgow University). It had only been a brief four minutes since they had left the court and there were only about that number of minutes left before they would be going along Drygate and up to the prison doors.

There was a total of eight men inside the vehicle, which contained separate, single-man cells in the rear for prisoners. Carty, aged 32 and stoutly built, was in one cell, while the other prisoner, a man on an indecent assault charge, was in another, and each was accompanied by a police officer. In the front were the remainder of the van's occupants, the driver and three escorting armed policemen: the officer in charge, Inspector Robert Johnston from Shettleston, Detective Sergeant George Stirton, who lived in Petershill Road, Springburn, and a Detective Constable Murdoch Macdonald.

Just yards past the historic spot where Wallace had so valiantly battled, the driver double-clutched the crash gearbox of the van putting it into first gear as he slowly turned into the Drygate. The prison gates were in sight now and the police van was just passing that point in the old prison's walls on the other side of which executions were regularly carried out. It was also the narrowest section of the street which the attackers had chosen for their carefully planned and well-rehearsed trap. One minute the little narrow street had been quiet and virtually deserted; the next, groups of men appeared and with frightening speed and menace, instantly made known their intentions, a hail of bullets coming from the weapons they flourished.

There were three groups of them, ten men in all, among them Sean Adair. He, too, was on the run from Irish police and like Carty a member of the Sligo Brigade of the IRA. Adair was, in fact, their Quartermaster, the Republican Army's term for the provider of guns, bombs, ammunition and other weaponry. All of them were madly firing hand-guns, their bullets flying everywhere, one hitting the van's windscreen, another smashing into the engine, which erupted in an explosion of steam, others 'pinging' as they ricocheted wildly off the side of the van and the high stone walls on either side of the street.

Officer in charge, Robert Johnston, was the first to be hit, falling in a pool of blood on the cobbled street in front of the van, a bullet having sliced off part of his head, another going through his heart. Detective Sergeant George Stirton, gun in hand, leapt from the vehicle to defend his dying colleague, pumping round after round at the attackers as he stood over him.

It was like World War I all over again for him, for the detective had seen considerable action as a sergeant-major in the Tank Corps and subsequently received two of the highest bravery honours, and been mentioned twice in despatches. Eye-witnesses lavished praise on him for the plucky way he stood, legs astride over his mortally wounded senior officer, ready to defend him to the last. Detective Constable Murdoch Macdonald then leapt from the van, shooting as many bullets as he could at what seemed like a small army of assailants.

Despite their valiant stand, however, they couldn't beat off the men trying to unlock the bolted rear door of the van to free Carty. The gang had got round to the rear of the vehicle and their shouts and curses filled the air as they fiercely struggled with the van's heavy door. They attempted to lever it but the stout lock held. Then they tried shooting it off but still the lock remained secure while the gun battle continued to rage between their comrades and the two beleaguered policemen. Sergeant Stirton was next to be hit, a bullet smashing into his wrist while firing his gun. Then another bullet slammed into his arm. Despite these injuries, from which he was bleeding profusely, he courageously continued to guard his commander on the ambushed escort mission.

Still the attack continued, more bullets criss-crossing the narrow road and even more desperate attempts being made on that lockfast van door. As the shooting continued, the driver of the vehicle, a Constable Ross, who had ducked behind the dashboard when the first hail of shots had smashed the window, was able to get the vehicle started again and slowly drove the remaining few yards to the prison gates. Just at that point, one of the ambush party made a last frantic bid to blast open the rear door of the van and one of his shots this time released the lock and the door swung open. It was only then that he must have realised that the prisoners inside were each in separate and locked cells and that even with the main door open, there was no further chance of rescuing the incarcerated Carty.

Out of frustration, he pumped some more shots inside the rear of the vehicle then turned to join the other attackers who by now had unanimously accepted capitulation in the recognition their bid was hopeless. There was an imperceptible nod of acknowledgement between them and, as suddenly as they appeared, all ten of the attacking Irishmen made off, some running towards Rotten Row, others towards Cathedral Square, melting into the morning crowds heading for the busy shopping areas of Cathedral Street, Castle Street, George Street and High Street.

Most shoppers were unaware of the amazing events that had just taken place so close by – only those few pedestrians at the nearest point in High Street witnessed the amazing battle.

It wasn't till some hours later that Glaswegians were to be horrified when the three evening papers, the *Times*, *News* and *Citizen* splashed news of the sensation, some calling it 'The Glasgow Outrage', others 'The Glasgow Atrocity'. The description of what had so dramatically occurred was given in full, under such subheadings as 'Grim Fight under Shadow of Gallows'.

Startled eye-witnesses gave accounts to reporters. 'Everyone seemed to be thunderstruck at first,' said one woman. 'We all stood still at the start but once we realised what was happening, everyone scattered. I saw the blood dripping from the policeman [Stirton] who was guarding the other one who had been shot. And the van itself had bullets everywhere on it.'

A man told the *Record* reporter, 'They were all young men and I could see quite clearly that each had a revolver in his hand. They were dressed in mufflers and tweed caps and were shouting at each other excitedly as they ran off. One of them had bright ginger hair. They were running fast as they headed for Castle Street, putting their revolvers away as they did so and then once into Castle Street they reduced their pace to a quick walk. The last I saw of them was them disappearing into the crowds of shoppers.'

These were most fractious times at home and in many parts of the world. In Europe, still reeling from the Great War, there were problems in Poland and Silesia. Workers were unhappy throughout Britain and in Glasgow there were strikes in the docks and on the tramcars. Crews of ships, gas supply workers and railwaymen were all on strike, and on the day of the rescue bid, it was the 37th day of a miners' strike.

Ireland was enduring some of her bloodiest days. The Anglo-Irish Treaty was still unsigned (that didn't happen till seven months later) and there were daily battles between Republicans and the new reinforcements from England brought over to bolster the Royal Irish Constabulary, the RIC. They were mainly former soldiers and because of the odd mix of uniforms with which they were issued, they became known as the Black and Tans, one of the most detested forces of military police Ireland has known.

The country was in turmoil, and ambushes, murders and bombings were the order of the day. Specific Republican targets were those Black and Tan officers, some of their homes in England being bombed and fired by comrades stationed on the mainland. On the very day of the

Glasgow High Street attack, there had been a spectacular and deadly ambush of a nine-man RIC patrol in County Kerry. Only one of the officers survived. The same week, at Drumreilly, County Leitrim, John Harrison, described as a 'loyal Protestant farmer', and the father of 12 young children, was taken from his home and shot dead by IRA volunteers and his body thereafter, as the newspapers described it, 'chopped with an axe'. When the doctor saw the corpse, it was in such a state that he promptly fainted. And in Dublin a bomb missed its target and 14 pedestrians were injured.

Relations between Glasgow's two main communities were much more terse and troubled then. Many remembered the riots over the new arrivals from Ireland not many years before in various parts of Lanarkshire, Renfrewshire and Glasgow.

Although immigration by now was considerably less, in fact just a steady trickle, there was still friction on several counts, well to the forefront being that of the oldest of resentments for the immigrant, no matter their country of origin, that they would take work away from the native community. There had been considerable exception, too, over the recent 1918 Education Act which was to give Catholic children their own state schools, and even at the Assembly of the Church of Scotland they had openly spoken of 'the menace of Romanism'.

Support for the IRA from the Irish/Catholic community in Glasgow was a lot less tacit than it was to be in later years. In those days, the IRA to the Irish were universally 'the bhoys'. They were out fighting for the kind of freedom their nationalism wanted and at that time, despite the axing of that poor Protestant farmer in County Leitrim, their warfare hadn't degenerated into blowing up wee schoolboys in Warrington or pubs full of innocents in Birmingham or the other deeds that later generations were to perpetrate.

The attitudes of extremists from both camps in the city were in a permanent state of a barney waiting to happen. Turn the pressure by the tiniest of fractions and that barney really did happen. And the 'Glasgow Outrage' of that day in May was like turning up that pressure to full blast.

The series of riots that were to break out on that Wednesday evening were a predictable ingredient of the day's agenda. Sectarian gangs clashed in the East End and posses of police out hunting the attackers were themselves attacked by Irish sympathisers in various parts of the city. At one time a crowd of more than 2,000 were milling around in Gallowgate where a tramcar was stoned and immobilised. Much of the trouble centred on Abercrombie Street, dividing Calton from Bridgeton, and where seven men, including a priest from the St Mary's Presbytery House, were arrested after a cellar there had produced a huge and deadly haul of guns, hand grenades, gelignite, bomb equipment and ammunition.

The Abercrombie Street incident had been particularly nasty, tempers exceptionally roused because the police had gone into St Mary's Catholic Church during benediction and had arrested the priests from their confessional boxes. Coppers in a Glasgow East End chapel on such a mission! Sinn Fein trying to join in an Orange Walk is a rough equation of the welcome on hand. It was also noted that one of the raiding party of police was a Roman Catholic who was subjected to particular abuse, words like 'Spy' and 'Traitor', accompanied by the usual unprintables, being hurled at him.

They had initially detained two of the priests, but had allowed one of them, a Fr. Fitzgerald, to go free and he helped considerably to calm the crowd there. However, the situation became so ugly later in the evening, that the police had to request help from the military after 46 suspects, including some of the rioters, as well as the priest, a Fr. Patrick McRory, were detained at the Central Police Station. Such was the authority's fear of further serious trouble, that armed troops had to be put on guard at the station to defend it from any assault.

The newspapers were obviously full of the story the next morning, one of them headlining the riots in the quaint reporting style of the day with the words . . . 'East End Hullabaloo', then describing what had gone on as . . . 'Much excitement prevailed the previous night'.

Some hullabaloo! Some excitement!

Of those arrested overnight, 32 appeared at the Central Police Court the next morning, 20 of them charged as participants in the attack. Six of those were women. After the names of each of the accused listed in the evening papers, was either the initial 'I', meaning that they were Irish (of which there were 15), or 'G', indicating that the remaining five came from Glasgow.

'The prisoners were all responsibly dressed,' noted the *Evening Citizen* reporter, somewhat condescendingly, 'most of them wearing overcoats [was that the responsible bit?] and some with soft collars. The priest was in ministerial garb and one of the women was in mourning.'

The arrest of the young priest, Fr. McRory, had especially incensed his community, instigating a variety of rumours, one of which was that three priests had been taken away that night by police. That one of their very own church officials should be apprehended as he was and taken away was to have a profound affect on the local community. There were all-night vigils of prayer for the imprisoned priest's release, a young and very popular man in the parish, and feelings continued to run high in that predominantly Catholic-Irish part of the East End.

It was to be in the third week of July, some 11 weeks later, before St Mary's were to get the first word of Fr. McRory's imminent release – it was considered by the authorities that there was not sufficient evidence to proceed with charges against him and a number of the others.

There had been rumours late on the Thursday that there may be some good news the following day, on Friday, 22 July, and crowds began milling around St Mary's just after dawn in the hope of hearing something. Early in the afternoon, Fr. Fitzgerald, the priest who had initially been arrested with McRory, appeared at a window of the Presbytery to give them news for which the crowd had been longing. The din outside in the street was such that he had to appeal for order before telling them: 'I have just been telephoned by the Governor of Duke Street Prison to say that Father McRory is being released.' There was an enormous cheer in response from the crowd and the word flashed round the district of the impending homecoming of the popular young cleric. With the prison only about half a mile away, hundreds immediately began marching there to give the 18 detainees, including the priest, their first welcome to freedom.

Meanwhile, Abercrombie Street and all the surrounding streets got ready for Fr. McRory's return and what was to be the biggest day of celebrations in that part of Glasgow (until, of course, that other great day in May 1967, when Celtic became the first British team to win the European Cup). Hundreds of children, all in green, appeared as if from nowhere. A huge 'Cead Mille Failthe' (a hundred thousand welcomes) banner was unfurled and raised, its ends attached to the windows of houses on opposite sides of the street. Flags and bunting were everywhere – even the chapel house was sheathed in them, and houses which had neither flags nor bunting made do by draping their husband's Hibernian sash from the kitchen window. The Ancient Order of Hibernian pipe band quickly assembled and warmed up. They were determined that this really was going to be a great day for the Irish.

In honour of the event, the Catholic newspapers devoted the kind of coverage reserved for the most outstanding of occasions, outstandingly great occasions, that is. Just like that street banner, the *Catholic Observer* also resorted to the vernacular Cead Mille Failthe as their main headline and together with the *Catholic Herald*, their enthusiastic writers became quite lyrical in their descriptions of the day's celebrations, all the more so as their reports read on.

'The all-night vigils of prayers for the release of Father McRory have borne fruit,' said the *Catholic Herald*'s man, noting that 'in the far-flung net of their inquiries, the authorities thought fit to detain Fr McRory . . . on what grounds, goodness only knows. The news seemed to have spread far and wide and Calton joyfully set itself the task of preparing a suitable welcome for its Soggarth Aroon.'

Soggarth Aroon! Now there's an expression! It goes way back to verses of the same name by the early nineteenth-century poet John Banim, and is an Anglified version of the Irish Gaelic 'sagart a rùn', which simply means 'my dear priest'.

So caught up were they with the elation of the day on the return of their very own Soggarth Aroon, that poetry seemed the most appropriate way of expressing their feelings. And so the *Herald* report went on:

> Unroll Erin's flag, fling its folds to the breeze,
>
> Let it wave over the land, let it float over the seas.

Which it most certainly did, in such abundance that the *Catholic Herald*'s description of the area was that 'the green, white and gold of Ireland simply obliterated Abercrombie Street and the adjacent network of thoroughfares and it was through an avenue of Sinn Fein flags that one approached St Mary's Presbytery around which had congregated thousands of Irish people, almost frantic with joyous exuberance at the prospect of welcoming their beloved priest back among his friends once more'.

Being a newspaper of the devout, the report was also interspersed with some befitting pious lines, such as . . . 'Homeless in their hour of pain, Mary bring him home again. Our Lady had not failed her suppliants.'

By the time the open car carrying the newly released priest reached Abercrombie Street, the crowds were so dense the car was halted and a group of other priests, some waving Sinn Fein flags, raised their hero on their shoulders and carried him into the Presbytery. At that point, the crowd accorded the radiantly smiling priest their favourite anthems, 'God Save Ireland' and 'A Soldier's Song'.

And for one young Catholic baby girl being christened that following Sunday morning, there was a special treat. She was given the middle name of McRory in honour of their local hero.

Meanwhile, three months after their thwarted bid to release Frank Carty, who was now said to have been the commander of the Sligo

Brigade of the IRA, 13 accused pled not guilty at the High Court in Edinburgh to a list of serious charges, including that of killing the police inspector and conspiracy.

Defence counsel produced alibis and questioned police methods of identification in such a manner that no one was ever convicted of the attack.

The High Street ambush on the police van carrying Carty had all been in vain and the death of the police officer another terrible waste of life. Three days after the incident, the IRA man was returned to Ireland without further trouble.

Back home, however, Carty was not to be out of the news for long. Following the Treaty with the British in which the latter agreed to quit all of Ireland, except for the the six counties of the North, a smouldering and bloody civil war burst into flames in June 1922. Carty by then had been released from prison and was to be found in the thick of it all. One well-documented skirmish in which he was involved was to have a striking similarity, albeit with a bizarre twist, to the one which had taken place in Glasgow the previous year. It occurred at a place called Dooney Rock, not far from Sligo. An armoured car of the Government forces had been patrolling in the area when it was halted at a road block. As soon as the vehicle stopped, groups of men appeared and it was ambushed. Two Government men were killed in the first volley of shots and there were to be other casualties in the fierce battle which ensued.

Eventually the ambushers, with better luck than they had in Glasgow, were victorious and the armoured car was theirs. Their leader was none other than Frank Carty. Among the men on the opposing side who were killed was one Sean Adair, IRA Quartermaster and the man who figured in the attempted release of Carty in Glasgow.

Two years later, Fr. McRory, the arrested priest and the endeared Soggarth Aroon of the people, was to die, sadly, from a ruptured appendix.

12

THE REBEL JOHN MACLEAN

≈≋≈

'The most radical elements of the contemporary British Labour Movement are mostly of [the] Scotch or Irish race.'

Leon Trotsky, 1925

In the case of the Scotch race to which the legendary Russian revolutionary referred, there's no doubting the existence of a rare quality in that unique and rather marvellous miscellany of Homo sapiens which occupies Central Scotland . . . a glorious ragout of Pict, Viking, ancient Scot, Anglo-Saxon, Highland and Island Gael, Irish of various sorts, blended over the centuries with some exotic flavourings such as the Jew, the Italian, and a touch of the Baltic and the Slav. It's a heady racial cocktail and has produced that special brilliance witnessed in those who lead, who challenge, who explore, who stand up to be counted. Splendid parliamentarians, leaders of trade unions, the best managers of the best football clubs – just think of that breed alone! – and those who are willing to fight, defending their views in doing so, regardless of the consequences, taking no account of the sacrifices, for the betterment of their fellow man.

John Maclean was a Glasgow man of that latter sort. He never became a great union leader or parliamentarian, but as a fighter on behalf of the working class, he was an outstanding legend and a pioneering champion in the days when workers were sorely in need of people to defend them, to question governments' demands on them, and to campaign for peace instead of war. For the best part of the first quarter of this century, Maclean was to agitate, write, lecture, teach and spend most of his time with the working-class people of Glasgow to whom he was utterly devoted. He was to sacrifice his marriage for his work, give up his liberty for his beliefs, suffer the horrors of solitary confinement and have an untimely and unexpected death, all for his cause.

The story of John Maclean is a stark reminder of just how recently achieved have been our present freedoms. Maclean experienced the kind of indignities and treatment we imagine only happen in the most repressive nations. Shamefully, such events took place on our doorstep: in Glasgow, not all that many years ago.

John Maclean was born in Pollokshaws in 1879, hard and troubled days for working people. Masses of the dispossessed were still arriving from the Highlands and Ireland. There was no Government relief or welfare assistance for the thousands of unemployed. If the poor protested, they called out the Dragoons from the cavalry barracks just off Eglinton Street and foot soldiers from the Infantry Barracks along the Gallowgate. Courts did the rest with the customary transportation sentences, a godsend of a solution for putting people who protested out of the way.

Young Anne MacPhee and Daniel Maclean, her husband to be, had been two of the countless victims of rapacious Highland landlords, driven with their parents from homes and crofts, one from Mull, the other from near Fort William. Glasgow was the only salvation for these deprived Highland, Island and Irish hordes left with nothing by their lochsides and in their glens and straths. For all of them, Glasgow was their city of hope. It didn't matter that it suffered from mass unemployment, that it had the most deplorable of housing conditions, with a fifth of Scotland's population crowded into it and its suburbs – roughly eight square miles in all – Glasgow was the only place that offered them the chance to at least survive.

After marrying at Nitshill, the Macleans settled in Pollokshaws, a thriving industrial town before the turn of the century. It was on his grandmother's knee there that the young John Maclean was first to hear of the terrible deprivations working people suffered, their land, their homes, their livelihood snatched from them, the authorities assisting the landlords to hound them from their native soil, burning their humble houses to ensure they could never return.

The seeds of hatred for capitalism and the aristocracy were to find extremely fertile ground in the mind of the young John Maclean, the sixth of seven children from the union between Daniel Maclean and Anne MacPhee.

He was just eight years old and one of the four surviving children when his father, a potter, died. His mother was to spend the rest of her life 'making ends meet', with no widow's pension, no form of income support, rent allowance, subsidised rent, heating or medicines. Working as a weaver in Pollokshaws, she also ran a small shop and took in lodgers. As soon as he was old enough, the young Maclean had to do his bit, too, and worked as a message boy before and after school hours, as a caddie at the nearby golf course in Thornliebank and as errand boy at the print works, where he also worked during school holidays.

Schooling was at Pollok Academy, then Queen's Park Secondary, the latter noted for its academic record and where he gained sufficient standards to be accepted as a pupil teacher at Polmadie School and later at the Free Church Training College from which he gained his teacher's certificate. His first teaching post was as an assistant master at Strathbungo School, during which he attended classes at Glasgow University, graduating with an MA in 1904.

Glasgow was a political hotbed at the time. It had gained an international reputation as Britain's most notable city of socialist culture. And that wasn't just another label presented on a yearly basis to various cities. It was what Glasgow really was. The city abounded with anarchists, radicalists, revolutionaries, socialists of varying degrees and various other political activists, all determined in their own way to bring changes to the way life was conducted. Whatever way that might be done, whatever outcome might be achieved, they were mainly unified in the central principle of their beliefs, that the burden of the downtrodden working class had to be alleviated. Their weekly meetings in the streets off Argyle Street in the city centre and around the main gates of many of the city's parks were a feature of city life at the time. Debate and argument at home, the workplace or any venue in which people gathered was the stimulant of the day. The merits and otherwise of atheism, communism, socialism, capitalism, secularism, nationalism, republicanism and anarchism were among the fodder of their talk.

The stories of his grandparents, the deprivations of his parents, and the arduous labours of his own life to gain his degree, working as farm labourer and postman, walking miles every day to and from college, were all factors in John Maclean's own political formation. One of his first affiliations was with the Progressive Union, whose aims were 'for the social intercourse and mutual improvement, materially, mentally and morally, of members as well as the discussion of philosophic, scientific and literary subjects and all problems of present-day interest, especially those which concern the social and religious life of the people'.

Socialism and anarchism were contemporary and regular topics discussed at their meetings and Maclean, just 21 and a convinced socialist, was one of the keenest debaters as well as lecturers on a wide range of subjects, including poverty, drink and crime. Within a year, the socialist had become Marxist, exposing his innermost feelings in a long letter to the *Pollokshaws News*, part of which read: 'That the class struggle is bitter, we need only reckon the annual death roll of the workers, the maimed, the poisoned, the physically wrecked by overwork, the mentally wrecked by worry and those forced to suicide by desperation. It is a more bloody and more disastrous warfare than that to which the soldier is used. Living in slums, breathing poisonous and carbon-laden air, wearing shoddy clothes, eating adulterated and life-extinguishing food, the workers have greater cause for a forcible revolution than had the French in 1789.'

Regardless of that greater cause, there was to be no rousing call to the barricades: Maclean refrained from advocating revolution holding out that a 'new Labour Party' —but not 'new' in a much latter-day's sense! – could bring about those better conditions democratically, through Parliament.

The political orator and lecturer had already committed his life to spreading the word of his beliefs and helping the workers wherever and whenever he could, not just by encouragement but in many varied practical ways as well. In Greenock, for instance, where he had become particularly active and well known, he wrote a pamphlet on the highly disreputable practice of some local butchers selling meat which came from diseased carcases. His sensational revelations caused an uproar. Better still, it instigated a health board inquiry and the appointment of a meat inspector at the local slaughterhouse. And E Coli and BSE weren't even on the horizon.

Actions like this not only had an inspirational effect on his followers, but were to galvanise his own efforts in spreading the word of his beliefs. He spoke at every meeting-place in Glasgow, in the hundreds of venues for such gatherings which were more commonplace then than, say, any form of local sport is today. And better attended.

On long summer vacations from his work as a teacher, he accepted speaking invitations from all over the country: encouraging transport workers in Belfast to strike, organising dockers in Glasgow, inspiring fishermen in Aberdeen, and lecturing others in Lerwick.

Virulently anti-war, Maclean was to campaign more and more against the growing militarism and talk of conflict with Germany. Only on the Clyde had workers in Britain resisted the war propaganda and it was to become a focal point not only for the working-class struggle but for the anti-war movement. When war did break out in 1914, Maclean, hailed by the legendary Red Clydesider Willie Gallacher as 'that indomitable and irrepressible revolutionary fighter', was to publicly and repeatedly reattest his Marxist faith. He would tell them at his public meetings that he too would be going to war . . . 'war that is, against the war-makers'.

As more and more young men went off to the trenches, many of the anti-war campaigners had second thoughts, being engulfed in the sweeping tide of patriotism. But Maclean never wavered in his stance, arguing his case day and night, and rallying the diminishing faithful around him. Because of the growing public feeling against the pacifists and anti-war campaigners, they no longer held their big public meetings at places like the Metropole Theatre in Stockwell Street which had been one of their regular Sunday night venues. They considered it more prudent in light of the patriotism which genuinely did exist, to retreat to local halls where they felt safer from those who might think of them as cowards, or even worse, traitors.

Maclean continued in his refusal to contemplate any form of abatement in his beliefs, regularly speaking at the main meeting point in Bath Street and sending delegates to try and convince munitions workers that they should be turning their labour to more peaceful pursuits, no easy task to a workforce earning bigger wages than ever they had in peacetime. By the end of the first year of the war, however, John Maclean had become a household name in Glasgow for his resistance to the slaughter and the growing support he was receiving for his regular Bath Street meetings, so popular by then that they were virtually the heart of the revolutionary movement in Glasgow and Clydeside.

Maclean preached about the capitalists taking advantage of wartime conditions, making even more money through increases in rent, food and household coal prices. When he heard about the unrest in Govan over rent increases, he immediately diverted his energies towards a rent strike that had been initiated through the Women's Housing Association.

By the end of 1915, unrest had escalated among Glasgow workers regarding the numbers of men being killed and the deterioration in their own conditions. The Bath Street meetings had become even bigger, troubling the police authorities sufficiently for them to consider ways in which they could have them either curtailed or stopped. But the clumsy and amateurish subterfuges they initially employed met with the success they deserved and the meetings went on. So, however, did the police monitoring of them.

The fountain at Shawlands Cross was another of Maclean's regular meeting-places and one evening just after 9 o'clock – the pub closing hour – a well-refreshed soldier with some mates abused Maclean and those attending the meeting. They then complained to the police, and when Maclean refused their request to call a halt to the proceedings, he was arrested and taken to the nearby Southern Police Station at Craigie Street and charged with that handy and multi-purpose standby of Scots law, breach of the peace.

There was further trouble the following Sunday at the Bath Street meeting, this time inspired by police using provocateurs from an opposing political stance. Again, their ploy was to backfire, the Maclean followers being too loyal, and on this occasion too numerous, to be thwarted by such maladroit manoeuvres.

Maclean's popularity and the farce of crude police tactics to stop him became too much for the authorities. There were better ways of stopping him than the local police court . . . the Defence of the Realm Act for one. DORA, as it was known, was one of the harshest anti-freedom laws known this century, the sole intention of which was to deter any form of interference in the war effort. Maclean's writings in a variety of pamphlets and socialist journals had not gone unnoticed. Witnesses had observed and noted the fiercest of them: 'It is the duty of every man of the slave class to rally round us in this bitter fight to retain the freedom won by our fathers from the fathers of the Junkers who today ask us to die for them . . . No man has the right to be any other man's master . . . It is because we object to the slavery implied in mastery, the mastery over land and the capital of the world, that we are socialists and nothing but socialists . . . I have been enlisted in the Socialist Army for 15 years. God damn all other armies! Any soldier who shoots another soldier in the war is a murderer.'

That, considered the Crown, was interference aplenty, and Maclean was summoned under the dreaded DORA for making statements 'likely to prejudice recruiting'. After a brief trial at the Sheriff Court, which had bordered on farce, he was fined five pounds. Worse than that, however, was the fact that his actions were to cost him his job as a teacher, Govan School Board ordering his dismissal. Although more than the average man's weekly wage, the tolerant five pound fine irked the authorities as much as his speeches, making them more than ever determined that in some way he should be effectively silenced.

Two months later they pounced again, armed this time with the benefit of an amendment to the Defence of the Realm Act which now made interference in the war an offence punishable by prison with hard labour. And John Maclean was to be their first victim.

On Sunday, 6 February 1916, while returning home to Pollokshaws from one of his Bath Street rallies, he was arrested, taken to the Central Police Station and from there to Edinburgh Castle to be held in the category of a prisoner of war, with the choice of appearing before a military court martial or the High Court. He chose the latter, the Crown turning out the Lord Advocate, the chief prosecutor in the land, to conduct the case against him, convincingly performing that role for the jury to return a verdict of guilty of four of the six charges laid against him.

That judgement in the High Court on Thursday, 13 April 1916, had been calmly anticipated by Maclean. But not the savage sentence of three years' penal servitude.

They made sure there would be no special treatment for their star political prisoner: the first month of the sentence was served in solitary confinement in the ancient and castellated Old Calton Jail, in Edinburgh, now demolished but at the time reckoned the worst prison in Scotland. Its staff was specially selected from the army and mental hospitals, and its food the lowest order in slops. No form of reading material or speech with other prisoners was permitted, every inmate incarcerated alone in a cell in which the only furnishings comprised a stool, a mattress and toilet bucket. Their only daily break consisted of half an hour in the small exercise yard. It was the same harsh regime throughout Scottish prisons at the time, the general rule being that males under 60 had no mattress for the first 30 days of confinement, that work and exercise were performed in enforced silence and only one letter and one visit were allowed every three months.

John Maclean, now labelled as Convict 2652, had been silenced. How they wished they could have done that to his huge army of supporters. There were rallies and meetings of protest at the sentence, numerous campaigns mounted to agitate for his release, while deputations and delegations demanded that MPs and various organisations take immediate action to fight for his freedom.

When Prime Minister Lloyd George came to Glasgow at the end of June, 14 months after Maclean had been sentenced, the thousands who lined the streets weren't well-wishers. He faced one of the biggest and angriest remonstrations the city had known. While the Corporation lauded him, honouring him with the Freedom of the City, an enormous crowd of around 100,000 met at Glasgow Green demanding freedom in its truest sense for Maclean, by now the hero of the revolutionary movement throughout Britain. And as Lloyd George drove through the streets, his car surrounded by more police and troops than for any other Prime Minister in history, crowds along the route demonstrated their solidarity with the incarcerated John Maclean.

The message conveyed that day and the general mood of the nation was not to be ignored, and Maclean was given early release from prison. The sentence had made its mark on him physically, but was not to affect his determination to help in the struggle of the workers. If anything, he was even more enthused and immediately embarked on a whole series of plans he had been formulating while in prison, beginning with the foundation of a new educational programme for workers and lending his support to the men who were known as the 'conshies', the conscientious objectors who refused to take part in the war.

The legend of John Maclean had spread throughout Britain where he was the star attraction at rallies and meetings, propagating his gospel of praise for all that was happening in Russia and condemnation for all that was not happening in Britain – vehemently denouncing war and the warmongers. His fame spread to Europe where he had become a byword among other socialist leaders fighting for the workers. In Russia, fresh from its own sweeping revolution, he was being hailed a hero of such magnitude that they not only elected him an Honorary President of the first All-Russian Congress of Soviets, together with Lenin and Trotsky, but made him their first Consul in Britain and Maclean opened an office for this purpose at 12 South Portland Street, Gorbals. John Maclean, the prickly thorn the authorities thought they might have silenced, was being seen and heard more than ever before. He had become a notorious Bolshevik and a monster they feared.

The Great War was by now in its final year but that was no excuse to let the work and continuous agitation of Maclean go unchallenged. Special Branch and army intelligence officers continued their watchful note-taking at his meetings, the most recent of which had been among miners in Durham where he was given a most enthusiastic reception. It was on his return from there that detectives were yet again to arrest him at his consular offices in the Gorbals, ignoring all forms of diplomatic immunity by doing so. And this time the Crown had conceived an even better way of getting rid of him, namely by charging him with sedition, a very grievous offence. He was arraigned at the High Court on eleven charges accusing him of making statements at various meetings 'likely to prejudice recruiting and cause mutiny and sedition among the people'. He scoffed at the indictment and refused to plead, the Lord Justice General informing him that in Scots Law that would be interpreted as a plea of not guilty. He then remanded him for trial to begin on 9 May 1918, at the High Court in Edinburgh.

They really gunned for Maclean this time, witness after witness giving sworn testimony of the seditious nature of his speeches at numerous meetings: they told of how he had harangued workers that they should take over the City Chambers, take control of the Post Office and the banks and that the House of Commons should be superseded by a Soviet.

The one-and-a-quarter-hour address Maclean gave at the conclusion of the trial was one of the most impassioned speeches ever heard in a court in Scotland. He rounded on the legal authorities for having brought him to trial. 'I am not here as the accused . . . I am here as the accuser of capitalism dripping with blood from head to foot.' Nor was he to show any remorse or guilt for any action he had taken, any speech he had ever made. 'I am a Socialist and have been fighting and will fight for an absolute reconstruction of society for the benefit of all. I am proud of my conduct and have squared my conscience with my intellect and if everyone had done so this war would not have taken place.'

The brilliant oration did not impress the jury, who were so convinced by his anti-war speeches and agitation among the workers that they didn't even request to retire in order to make up their minds. The sentence was to be even more vicious – five years' penal servitude.

As in his previous jailing, Maclean was again to be an even greater source of agitation as a prisoner than he had as a free man. A wave of protest meetings began throughout the country, a regular one being held each month at Glasgow Green.

The revulsion among the workers at the severity of his sentence was not to be shared by much of the Press of the day. The revolutionary among them represented Bolshevism and that was the bitter enemy of all of the Press barons. One article observed that had Maclean acted the way he had in some other countries the sentence would have been death, an observation which was probably quite accurate.

Scotland may not have behaved quite like that towards its twentieth-century revolutionaries, but it was most certainly not the home of the free. When militant socialists were organising workers for better hours, the authorities had eight of the leading campaigners seized, a court ordering they be banished from Glasgow. Among them was David Kirkwood, the legendary shop steward at Beardmore's Parkhead Forge. When he was caught for breaking the banishment order, they locked this respectable, church-going socialist in a vault, deep in the bowels of Edinburgh Castle, where the only light was a small grating high in the roof and where, he said . . . 'My mind refused to think . . . I was a done man.' That was just the way it was if you bucked the powers not all that many years ago.

That same attitude towards those with extraordinary political beliefs was doubtlessly the reason for a shameful episode to follow in Maclean's treatment by the authorities. After about five months into his sentence at Peterhead Prison, Maclean was visited by his long-suffering wife, Agnes. She was shocked at the sight which greeted her. The last she had seen him he had been his normal self, the stockily built man with broad facial features, the Gael's high prominent cheekbones, the cheery smile and glowing eyes. The person now before her appeared emaciated, his hair had turned white and he had all the appearances of someone who was either seriously ill or suffering in some way. He told her that as he was convinced the food given him on his last sentence had been drugged, he had been given the rare concession of having his own food, prepared by friends outside the prison. However, this had not worked out as the food did not suit him. So he had asked to be transferred to Barlinnie Prison in Glasgow in order to get the kind of food to which he was accustomed, that is, prepared by his wife, but this had been rejected. He had therefore gone on hunger strike in protest and for the past three months had been enduring the indignity and torture of being force fed, two warders holding him down while another poured liquidised food through a tube which had been forced down his gullet. It was the cruellest and most degrading of treatment and his body had been ravaged by it.

As a medical practice, feeding patients in such a fashion was a well-established treatment in hospitals for those unable to intake food orally, and when done by caring staff, although uncomfortable, it was perfectly safe and more helpful than harmful to the patient. It was a different matter, however, when such feeding was done forcefully, the thick rubber tube rammed with neither care nor attention down the gullet of a struggling inmate. Just a few months before being administered to Maclean, it had been amply demonstrated how tortuous and dangerous it could be when the prisoner Tom Ashe, one of a group of hunger-striking nationalists being held in Mountjoy Prison, Dublin, had died as a result of the revolting treatment. The fluids they had been thrustfully administering him entered his lungs via his windpipe and he died, due to drowning.

When word of Maclean's situation got out, there were questions in Parliament, the Home Secretary vehemently denying allegations of drugging and torture. Nevertheless, the startling claims about what they were doing to him in prison was to compound the Government's embarrassment over their celebrated political prisoner as well as cause even greater resentment among protestors. Their meetings grew in fervour, one of the biggest being held at the Albert Hall in London where huge banners proclaimed, 'Release Maclean'.

The protests escalated to the extent that the Government was forced to capitulate. There seemed little point in detaining a man for dissuading others from enlisting when hostilities were virtually over. Five days after the armistice was signed on that memorable 11th of November 1918, Maclean was informed he would soon be freed.

Tuesday, 3 December 1918, was to witness one of the biggest welcomes anyone has ever received in Glasgow: every street between Buchanan Street Station, where his train had arrived from Aberdeen, all the way to George Square was jam-packed. Only the boxer, Benny Lynch, another Scottish champion, was to equal such a welcome, when he returned to the city having won for Scotland its first-ever world title. And, curiously, it was around those very same streets of the Gorbals where that future world champion, at the time a wee street scallywag of five years of age, spent his childhood – and where John Maclean was to spend every available minute of the first weeks of his freedom. He was campaigning to be the Gorbals Member of Parliament in the forthcoming general election. Despite his ill-health, still suffering from the humiliating treatment at Peterhead, he canvassed night and day for votes, knocking on doors, speaking at street meetings, addressing those groups of the day known as corner boys and having words with men in pubs. Perhaps they may not have fully appreciated the teetotal, non-smoker's message that under a truly socialist government there would be less need for drink which in turn would mean less crime. But while they loved and admired their John Maclean for his dedication to them, the working-class people of the Gorbals were not ready for this uncompromising revolutionary as their Member of Parliament, and he only received just a little over 7,000 votes. Despite their own conditions and deprivations, the days of revolt were not to be at hand.

The Marxist John Maclean was only 39 years of age when he fought the Gorbals seat as a Republican. He looked a man twice his age. Whatever the cruelties he had suffered in jail, it had taken its toll and he was never to recover the full health he had enjoyed as a younger man. His wife Agnes had for years been without the company of a husband who was not only married to his cause but appeared now to be committing suicide for it. She had coped well to look after their two young daughters Jean and Nan, but was now planning to leave him and return to her home town of Hawick and her career in nursing. As Maclean's first biographer, Tom Anderson put it: '. . . John should never have married; his life was so entwined in the pursuit of socialism that he had no time to spare for mere mundane matters.'

There was nothing everyday or ordinary about John Maclean's ideals and the split up of the family made no effect on his continued dedication to his faith – a faith which was so great that when he was asked for a donation to a miners' appeal, he handed over £5 earmarked for a much needed new suit and which had taken him an age to save.

Despite it being peacetime, John Maclean still concerned the authorities. They had him constantly watched and, when he spoke, police officers in plain clothes would be listening and taking notes. The land that proclaimed it was the Mother of the Free drew a line when it came to people like him, even fining one of his comrades . . . for selling socialist literature on Glasgow Green.

They were watching and noting him yet again when he addressed a street corner meeting in Airdrie and because they said he used language 'calculated and likely to cause sedition and disaffection among His Majesty's Forces and among the civil population', they jailed him once more, this time for three months. To avoid the prospect of having to force feed the man for which they had no answer except prison, he was given the unprecedented privilege and status of political prisoner, being granted his own clothes, books, food, newspapers and regular visits.

He was only months out of Barlinnie when they were to pounce once again, this time for telling Gorbals unemployed that they should take food rather than starve. For that heinous suggestion, they bunged him up once more, this time for a year. But again they were to grant him the unique political prisoner status and there were no hunger strikes.

John Maclean was released from prison for the last time on 25 October 1922, but there was no euphoric welcome this time. Even the need for the authorities to hound him was over. The days of his envisaged Scottish Workers Republic had passed, just as the revolutionary thoughts of the workers had, now convinced by an active Labour Party that they could bring about the necessary changes by constitutional means. Few feuds are more bitter than those of politicians at variance on dogma, and even the Communists – his heroes, their hero – were to turn against him because he had held out for a separate Scottish Communist Party. That had been against the wishes of those in

Moscow, Lenin himself decreeing that there should only be one united Communist Party in Britain. Ironically, the workers of the world who wanted to unite were unable to be united themselves.

Alienated politically more than ever, without a wife, and virtually penniless, his face deeply lined, his hair even whiter, it was a mark of the man that the zeal for all in which he believed remained. His lack of funds showed in his dress, the well-worn suit as shabby as that trademark of a black nap coat, its sagging pockets stuffed with pamphlets and papers. But his spirit was undaunted and he continued to fight for the same causes he had all his life. Despite deteriorating health and developing pneumonia, he campaigned right up to the very last, which towards the end included a viciously bitter mid-winter canvassing for yet another Gorbals election. That very last election address, in fact, was dated 30 November 1923 – the day he died. He was 44 years of age.

The funeral of John Maclean from his terraced home in Auldhouse Road, Newlands, was one of the biggest-ever of its kind. Thousands took part in a march from Eglinton Toll to Eastwood Cemetery, the *Pollokshaws News* reporting that between 10,000 and 15,000 had packed into the grounds. Another report said: 'There was a greater crowd at his funeral than had ever been seen in Glasgow before, and all the leaders of the working class were at the graveside. But not the leaders only, the rank and file were there in thousands and many people wept that day who had never wept in public before.'

The Red Flag covered his coffin which was borne from the cemetery gates by leaders of the Scottish Republican movement. They buried him together with the great expectations, the impassioned ambitions and dreams he had for the workers.

13

WHEN GLASGOW WAS CINEMA CITY

At the turn of the century Glasgow was one of the liveliest cities in Europe – there was much more to the evening street scene than there is today. Walking was the principal form of transport and bustling streets were filled with groups and parties heading for the theatre, the music hall, smoking concerts and banquets, billiard rooms, pubs and penny-geggies (more about them later). There were no plastic hamburger shops, pizza take-aways or doner kebabs on offer; yet there was no shortage of our very own appealing alternatives. Windows of restaurants and chop houses attracted hordes of people with their tempting trays of tenderly roasted sirloin, large brick-sized lobsters and tubs of the freshest oysters, and where you could still get the popular traditional fare of the day, like sheep's heid and pig's trotters, appetites were stimulated by the long-lost and thoroughly unique street aroma from the charcoal braziers of the roast chestnut sellers, a threepenny bag of which was as good as a restaurant feast . . . for two.

Some restaurants specialised in finnans and toddy (now there's a mix!), others in fish and pastries washed down with big jugs of Chianti, no less, and there was even an American bar where they served Bourbon, the way they served it in its home state – with the bottle plonked in front of you and bowls of olives and crackers. Aye, there was some style around.

As for entertainment, there was plenty of that going on, much of it free by just taking in the theatre of the street: the busy and lively thoroughfares of the city were a magnet to performers and performances of all descriptions. There were escape artists and strongmen who did miracles with their muscles in freeing themselves from canvas strait-jackets and padlocked chains or used their bare chests on which to rest big boulders which other men sledgehammered to smithereens; there were singers and dancers of all descriptions – soft-shoe, boot or clog – one-man bands and men who played saws or Jew's-harps, and enough conventional musicians to make a full-blown orchestra.

It was into this robust and rumbustious scene that yet another form of entertainment was to arrive . . . the cinema. And just as it did with so many other aspect of life, Glasgow was to embrace this infant of the entertainment world with a fervour and passion unequalled anywhere else in the United Kingdom. For Glasgow in its picture house heyday *was* Cinema City. Pre-war newspapers carried page after page of advertisements for uptown and suburban picture houses. Column after column displayed programme details of the 130-plus cinemas, more per head of population than any other city in Britain. Only in the US, in fact, were there cities that could rival Glasgow for its number and its variety of movie halls.

The city's very first 'picture houses' were a far cry from today's multiplex, multiscreen, dolby-digital, stereo-equipped, hot-dog-and-bucket-popcorn, state-of-the-art film centres where screens are queueing to greet the customers. Our very first picture houses were opened up in converted shops before the turn of the century or were a sideshow feature of the bands of travelling showmen who introduced the novelty of the film along with their shows. Travelling and resident circuses began screening them as an added attraction to their performances and so too did the skating rinks when they were staging variety shows. Few thought they would become the major player in the city's entertainment scene, believing that these little 'flicker shops' would just be another passing fancy. But those pioneer movie audiences put up with old wooden church pews for seats and draped linen sheets on the far wall to act as screens. Despite all that, and the fact that what they were watching was a shaky, silent and scratchy black-and-white film, they were voted a great night's entertainment. They were certainly a step up from the penny-gaffs, or penny-geggies as we called them, the mini theatres set up in sheds with benches where the show was often a hastily scrambled adaptation of some popular play. Sometimes even a lecture on the evils of drink would be thrown in, with an 'orchestra' of three quasi-musicians scratching out what they could.

The film star hadn't been created yet, neither had the full-length movie, so the programme for a night's entertainment at those early flicks consisted of a series of half-a-dozen or so shorts with a variety of themes ranging from comedy to drama and news to general interest. And at the best of them the 1½p to 3p admission price even included a cup of tea and a biscuit.

It wasn't till the early years of the century when the American film *The Birth of a Nation* was screened at the Theatre Royal, and for which they charged the customary theatre prices, that it was appreciated that films were to be no passing notion. The enormous success of its screening and the money that it made showed quite clearly that films had come to stay. Local showbusiness entrepreneurs quickly got the message and moved fast. *The Birth of a Nation* heralded the birth of a new entertainment child along with it, and planners and builders were hastily consulted.

The Skating Palace in Sauchiehall Street was to become the venue for the first commercial showing of pictures in the city and probably Glasgow's most historical showbusiness site – skating, dancing, a circus and latterly films all being performed at one time or another on that location. It was to last longest as a cinema, as films were shown continuously there for the best part of the century. In fact, it wasn't until the writing of this book that its owners decreed that for that particular site at least, the time had come for the premises to be put to some other use.

Known for most of its lifetime as the Regal, some old-timers say that when it was known as the Skating Palace the speciality had been roller skating. Perhaps that form of skating was practised there at times, but it was skating with blades for which it was really known and reckoned to be the modish place in the city for the popular pastime that drew huge crowds to various rinks. When the skating boom passed, it was then taken over by the famous Hengler's Circus, or, as they billed themselves, 'Hengler's Cirque', touring performers who came originally from Denmark but had been on the road throughout Britain for more than a hundred years. Like others before them, they had originally come to Glasgow as a travelling circus, setting up their tents on Glasgow Green. A lioness belonging to one of these previous shows had even given birth to cubs right there on the historic Green.

After establishing themselves as one of the most popular of these tented circus shows, Hengler's moved to a permanent location, first of all in West Nile Street then to premises at the corner of Wellington and Waterloo Streets, the site which for several decades would become a major post office building. Hengler's final venue was when they moved at the turn of the century to the Ice Skating Palace in Sauchiehall Street. In the late '20s, the changing showbusiness scene was to see this building, after reconstruction work, become a dance hall with the grand title of the Waldorf Palace de Danse and in 1929, when sound was added to moving pictures, it was transformed yet again, with movies returning to the venue when it became the 2,309-seat Regal cinema. For years it was one of the most popular picture houses in the city, undergoing more modernisation to a multi-screen unit in the '60s and '70s.

Much of Glasgow's cinema history was founded in Sauchiehall Street. It was the home of Pringle's Picture Palace, the first building to be opened exclusively for the showing of films in 1907, and the Electric Theatre, the first purpose-built cinema in the city and where they were showing colour films – that wonder of wonders of the new industry – as far back as 1910. Not long after that, yet another, the Vitagraph, had settled into the street and in years to come even more were to come to Glasgow's most fashionable shopping street.

Such was the popularity of the new medium, that by 1917 there were over 100 establishments throughout the city in the role of these early-day cinemas. Most of them had previous lives in a variety of functions as diverse as a roller rink, a coach-house and stables, a disused cork factory, a portion of an old warehouse, a former tea room, a church hall and a 'Wee Free' church – all of which had taken a new lease of life as flicker houses.

Because of their easy conversion, however, most early cinemas were former music halls or theatres, their vaudeville shows and live productions giving way to the moving film, although many continued in the dual role of presenting live shows as well as film entertainment.

Some were to become the height of luxury, like the The Picture House in Sauchiehall Street with designer tea rooms and a 'palm court display' with ornate fountains, an elaborate goldfish pool and spectacular cages of singing birds. The Picture House was *the* picture house, becoming the leading cinema in Scotland, a place to be seen in, to say that you had been in it, a treasure house of '30s trendies with the cachet that certain lounge bars and discos were to assume in the latter part of the century.

There was esteem of a different sort at the nearby La Scala where you could really impress your partner by having an evening meal and watch the programme at the same time. A section of the stalls there doubled as a restaurant serving meals throughout the programme, each white naperied table with its own small, dimly lit lamp. Which meant you could have Claudette Colbert, Myrna Loy or Jean Harlow making love (in the formal way they did with their leading man in the '30s, that is), together with the aroma of fish and chips, the rattling of tea plates, the clattering of cutlery, the scurrying of waitresses, followed by a full-strength Capstan with your Camp coffee, all in the one place. You better believe it. It really was different in those days. Incidentally, these lunch or high tea outings together with the hit film of the day, was no passing phase. The unique dining facility lasted for 40 years.

Glasgow took to its cinemas very seriously right from the start. The Film Society of the Cosmo, now known as the Glasgow Film Theatre, was probably the first such grouping in the world. City cinema pioneer, John Maxwell, who rented Corporation halls for picture shows, formed a circuit known as Associated British Cinemas which became the biggest of its kind in Britain and the second biggest in the world. He commanded a vast chain of over 340 cinemas, virtually every city and town in the country having its own theatre.

George Green was another Glaswegian who could think really big when it came to cinemas. And if ever anyone typified the entrepreneurship of those early cinema pioneers, it was George and his family. Whether the material came in a can or not, the new flicks were showbusiness and George Green had been at the sharpest end of one of the then most popular forms of showbusiness for much of his life. George, the son of a master cabinetmaker and whose family originally came from Lancashire, toured the country with those legendary bands of travelling showmen. He had various forms of entertainment booths which he staged together with the other travelling showmen at local fairs and holiday carnivals.

Just like the other showmen, he was always on the lookout for new gimmicks to attract the customers to his show, each claiming that what they had to offer was better than what was next door. When the first of the new films appeared – scratchy, shaky, silent and skittish as they were – they were nevertheless the greatest novelty of the day and George got immersed in them. Just after the turn of the century, he commissioned the building of a mobile cinematographic booth (they used the full word in those days) which had all the glare and gleam of the normal travelling showman's booth. Those old enough will remember them: flash on the outside, trash in the inside. It measured 50 by 30 ft and the attraction was 'an exciting evening of the world's newest and greatest showbusiness attraction . . . moving films'.

They flocked in to share the great new experience, an evening of wonderment which lasted a mere 20 minutes. But then some of the movies themselves only lasted for a little more than one minute. They were the usual mix of the day: miniature dramas, woefully acted and weirdly directed. Others consisted of poorly shot scenes of beauty spots, not that they looked all that beautiful in dissolving and dissipating sepia. But the realism was apparently there. Startled front-row audiences were known to withdraw to the rear of the booth, fearful they would get wet from the celluloid waves lashing the rocks in one of those one-minute scenic spectaculars.

George could get 500 customers per show into his travelling booth and at one old penny (equivalent of a ½p) a time, that was making roughly £2 every 20 minutes. If he made £20 or more in a day, then at 1902 standards, George was really in the money. Later he added wooden forms for the front few rows of his travelling theatre, but they were double the price of standing customers. Eventually George brought his 'Theatre Unique' to Glasgow and parked it in the Gallowgate for shows. George Green died in 1915, but his sons Bert and Fred carried on the business, converting the Whitevale Theatre just off Gallowgate for the regular showing of moving pictures, one of the first of its kind in the East End of the city. The whole family were immersed in the Whitevale and the other theatres they were acquiring for their expanding cinema empire, their sisters and mother all taking part in running the business, which meant staffing the payboxes, acting as usherettes as well as 'chuckers-out'.

By the end of World War I, the Greens had a small chain of seven cinemas all well established in the city. Their circuit was to become the third largest in Scotland and was to include the biggest picture house in Europe, the legendary Green's Playhouse at the top of Renfield Street.

The Greens sent architects to America to study their huge cinemas, the result being the massive building that was to be a Glasgow landmark for years. The Greens thought big: their cavernous cinema was able to seat 4,400 and the balcony alone was bigger than many cinemas with room for 1,300, topped by an upper balcony with 1,000 seats.

It wasn't just for its size that the Playhouse was famous. A big attraction was its red and golden divans, the latter more expensive, giving courting couples the luxury of double seats minus a central armrest, which would give that area of the huge cinema a sort of love-in look about it. The stories emanating from those double seats known as the Playhouse's divans are part of Glasgow folklore.

Not content with creating Glasgow and Europe's biggest cinema, the

Greens incorporated the city's largest dance-hall in the same building. It was situated on the top floor of the monstrous building and when doubtful city planning officials expressed concern about the structural wisdom of a ballroom positioned above the cinema, the Greens had six large cement mixers hauled up and rolled from side to side on their proposed dance floor to demonstrate its strength. The floor held and they got their dance licence.

When the Green's Playhouse ended its days as a cinema in the early '70s, it was converted for another form of showbusiness, one which was to make those two huge balconies bounce with the fervour of the people in them, albeit a different kind of fervour which made them shimmer back in the days of the love divans. The Playhouse was to become one of the most famous rock venues of all time: the legendary Apollo. World renowned bands like The Who, Queen, the Rolling Stones, Status Quo, the early-day Elton John, all the top American rockers and many others all concurred that playing there was an experience unequalled anywhere else in the world. The Apollo was to last for nearly 15 years, closing in 1985. Two years later, the building that gave Glaswegians and others a million memories, was sadly demolished.

Glasgow's suburbs gushed with scores of great cinemas, each with its own architectural identity, all of which were to become household names in their own communities. They left generations of cinemagoers with the happiest of memories, of nights where they were carried off from their more sepia surroundings by the fantasy of film land and its beautiful people in a New World where everything, it seemed, was wonderful and fantastic, and reality never happened. Or, if it did, you wept your eyes out.

The '30s were to see the biggest boom in the movie-building years, some of the constructions coming with the strangest designs, jarring with all other forms of surrounding architecture. The design miscellany of many of them, particularly when viewed today, ranged from the bizarre to the weird – and some were downright oddball. But at the time they were considered daring and contemporary. Movie madness had got to the designers of these new picture theatres who reached for the far-out in their building plans. The movies were new and exciting, the very latest form of showbusiness, so it was therefore appropriate that the places in which to see and enjoy the romance of cinema should be of a design which was also ultra-modern.

A new wave of consumer art deco was sweeping the city at the time, mainly in the design of cafés, pubs, restaurants and shops, several of which, thankfully, still survive. So the new cinemas joined the style vogue and all that came with it, such as straight lines, lots of chrome, inlaid woods, geometrical shapes, stylised natural forms and symmetrical utilitarian designs. And if you ever wondered why your local flicks came with the most freakish outlines, a touch of Spanish/Moorish perhaps, blame the influence of Continental Modernism which was part of the art deco craze. It also explains what to many was the mystery of the Egyptian appearance in some of those custom-built cinemas. What on earth had Cairo to do with what was coming mainly from California? The bizarre trend started with the captivating discovery of Tutankhamun's tomb in 1922, arousing tremendous interest in Egyptian art. This in turn was to be the influence for the trend in quasi-Egyptian art deco. And being trendy, it was just the design for these new homes of entertainment, each suburb throughout the city having at least one of them.

The new cinemas being built in many suburbs of Glasgow were the largest Moderne/Art Deco buildings in the city, and those which remain are now landmarks of an era when architecture was boldly reaching out to new frontiers, even if they did border on the frivolous. Among the outstanding and perhaps best remembered of this genre are the Astoria at the Round Toll, Possil, second only in size to Green's cavernous Playhouse, with its cubist ceiling lights and futuristic auditorium decor; the State at Shettleston and King's Park; the Vogue in Langlands Road, Govan – the external coating of its striking moderne styling had a special rendering of faience, a form of tin-glazed earthenware; the Lyceum in nearby Govan Road, on the site of an old music hall, cutting a conspicuous dash among the adjoining sombre tenements with its use of moulded and Vitrolite glass cladding and neon lighting; the Ascot at Anniesland, its entrance façade flanked by two semi-circular towers finished in a cream, red and black faience; the Mayfair in Sinclair Drive, Battlefield; the Embassy in Kilmarnock Road, Shawlands; and the Aldwych in Paisley Road West.

Glaswegians who lived through the heyday of its cinema city days have their own special memories of their local or favourite picture house. Invariably, however, it would be one of the local flicks they would remember best, and not especially for the films that they saw there. Typical of these could be, say, a place like the Paragon, an old converted church in Cumberland Street in the Gorbals. The old Glasgow suburb might have been one of the most deprived places in Europe, but when it came to the social events of the day, the Gorbals had plenty of everything . . . pubs, dance-halls, theatres and cinemas.

Just as in every other part of the city, the local picture house had a special place in the hearts and minds of the Gorbals community, most being known by an endearing nickname of one sort or another. Old residents might not even remember what some of their official titles were, but they can certainly rhyme off the names by which they knew them, like the Crownie and the Bees, the Collie and the EE, the Palace, Green's, Bedford, Ritz, and, of course, the Paragon, an old United Free Church in Cumberland Street, which from its opening in 1912 was to achieve legendary status for the 40 or so years of its existence in the heart of the Gorbals.

There were many like the Paragon scattered throughout Glasgow, little establishments where the commissionaire at the door would be kitted out in the gaudiest of uniforms, usually a bilious blue or malignant maroon which, when new, would have been appropriate on the back of some Ruritanian field-marshal, but was now so stained and shabby you would think he had either just returned from the trenches or else was some sort of pre-existent Benny Hill. Mind you, on the subject of uniforms, not all cinema commissionaires looked like that: some of the uptown, front-of-the-house men were sergeant-major smart, although their uniforms with gold-fringed epaulettes and brocade lanyards were more ornamental than regimental and the colours more fashion house than guardhouse. Pastels were the mode – shades that no army would ever wear, or even *dare* to wear, lest they be known as Dandys' Army instead. They were so finicky about these uniforms in some city centre cinemas that they conducted daily, before-work parades to check that everything was in order. At the Regal in Sauchiehall Street, for instance, the 12 usherettes would line up each working day for inspection at 12.30 p.m., half an hour before the show commenced, the brass buttons of their snappy tunics highly polished, their Spanish hats freshly brushed and they got a ticking-off if they weren't. And, in the early '30s, that was all in return for a weekly wage of £1.60 for a six-day week, and ten-hour daily shifts.

As you can imagine, however, there were no daily parades, or kit inspections at places like the Gorbals Paragon where the man out front in the semblance of a uniform might also be the projectionist, the cleaner, the maintenance man, maybe even the interval ice-cream seller. Yes, these little halls could be that hilarious! They were more a vital part of each area's folk culture, not so much for the films they showed, but rather for the happenings which occurred in and around them. Places like the Paragon were a happening in themselves.

When the Singleton family, well known in the cinema trade, acquired the Paragon in 1920, the seating capacity was 800. With some rebuilding, however, they were able to increase this to 1,400, managing the considerable number by retaining the original church pews for seating. If you weren't sitting on one of the old church pews, then you'd be sitting on something similar to a park bench – and when the ushers became too enthusiastic about cramming more and more people into the hall, getting your seat on bench or pew was often at the expense of the person sitting at the furthest end of it who, as often as not on crowded nights, would get shoved off. Overloaded benches collapsed with such regularity that customers had the collective knack of righting them again without as much as taking their eyes off what was happening on the screen.

A former manager I once interviewed remembered some of the more hectic times at the Paragon, such as Friday nights when the drunks would abuse the doorman and the local hard men would walk in without paying. They would simply defy the pleas of the cashier and the threats of terrified usherettes to call the police met with truculent ridicule. The commissionaire was also reluctant to intervene, perhaps relating to the fact that he had once been coshed at his post on a Friday night, then stabbed on the Saturday. Which helps explain why those tattered uniforms looked the way they did. Burglars were another problem at the Paragon, the cinema's safe being such a regular target that they were forced to install an elaborate burglar alarm system linked to the local police station.

Audiences could be unpredictable at times, as you can imagine, and this particular manager remembered one such night. 'Regulations forced us to show a quota of British films which, at the time, were not very popular to say the least. One night, everyone had come along to see a film starring Jeff Chandler, a big hero at the time. But first of all, for quota purposes, we had to screen an English film starring Margaret Rutherford and as soon as it came on the entire stalls audience began stamping their feet and refused to stop. Then the balcony audience, paying a couple of pennies more, descended on us demanding their money back. Luckily we happened to have another Jeff Chandler film, so we replaced the Margaret Rutherford one, giving the audience a double feature programme of Jeff Chandler. It was anything for peace at the Paragon.'

When the Odeon group acquired the Paragon they introduced a kids club with such lures as birthday presents, such as getting your name shown on the screen and being presented with a couple of complimentaries. And everyone knew the club song which they chanted as loudly as they could: 'Is everybody happy? YES! . . . Do we ever worry?

NO! . . . To the Odeon, we have come; now we're all together, and we'll have some fun; do we help our neighbours? YES! . . . Do we ask for favours? NO! . . . We're a hundred thousand strong, and we welcome you along, as members of the OCC we stress . . . Is everybody happy? YES!'

Those who remember the Paragon swear there was no other place like it among Glasgow's numerous cinemas. But there were favourites, some of the more popular and best remembered of which were the Picture House, Dennistoun, with its tiled pillar entrance; the wee Govanhill in Bankhall Street, Govanhill, and its Egyptian-styled frontage which was sited almost back to back with another cinema, the functional and moderne Calder, in Calder Street; the Waverley in Shawlands, with its domed entrance and very popular tea room; the Kingsway in Cathcart, all Spanish-American in appearance; Crosshill's famous BB Cinerama in Victoria Road (the BB stood for Bright and Beautiful), a welcome favourite in winter because its entrance hall was so huge it allowed you to queue inside. It also had an enormous electric organ, brilliantly lit in multi-colours, which at the interval ascended from the orchestra pit in front of the stage, blasting out as it did so the latest hit tunes which made everyone and everything seem really . . . BB.

The great days of the cinema have long since gone as have most of these one-time favourite halls – most of them replaced with everything from service stations to housing and shopping developments. You have to remember them as they were and precisely where they stood to recognise those which still remain in some other guise. Some for a time were converted into successful bingo halls and when that diversion was to take on a new aspect with the advent of the super bingo halls, many were reduced to lying sadly shuttered and dormant. Others became warehouse and storage facilities, one an Irish folk club, another a snooker hall; but there's not much you can do with a cavernous structure with strange geometrical shapes that confuse with another age. And wee places like the Paragon along with so many like it, full of character and characters, are just a fond memory.

14

THE BARRAS QUEEN

❧❦

She looked very much like any other wee East End woman, the kind that proliferated around Gallowgate and the London Road in Calton – energetic little bodies that in hard times did everything to keep the family together on the kind of budget that as long as they made it through till that night, everything would be fine. And tomorrow? Well, tomorrow was another day. Maggie McIver was just such a woman, as anonymous as they come. And just like the others, she looked after her pennies and ha'pennies with as much care as those whose purses held their entire fortune. But it would have needed more than a purse to look after what Maggie McIver was worth. For Maggie was one of the most legendary characters to come out of the East End. She bequeathed to the city an institution the very name of which is synonymous with Glasgow; it is more famous than the Burrell; it sees more people in a year than Ibrox or Parkhead put together. To refer to it as just some street market is like calling Disneyland a funfair. What takes place in and goes on all round about that part of the East End of the city is the very heart and soul of Glasgow. There is nothing like it anywhere else in Scotland. In fact, there's just nothing like it anywhere. It is, of course . . . the Barras.

The outwardly ordinariness of Maggie McIver, the woman who founded the most famous institution in Glasgow, belied the business genius which marked her as one of the shrewdest entrepreneurs the city has known. She had all the hallmarks of the successful, big-time, business tycoon. She knew potential, she never shirked risk and problems were other people's worry, not hers – she was too busy getting on with things to stop and care about problems.

Maggie McIver knew and appreciated the merits of hard work, something in which she was immersed virtually till her last days. She died in 1958 at the age of 77, and the Barras empire, including the famous Barrowland Dance Hall and pop venue, are being carried on by her family to this day. And it was to that very same Barrowland building that she would nod whenever she was asked how she would like to be remembered. In the broadest of Glasgow accents that wealth never dented, the reply would be: 'That's ma tombstone there. They'll aye mind me because o' that.' And they do.

Maggie McIver, the Queen of the Barras. was born Margaret Russell in Galston – she would say 'Gawst'n' – Ayrshire, in 1880, the daughter of a local policeman. When she was just seven years old, her father was transferred to Glasgow, to one of the toughest assignments in the force, a beat policeman in the East End. The family stayed at first in Greenhead Street, Bridgeton, where the young Margaret went to Boden Street School. There was no help of any kind for the unemployed when she was set to leave school. You either worked, or you starved. For young people, finding a source of regular income was an imperative not an alternative. Margaret's mother was a French polisher, a popular and competitive trade in the pre-polyurethane days of Victorian Glasgow, and, like so many, Margaret's own working life was initially to be in the footsteps of a parent, until the day a friend asked her to look after her trader's barrow.

Although it was just 100 years ago, the Glasgow of the teenage Maggie Russell was another place with a completely different set of daily familiarities. The street scene had all the sounds of a sadly lost world and breathed of vitality and a long forgotten individuality. There were traders with barrows everywhere in the city, most of them hand-carts, the others horse-drawn. And the noise and bustle of the day was dominated by vendors' cries, fruitmen hollering their 'honey perrs', fishmen crying their 'Loch Fi-yenn herrin'', offalmen with huge, slopping vats announcing the freshness of their 'tri-yepp', coalmen's yells competing with briquette boys' bawls, stickmen with chants about their bunched kindlers, bugle calls and ricketies announcing the ragmen had arrived – not forgetting, of course, the street entertainers who danced and sang amidst swarms of children at play. These were happy and memorable moments in an era of hardship and utter deprivation.

That fateful day when she looked after the hawker friend's stall was to determine the future life of Maggie. The friend had merely asked her to guard the barrow and its supplies, not to actually trade from it. But when customers began approaching, there was to be no casual put-off from this stand-in barrow minder. She sold goods to one, then another, and yet another and almost instantaneously, the spirit of competitiveness and the energy that could be generated by enterprise had been unleashed in the Brig'ton beat policeman's young daughter. French polishing had never been like this. As she herself described to her friend that first trading experience, 'It was just great.' She spoke in detail about it years later in a rare interview. 'It was at Parkhead Cross and it was nae bother at a'. When ah started selling from it that was when it gave me the idea of running a barra for masel. So I did just that. I bought masel a set of scales and hired a barra but I didnae know where to buy ma supplies and they had to show me the way to the fruit bazaar. At first I sold fruit during the day and at night I would go round the cinema queues selling what I had left. Then I began to vary my sales, buying fish which I sold in the morning and went on to fruit in the afternoons.'

Her enterprise paid off. Teenager Margaret Russell quit being a French polisher and became a street hawker. And it was a fellow trader who was to become her boyfriend, then husband, the pair of them meeting when buying their early-morning supplies at the wholesalers' fruit bazaar. Just like Maggie, James McIver traded from a hand-cart and, like the girl he was to marry, was an enterprising individual, keen to expand and progress. And what better way of doing that, the young newlyweds thought – Maggie was just 17 at the time – than by pooling their savings. They invested their few pounds in a pony and small float at first, then opened up a shop in Bridgeton. They soon moved to another in Marshall Lane, just off Gallowgate, then added another. They moved on from retail to wholesale, constantly on the search to improve their business activities and make a better living for themselves.

Having the use of a hand barrow was the first business move in Glasgow at the time. But most who wanted to be street traders couldn't afford their own barrows or, if they could, they had nowhere to store them at night. Owning a few barrows and renting them out, therefore, was an active and flourishing business, and this was to be their next venture. Maggie and James invested in a fleet of barrows which they hired out from a yard they rented in Calton, around other shops and premises such as Tortoloni, the cabinetmakers, Mary Dale's fruit shop, Maggie Divers' oyster shop, a pawnshop and the Lucky Midden, the part of an old sweet factory where they used to toss old and reject sweets and which was so aptly and fondly nicknamed by Gallowgate weans. The term was to become part of the city's patois.

Business in the hiring trade boomed and soon they had over 300 barrows on day, weekend or week-long lease. It meant good money, but not the easy life. The traders needed their barrows very early in the morning. On weekdays they had to be at the markets promptly in order to collect their supplies and at weekends, when the clothing traders were active, so many wanted barrows that the early birds would be there to ensure they would get one. To cater for them they had to open their yard at 4 o'clock on Saturday mornings, their barrows being on hire at 3p a day, or 8p for the week. The traders were so numerous that police had to supervise the queues.

Life for the clothes hawkers was particularly hard, trading as they did in the open. They and their goods were constantly at the mercy of the weather, their pitches often subject to the tolerance, or lack of it, of the local beat policemen. This was particularly the case after the closure and demolition of the Corporation Clothes Market in Greendyke Street in 1922. Opened by the City Council, this had been on the go for nearly 50 years. It was described as 'an outcome of purely humanitarian care for the very humblest stratum of the population'. Maybe a better description was the one which likened it to Dickens's masterly illustration of Krook's rag and bottle warehouse in *Bleak House*. Krook being a cadaverous, withered old man, 'a buyer of bones, old iron, wastepaper, men and women's wardrobes, and to be found surrounded by piles of old bottles, litters of rags, heaps of bones, sacks of human hair and bags of cat skins'. Aye, say the grizzled few who remember the old Greendyke Street market – it was just like that.

It was in 1920, during the decline of this old trading place, that Maggie and James saw the opportunity of opening their own market ground, and when some property became available in the Calton just off Gallowgate on the site of the present Barras, they snapped it up. It was a nostalgic site for the McIvers since it was where they had started their first successful business, the old Scotch Fruit Market.

It had poured for six successive weekends that first winter, the rag traders having to return to their homes with soaked and, as often as not, ruined clothing.

'Just think of it,' said Maggie at the time, her sympathy with the doughty traders. 'They craturs have to go oot hawking' for the stuff. When they get it hame they take it tae the steamie tae wash it oot and get it ready for the public. Then they take it to the barras, put it on display and the rain comes on and it looks like the washin' again.' It made Maggie all the more determined to roof the barrows and she and James decided to go ahead with the project. What they envisaged was drawn up as a plan on their dining-room table for the architects and builders P. & W. MacLellan.

There were problems, however, over the titles for the property. Some of it had been owned by an elderly woman who had lived in the West End of the city, and in any biographical material about Maggie McIver, the only reference to this person is that she was an unfortunate soul named Marion Gilchrist, who met her end by being murdered in Princes Street. But no mention is made anywhere that the unfortunate soul was the victim of one of the most sensational murders to have taken place in Glasgow this century. For Marion Gilchrist was the elderly spinster whom the famous Oscar Slater had been accused of murdering and for which, as a completely innocent man, was to serve 18 years in prison, a full account of which is told in another chapter in this book. Nevertheless, it brings a bizarre twist to the story of Maggie McIver and that ever-so-tenuous link, between her, one of the city's most endearing characters, and the legendary murder case.

Marion Gilchrist left an estate valued at varying sums, ranging from £60,000 to £100,000. Whatever the figure, she was today's equivalent of a millionairess and the changing of her will, eliminating certain members of the family, was undoubtedly the cause of her savage killing.

The murder had occurred in 1908, and estate procedures being estate procedures, the legal formalities of what she had left still hadn't been cleared up by 1926, when Maggie and her husband were trying to buy the East End plot she had owned. This was to delay their final takeover of the property and the negotiations, apparently, would have dragged on for some time more had it not been for the fact that legal men's dilly-dallies were not Maggie's way, and her harrying of them was such that they were to achieve within months what they hadn't been able to do in 18 years.

With the property safely and legally theirs, the McIvers could go ahead with roofing it, but even *that* process wasn't to be left completely in the hands of the builders who had said the first thing they would need to do was to level the entire site and cover it in concrete.

'Never heed about that,' the builders were told. 'We'll do it ourselves,' said the McIvers. And they did, for that was the way with them. Maybe their motto should have been 'Just do it' – it was certainly Maggie's motto. So, in order to speed the building process, she and James with others in the family rolled up their sleeves and prepared the site on their own. And in 1926, six years after they had bought the property, the Barras got its first roof, followed three years later with a walled structure. Sadly, it was to be just a year after this that Maggie's husband, James, died. He finally succumbed to the recurring malaria from which he had suffered since contracting the disease while serving in the First World War. Maggie, in her late forties, was left alone to raise her big family of nine.

With the Barras covered and thriving and having added more pieces of ground to her burgeoning business, ever-enterprising Maggie planned her next big venture. She had considered a whole variety of new ideas, but the one that was to eventuate came about as much by chance as by business acumen. It became that venue which today is one of the principal pop music venues in Scotland . . . the famous Barrowland.

Maggie had regularly hired public halls for stallholders' dinner dances. Rare, old-fashioned nights of soup, steak pie and peas, sweet, tea and two cakes, and a smashing night's dancing for 13p a head. Going over her books, Maggie made note of the various overheads, such as £36 for the dance masters as they were known, the professional organisers of such events, plus lighting, heating, taxes, and so on. Now, she thought, if only they had their own hall, many of these overheads could be considerably reduced. Then she had another look at what property she had in the Gallowgate and, sure enough, there was sufficient room there for a hall of their own.

Thus, the creation of Barrowland went ahead, the venue opening for its first dance on Christmas Eve, 1934. On that first night, the drummer of the band that had been hired couldn't make it and a substitute had to be arranged. He was Billy MacGregor, the bandleader for many years, later to become as much of a legend as the dance hall itself. And yet again this was because of another astute move by Maggie. The Barrowland's original band had been the Bluebirds, led by Billy Blue, who rented the hall from Maggie. The new dance hall, right on the doorstep of the East End, was an instant and sensational hit, with long queues forming every Saturday. When Maggie saw the extent of these it was obvious she had a real winner. It was also more than obvious that there would be more profit in running the dances herself instead of renting out the premises. So she asked drummer Billy MacGregor to form his own resident band. And the name MacGregor chose for his band (don't even dare to think anything into the name) was . . . the Gaybirds. Barrowland was born in an era when gay still had its original meaning, and that was happiness of a carefree and merry kind, and *nothing* else. It wasn't till years later that the word was to be hijacked.

There's no overemphasis in the use of the terms sensational and legendary when it comes to applying them to Barrowland, the Barras and the McIvers. So famous had they become by the Second World War, they even managed to get up the noses of the Germans. Word had reached them that too many people were having too good a time in and around that part of Gallowgate. There wasn't even the trace of a crack in their morale. Men and women home on leave from the armed forces together with others from Allied armies were all making a beeline for one of the best dance halls in Britain anytime they came to Glasgow. And that's the very message that was annoying the Germans who got their top propagandist on the job, the infamous traitor William Joyce, known as Lord Haw Haw for his anti-British broadcasts from Germany.

Joyce's role was to break the spirit of the British, instead of which he made everyone laugh. And they couldn't have laughed more in Glasgow on the nights he made jibes about the Barrowland and the dancers who went there. In a well-remembered broadcast one night he sneeringly told his large audience in Britain: 'I know how well the Barrowland people treat the French and American soldiers, and I hope they will do the same for the German victors when they arrive in Scotland.'

His broadcast had an effect on the city, all right. Listeners had never had such a laugh – and when the word got round, the spirit of wartime Glasgow soared, and with good reason. For the world was talking about their favourite dance hall.

The year 1958 was to be one of the saddest for the McIver family. In the space of only a few months they were to lose the matriarch of the family, Maggie dying peacefully at the age of 77, and the Barrowland dance hall was destroyed by fire. It was a devastating double blow to them. But with the same bounce-back determination of old Maggie herself, they rebuilt an even better Barrowland dance hall and the present structure opened for a gala Christmas eve dance in 1960. The *New Musical Express* voted it the third best venue in the United Kingdom.

The Barras itself as a market trading site has today been considerably reorganised, thanks to a Barrows Enterprise Trust which has improved and redeveloped the entire trading area, enhancing it with decorative entrances and establishing it as the busiest and most prosperous trading market in the country.

15

GLASGOW AT WAR

Unlike the First World War, it didn't take long for the early effects of the Second World War to be seen and felt in Glasgow. The Great War, as they had called it, the war they said was to end all wars, had ended just over 20 years previously and vestiges of it were still imprinted on the national psyche. Everyone, it seemed, had lost a brother or son, a father or uncle, and vivid recollections of it were still part of everyday conversation. Sepia pictures of uniformed men, the bloom of youth hardly gone from their young faces and who would never be seen again, decorated the walls of countless tenement homes.

Those men marching off never to return had perhaps been the most visual impact of the war on the city. There were regular farewell parades of the various regiments, one of the biggest and most memorable of which had been for Glasgow's own regiment, which, despite coming from Glasgow, was called the Highland Light Infantry. Thousands lined Sauchiehall Street as they marched down with fixed bayonets and cheery faces. But other than the cheering and waving to the new conscripts as they paraded through the streets on their way to the railway station and to what they thought was glory but in fact was hell, the First World War had very little visible impact on the city.

Food rationing had been voluntary at first, and not made compulsory until well into the war, although restaurants had instituted meatless days. There had been concern that perhaps one of the big airships they called Zeppelins, named after a German count, might be able to fly far enough to drop some bombs, so dimmed lights were enforced. As it was, their raiders didn't get this far, although they managed to reach Edinburgh where they dropped a few bombs on the High Street.

It was all so different in Glasgow in World War II. It was a mere eight hours after war was declared that fateful Sunday morning of 3 September 1939, that Glasgow was to be concussed with news that shocked the city. An innocent passenger ship belonging to a Glasgow shipping firm and which had sailed from the Clyde just days before, had been savagely attacked at sea without warning and sank. Crewmen and passengers, including many mothers and young children, were among the large casualty list. It was the equivalent in today's terms of some enemy fighter downing an innocuous passenger jet.

Just a few days before, the SS *Athenia*, belonging to the well-known shipping company Donaldson Atlantic Line, had sailed from the Clyde. It was a routine sailing like so many others, Glasgow and North American ports having the strongest of trade and other links. The *Athenia* would normally leave on a Friday, sail down to Liverpool then over to Belfast picking up more passengers at each before heading out across the Atlantic for Montreal and Quebec, arriving there nine days after leaving the Clyde. This had also been her intended routine that first day in September 1939, before the declaration of war on Sunday the 3rd. This time, however, the *Athenia* had more passengers than usual. Many, many more. Thousands of American and Canadian tourists in Britain and Europe were anxiously cutting short their vacations because of the impending war and every available west-bound ship was crammed with these anxious holidaymakers, eager to get home.

It wasn't just Americans and Canadians who were desperate to get to the safety of the other side of the Atlantic. Europeans of varying nationalities, including many Germans and Austrians, fearful of what was about to happen, were just as anxious to get to the peaceful haven that was the New World. So, too, were hundreds of young Scots children whose families, mostly with close ties in Canada, were taking the precaution of having them evacuated to friends and relatives there. Such was the make-up of the 1,101 passengers, more than twice as many as the biggest jumbo jet can carry, who packed the cabins and lounges on board the SS *Athenia* as she headed into the Atlantic that day. There were so many on board, the cabins couldn't hold them all and they were sleeping in lounges, even in the toilets.

It was just after 11 o'clock on that Sunday morning that the captain

received an urgent and dramatic message from the ship's agents . . .
Britain was at war with Germany. He ordered notices to that effect to be
posted throughout the vessel, the passengers happily contending with
their overcrowded conditions now knowing their decision to get as far
from Europe as possible had been totally justified. Little did they realise
what lay ahead.

It was just eight hours after the world-shattering announcement had
been made, as the ship left the coast of Ireland behind them and struck
a course of due west, that the SS *Athenia* came into the viewfinder of the
German U-boat's periscope. Who knows what was in that commander's
mind as he viewed the innocent passenger ship. Whatever his thoughts,
there was no mistaking what he could see, for there was absolutely no
resemblance between this ordinary-looking, civilian liner with its total
absence of any form of weaponry, and any form of battleship. No doubt,
his decision-making would have been on the basis that Britain had
declared war on them and this, therefore, was a ship of the enemy.

The order he gave to launch an attack was to put the Glasgow vessel
in a unique and tragic place in the history of the Second World War. For
that lethal torpedo streaking towards the *Athenia* in the chill waters of
early autumn in the North Atlantic was to be the first shot of the Second
World War at sea. It was just after 7.30 in the evening. With the target
being that harmless passenger ship, there was to be no mistaking the
message from the Germans; no misinterpreting their intended modus
operandi for whatever lay ahead. Quite starkly, it was that nothing and
no one would be spared in the conflict.

It was still light outside when the torpedo struck at exactly 7.40 p.m.
Inside the ship, however, all the lights had been on as one of the first
precautions of the ship's master had been to impose strict blackout
conditions, sealing every window, closing the deadlights on all
portholes. When the torpedo struck, every light went out and the
interior of the ship was plunged into instant pitch darkness.

Nineteen-year-old Thomas Ritchie from Possilpark was one of the
crewmen on the *Athenia*. He was an assistant steward with the
Donaldson Line on a wage of £8.75 a month. Many years after the war
I spoke to him and he gave me a graphic, first-hand account of what
happened after the high-explosive, underwater missile from the U-boat
thundered into his ship.

'We were serving the evening meal and I was in the pantry when there
was this enormous explosion followed by a sensation of great heat. All
the lights went out immediately and everything was in total darkness. It
was not so bad for the crew for we knew our way about the ship

blindfolded. But when I came out of the pantry into the dining-room there was screaming and panic.'

The scene with which the young seaman was confronted was of nightmare proportions, worse than anything he could ever have imagined being faced with at sea. The devastation caused by the explosion had fractured vital pipes, which criss-cross every bulkhead on a ship, and these were spurting their contents over passengers and crew. Some had been carrying thick oil, some scalding steam, others hot water, cold water and waste. Stairways had been blown away. Food and all the other contents of dinner tables had been scattered and everything was in a ghastly jumble amid passengers and crew, together with gushing oil and scalding steam. The screams of the burned and the dying were horrific.

'The first staircase we came to had been blown off and we had to climb to the deck above by little ledges. Crewmen were under orders to get to the lifeboats as quickly as possible in such emergencies, each man having a specific task so that the boats be made ready and lowered as safely as possible and with the correct number of passengers. Everyone knows the horrible mess seabirds get into with oil spillages. Well, that's the way we all were as we made for the lifeboats that night.'

It was no dignified sight that the young Glasgow seamen faced when they eventually did reach their respective boat stations. It was every man for himself in the unseemly scramble for the lifeboats, many men shoving women and children aside to clamber aboard the small boats.

'I had to grab one of the axes from the boat to which I was allotted and threaten the males who were trying to storm it, shouting to them that the first to put his leg over would get it chopped off.' It was only then that this particular lifeboat could be boarded with women and children, the davits lowering it safely to the water, despite being grossly overloaded with more than 100 passengers when it should only have taken 80.

The crewmen rowed right through the night and the passengers, with water almost reaching their knees, had to bale water constantly from the leaking craft. After a few hours, they tried to reach a ship with an illuminated Norwegian flag painted on her side which had been picking up survivors. But the sea was running against them and no amount of hard rowing could take them towards the potential saviour.

In the early hours of the following morning, and without any warning, they were startled to suddenly find themselves in the beam of a powerful searchlight. They were sure it was the U-boat or another enemy craft and feared for the worst. Then the shape of the ship hove into sight. In the fragile light of dawn, what they saw appeared to be the shapely lines of some luxury yacht. They were not wrong. It was a Swedish vessel which, it turned out, belonged to the multi-millionaire who owned Electrolux and who had been on a cruise to Miami at the time.

Safely on board, each survivor was handed hot soup and cigarettes. Tom almost had a relapse when he looked up at the man who was serving him with his ration: it was his very own father! Colin Ritchie had also been a crewman on the *Athenia* and had been picked up earlier from his lifeboat by the sleek, ocean-going Swedish yacht.

The ending was not so happy for many who had been on board the *Athenia* on that fateful voyage. Of the 1,101 passengers and 315 crew on board, 112 were killed, including 69 women and 16 children. Many more suffered horrific burns and other injuries. It was the first major story of the war involving death and destruction and Glasgow had learned in an instant what kind of conflict lay before them.

Within a week of leaving Glasgow, the first survivors of the stricken *Athenia* were back in the city again, a destroyer having landed them at Greenock. Many were taken to what was then the Beresford Hotel in Sauchiehall Street, now the Baird Hall students' residence. As many were American, the US ambassador in London immediately despatched his young son to Glasgow to comfort survivors and offer his condolences to Lord Provost Patrick Dollan. The handsome young American enrolled to perform one of his first public duties, endeared himself to those he met. Among those to whom he spoke was the young Possilpark survivor Thomas Ritchie who remembered how genuinely interested he seemed in the ordeal he and the others had faced. The engaging young American was in later life to become one of the foremost world figures. He was John F. Kennedy.

Glasgow Royal Air Force men were also to make an early mark in the history of World War II. At the time, Glasgow had its own Royal Air Force auxiliary squadron, composed of volunteers who served on a similar basis to the men of the Territorial Army. The 602 (City of Glasgow) Squadron, who had their headquarters in Coplaw Street, Govanhill, were to become a household name in the city during the war for the countless daring deeds of their dashing pilots in the skies over Britain. The 602, whose planes were based at Renfrew Airport, had been in existence since 1925, and was the first squadron to be formed in the new Auxiliary Air Force. And just to show how Scottish they were, they were the first air force men to introduce the kilt to their dress uniforms.

Shortly before the outbreak of war, the 602 had become a fighter squadron and was equipped with the new Spitfire, which later became one of the most legendary warplanes. Because of the need for air protection for the considerable activity around naval installations in the Firth of Forth, the Squadron had been posted to Drem, in East Lothian, which had its own rather unique place in flying history since it was near the starting point of the first two-way crossing of the Atlantic by the airship R34. It didn't take long for the move to be well justified. On 16 October 1939, a small convoy of ships, which had gathered at Gibraltar, were being escorted towards ports in the Forth when they were attacked by German bombers. The 602 Squadron from nearby North Berwick were scrambled and together with pilots from the 603 (City of Edinburgh) Squadron, dispersed the attackers.

It was in this engagement that 602 pilots claimed the credit of shooting down the first German aircraft of the war. However, true to form in traditional Glasgow-Edinburgh rivalry, the capital's fliers made the counter claim that it was they who bagged that first invader from the Luftwaffe. Whoever it was, both squadrons had triumphed on that day in October and what is not disputed in official records was that it was the first action of RAF's Fighter Command during the war. Between them, the Glasgow and Edinburgh men had brought down four German aircraft. But if you come from Glasgow, and especially if you had any connection, no matter how remote, with the 602, there was just no doubting who got that first enemy kill.

The 602 went on to undisputed glory as the war went on, being one of the most successful squadrons in the Battle of Britain which played such a decisive part in the immediate progress of the early years of the war. Throughout that legendary battle over the skies of southern England, they were to down a grand total of 89 German planes. On one day alone, 15 September 1940 – designated Battle of Britain Day – the 602 were responsible for destroying ten German planes without themselves losing one man or plane. They were to be in constant action throughout the war, taking part in the invasion of Europe and in action against German rocket sites. At war's end their total count of enemy aircraft destroyed was 150.

It was yet another Glasgow RAF man, but not a member of the 602, who was to become the first great solo hero of the war. John Hannah's name was to come as easy from the lips of Glaswegians at the time as would any of their top football stars. For John was the first Scot of the war to win the Victoria Cross, the highest, and rarest, of gallantry honours.

Sergeant Gunner John Hannah came from Scotstoun. He joined the

RAF at the outbreak when he was just 17, volunteering for aircrew and qualifying as a wireless operator/air gunner. Almost as soon as he had gained his aircrew wings and just a few weeks after his 18th birthday he was on bombing missions over mainland Europe in the role of an air gunner, the most precarious of duties on board bomber planes, not least because their posts are the first targets of opposing fighter craft.

In mid-September 1940, John was one of a four-man, light bomber crew on a night raid over Belgium, where their target was the docks at Antwerp through which vital German supplies were being shipped to their troops in North Africa. The Germans had the port ringed with batteries of deadly anti-aircraft guns which peppered the skies at the sight or sound of British planes. John's small plane, about the size of today's small executive jet, was riddled with shellfire from these guns before reaching the target, but that was not to deter them and they bravely pressed on with their raid. They had to fly over the same lethal curtain of ground fire on their return home, and once again suffered from the German guns, this time receiving both direct hits and shrapnel penetration. Such was the extent of these hits on them, that the floor beneath the pilot was completely blown away leaving him sitting on the bare chassis of the plane.

A serious fire then broke out and the captain ordered the crew to bale out. One of these men who safely parachuted was later to report that the last time he saw Hannah, he was at his post surrounded by the flames of a blazing fire and he presumed that he was either dying or dead. But the Glasgow man was still alive and, as that crewman had witnessed, was at his post where he continued to strafe the marauding German night fighters which had taken over the attack from the ground batteries. The fire in the plane became so severe that ammunition piled around him began exploding and he was forced to leave his Vickers gun post to tackle the flames. He beat at them first of all with his log book, then his flying helmet and finally his hands. Amazingly, his unbridled courage and sheer determination won through and the flames were eventually extinguished. As soon as they were out he crawled along the narrow fuselage, the wind screaming through its countless shell and bullet holes, to report the news to the pilot, a Canadian. As the engines appeared unscathed and with the fire out, the pilot changed his mind about abandoning the plane and with John taking over the role of co-pilot and navigator he decided they should try and make it for home.

Senior officers at their base in England were staggered when they saw the battered bomber circle the field before landing. They couldn't believe that a plane with so many holes clearly visible from the ground could fly.

And when it finally rolled up, they reported that they had never before seen such a badly damaged plane return to base.

The two flying heroes were immediately recommended for the highest bravery awards, Hannah becoming the proud recipient of the Victoria Cross, while the Distinguished Flying Cross was awarded to the Canadian pilot who, tragically, was to be killed on his very next mission. As a result of his severe burning injuries, Hannah had to receive extensive plastic surgery, an innovation in the medical world at the time. But the brave Glasgow man never fully recovered from his severe injuries. He was discharged from the RAF two years later and only lived a further five years. Glasgow, however, did not forget John Hannah, VC. His name lives on at his old school, Victoria Drive Secondary in Scotstoun, where each year the John Hannah Trophy is awarded to their most distinguished pupil.

16

THE GOOD TIMES
STOP ROLLING

While the war had such an immediate and dramatic impact on Glasgow, what with the savage sinking of the *Athenia* and men of the city's 602 Squadron going into such quick combat, it had all been so different and war so distant during those summer months just prior to the declaration. There had, of course, been all the prospects of a second world war breaking out, but irrespective of the direst of warnings about the grim times which they were being told could lie ahead, Glaswegians carried on with their lives with traditional zest and enthusiasm. And many of the events that concerned their life were much as they are today. Like football.

Aberdeen had kicked off the new season by beating Celtic 3–1, the Glasgow team featuring Kennaway, Hogg and Morrison; Geatons, Lyon and Paterson; Anderson, McDonald, Crum, Divers and Murphy. The other main Glasgow side, Rangers, got off to a better start, beating St Mirren 3–1. Their team starred the legendary goalkeeper Jerry Dawson, along with Gray and Shaw; Bolt, Woodburn and Symon; Waddell, Fiddes, Thornton, Venters and Kinnear. Nostalgic names, all of them, to older fans who, to a man, will wryly note the total absence of foreign names in their teams and wish their likes were around today.

That summer had seen other sporting highlights, like speedboat king Sir Malcolm Campbell skimming over Coniston Water at an incredible 141 mph; golfer Dick Burton from Sale winning the Open Championship at St Andrews, beating the American J. Bulls of Chicago; and 60,000 turning up at Ibrox but not for football. They were there to see one of the greatest athletic sports meetings in the country. That was the reputation of the annual Ibrox Sports, one of the major field and track meetings of the day, attracting champions from all over the world. And that summer of 1939, Sydney Wooderson, the bespectacled and unassuming English runner was one of the star attractions, justifying his presence by setting a new mile record. And note his time – 4 minutes, 11.8 seconds.

The prospect of a looming war certainly had no impact on the more nefarious aspects of Glasgow life. The city's notorious street gangs didn't need the threats of Germans or others. They had wars of their own to contend with, and the police that year had to reinforce their patrols in the Gorbals to contain the regular conflicts of two of the more infamous gangs, the local Bee Hive Boys and the Stickit from over the Clyde in Bridgeton.

Elsewhere, and in more peaceful pursuits, the Royal family were having their usual 'hols' at Balmoral; Colville's, the big steelworks at Cambuslang, had just set a world record by making over 7,000 tons of steel in a week; and nudist colonies were becoming fashionable, Glasgow's newest club advertising for members for their camp at Lugton in Ayrshire, of all places, far better known for golf rather than gall.

As always, it seems, the IRA were in the news. There had been sensational newspaper stories about the prospect of them launching a mainland bombing campaign, saying that they were being backed by 'foreign organisations', obviously meaning the Germans. The stories, it was to turn out, were no wild speculation, for just weeks after they appeared, a bomb went off in the left-luggage at King's Cross Station killing a young Scot and badly injuring his newly-wed wife.

But most people were concerned with the happier events of life. The popular Clyde towns, Glasgow's beloved 'Doon the Watter' resorts, had one of their boom seasons: a typical boarding house at Millport advertising bed and breakfast with porridge, ham and eggs and toast for 20p a night and the promise of an evening at one of their great wee pubs where half an' halfs were going for 5.5p . . . 4p for the whisky, 1.5p for the beer. And a packet of 20 Capstan cost another 5p, all of which were prevailing prices on the Clyde at the time.

Thousands of other holidaymakers, perhaps better heeled, headed for further-off places, such as Scarborough, Isle of Man and Blackpool and all the other fond Glasgow favourites. Mind you, they tended to be dearer than Millport. At Blackpool, the going rate for a B&B was 22.5p a day and full board was 40p, or £2.80 for the week. At Douglas, you could get what the Manx folk referred to as TBB . . . tea, bed and breakfast. And that would cost you 25p a night.

If those prices seem incredible, comparative High Street prices verged on the unbelievable. A business or lounge suit from a good city tailor cost £3.15. A sports jacket in the same shop, £1.25. Sports shirts were priced at 14p, boys' shoes 18p. And if you shopped around at bargain suppliers, they were even cheaper than that.

Lewis's in Argyle Street was one of the city's main stores and at their sale that summer 12ft x 9ft Axminster carpets were going for £2.50. Women's linen skirts with matching jackets at the same sale were 25p and an oak dining-room suite just £8.55. Or, if you wanted it on credit, £9.14.

Few had cars, but if you were affluent enough to afford such a luxury, year-old second-hand Ford 10s (with sliding roof and real leather upholstery) were on sale at £90, rival Vauxhall's (de luxe model) of the same vintage, £140. Just as few had the resources to buy their own home, although it was becoming increasingly fashionable. One of the big builders had a showhouse bungalow built on a site, now a service station, just across from the Plaza Ballroom at Eglinton Toll and they were selling new semi-detached villas for a £25 deposit, with repayments at just over £1 a week. And that £25 first payment also included the price of your removal to your new house. Try getting a builder to throw that in for your multi-thousand deposit today!

And wages! While prices may well be inconceivable, wages left little of the disposable. The average worker's take-home pay was between £3 and £5 a week (considerably less for women), and it was much more difficult then to buy that £140 Vauxhall or save a £25 deposit on a house than it is today, even by our comparatively astronomical prices.

Despite the fact that more than 150,000 Glasgow men and women were off to the fighting Services – four Victoria Crosses being among the hundreds of gallantry medals shared between them – the population of Glasgow grew to an all-time record after war broke out. From around 1,100,000 in 1939, the population soared to 1,300,000 in the early '40s, mainly due to workers being 'directed' to jobs in the armaments factories in the city. There was a 'you'll work where you're tellt' policy and it was to see nearly a quarter of a million being ordered from their towns and villages throughout Scotland to take up compulsory employment in Glasgow. They made up the workforce in the vital munitions factories and engineering plants engaged in the war effort, most of them within the city boundaries. There were jobs for everybody and everybody was in a job, huge workforces being needed by many of the plants. The scale of these workforces was colossal, like the new Rolls Royce plant in Hillington where there were 27,000 workers on the payroll of the one company.

Despite life carrying on virtually as normal that summer of 1939, there were some foretastes of the grim and dark days to come. In order to get the city's defences readied, the first blackouts were imposed. This meant showing no light whatsoever from any room in your house and bales of sombre black curtain material were snapped up from shops for the purpose.

Windows were taped to prevent splintering from bomb blasts and all sorts of designs, some bordering on art form, were being devised by householders to make the taping look as attractive as possible.

As soon as war broke out, the more casual aspect of these blackout trials quickly ended and the new lights-out rules imposed in real earnest. Air Raid Precaution wardens, together with police, patrolled every street, enforcing the strictest blackout policy – heavy fines were imposed on persistent offenders whose curtains exposed any light.

There had been a surge of volunteers for the new ARP, almost a million and a half of them enlisting in the civil defence force throughout the UK. Their patrol men's cries of 'put out that light' or the one that was to become a catchphrase, 'Mind that chink', the chink, of course, being any sliver of light showing from a window, were a regular part of nightly city ritual. And if you didn't mind your chinks, there was a bobby at the door with an opened charge book. But Glaswegians don't take to authority without a laugh back at them, and Dave Willis, one of the star comedians of the day, had everyone in stitches with his air-raid patrolman's stage routine. Willis, a Chaplinesque character from the Cowcaddens whose moustache also doubled for that of Hitler's, used the resemblance to full advantage to deride the German corporal to the great delight of wartime theatre audiences. But it was his Air Raid Precaution warden's song, 'In My Wee Gas Mask', that was to be Glasgow's own 'Lili Marlene' song of defiance, the simple and flippant words easily remembered and universally sung by everyone, it seemed, from weans to grannies: 'In my wee gas mask, I'm working oot a plan, and a' the kids imagine that I'm just a bogey man. Whenever there's a raid on, Listen to the cry . . .' and so on till it's final line, which was about Willis himself – 'The nicest looking warden in the ARP'. The bombers might be coming, but Glasgow was determined not to let that get them down and 'My Wee Gas Mask' was just one of their ways of showing it.

As well as house lights, street lighting was likewise doused or dimmed, city thoroughfares becoming so dark most pedestrians carried small torches to find their way around. Trams, trains and buses also had their interior lights either dimmed or extinguished, only the conductor having a small light to facilitate the collection of fares. And what few private cars that were on the road (only essential travellers engaged in war work were allowed petrol) had special masking shades fitted to headlamps with mudguards and bumpers trimmed in white paint so that they might be seen by pedestrians and other traffic. It was a muggers' paradise had there been any, that is. But that scourge of latter-day society had still to emerge.

Every available building contractor was called in to help prepare for whatever air onslaught the Germans had in mind for the city. Exhibitions of the available types of shelter for those lucky enough with gardens in which to have them built, were staged in George Square and main railway stations. One of the most popular was the semi-underground Anderson, made of corrugated sheeting and covered with earth, the occasional one still used to this day as a garden shed. And there was the locally made Hudson, 'giving admirable protection against splinter and high-explosive bombs'. Yours for just £30 . . . or the price of a good holiday in Morecambe Bay.

But as most Glaswegians lived in tenements there wasn't to be the luxury of a personal shelter. At first, householders were advised that if there were no proper shelters available, their closes were the best available areas for protection and that they should congregate in them during raids. As many as possible had stout wooden supports and reinforcement buttresses erected inside them.

These were to become instant play paradises for children who utilised them as climbing frames and a new form of wet-weather, adventure playground. Outside each close-mouth, brick baffle walls were erected to prevent debris and shrapnel from blowing into the building entrance. Occupiers of tenements that didn't have their entrances reinforced like this, or without nearby shelters, were advised to gather in the lobbies of ground-floor tenants. They would have a better chance of survival there, they were told – and a new meeting-place for evening parties was born.

Sites were set up in public parks either for anti-aircraft gun emplacements or for one of the RAF barrage balloon units which ringed the city as a further deterrent, the object of them being that enemy bombers would get ensnared in the balloon's hawsers. Every citizen was issued with a gas mask which had to be carried at all times and the main railway stations were packed with hundreds of children being evacuated for their safety to the country.

Glasgow was ready for whatever was coming, at least so it appeared. But despite all these visible precautions, the ARP patrol men and blackouts and the dire warnings from the Government to prepare for the worst, a survey surprisingly revealed that only 30 per cent thought there would be heavy raids. Most were either vague, indifferent or didn't expect them at all. Maybe it had something to do with Glasgow phlegm.

Alas, just as the Government had warned, the bombers did come, although not, thankfully, with the ferocity experienced by English cities like London, Liverpool and Coventry. That fate was being reserved for boundary neighbour, Clydebank, which was to suffer one of the most concentrated air attacks perpetrated by the Germans during the war. The town was so devastated, only seven of its 12,000 homes were left undamaged after two nights of ruthless air-raids. The vital Clydeside engineering and shipbuilding plants had been the target, but most were missed and innocent civilians suffered instead.

Glasgow wasn't completely eliminated from the Germans' plans. The first fearful sounds of the wailing air-raid sirens could be heard in earnest in a daring daytime attack on 19 July 1940. This was followed by a night raid on 18 September of the same year when a stick of bombs straddled George Square, but missed all the important targets. A building in North Hanover Street was destroyed, as was the corner block at Ingram and Queen Street, which is why the modern building there now is out of character with the others around it.

It was on this raid that one of the German bombs, a huge 500 pounder, directly hit the cruiser HMS *Sussex*, berthed for repairs at Yorkhill Quay. The bomb didn't go off, however, although it tore through three decks of the ship causing severe damage and putting it out of action for two years. Hundreds of families living in Yorkhill as well as the young patients in the Royal Hospital for Sick Children had to be evacuated until the bomb was defused. Had it gone off it would have detonated the huge armament supply carried on the vessel, devastating the surrounding area.

It wasn't till 1941 that Glasgow was to experience the worst from the German bombers. They had already flown over Clydeside on numerous reconnaissance flights, photographing all the essential heavy industry and shipyards which beribboned the river. These had been gone over in fine detail by the crack Luftwaffe Pathfinder unit, Kampf Gruppe 100, who were to lead the deadly aerial armada of hundreds of Heinkel 111 and Junker 88 bombers. This was to be a major blitz: so many bombers were required that they had to be culled from bases throughout parts of occupied northern Europe, from Beauvais in France, Aalborg in Denmark, Stavanger in Norway and others from Holland and North Germany. Their converging point, the Firth of Clyde.

The heavy, threatening drone of their engines, a chilling deep throb that was to become such a distinguishing mark of the German planes, could be heard all over Central Scotland, from Ayrshire to as far north, it was claimed, as Aberdeen.

Their precision navigation having found the target areas, the Pathfinders then dropped small incendiary bombs, and the flames from these ensuing fires gave the bomber crews all the light and target direction they needed. But despite their meticulous planning, their targets carefully labelled, it was to be houses not works, civilians not workers who were to bear the wrath of more than 430 bombers spewing out thousands of high-explosive bombs on two successive nights. They killed more than 1,200 and seriously injured another 1,100 in Clydebank and Glasgow. Although the most concentrated damage was in Clydebank, 647 were killed in Glasgow and 1,680 injured. Bombs were scattered in various districts of the city – a huge map prepared at the time by Glasgow Corporation under the War Damage Act, graphically showed just how much of a pounding the city had taken in various raids. The red parts of the coloured map pinpointed houses which were either totally destroyed or had to be demolished following a raid. The blue parts showed houses and buildings which were seriously damaged and the yellow areas were those which received slight damage, including broken windows.

Just one glance at the map shows the frightening effects of the German *blitzkreig* on Glasgow. Huge swathes of the city, including numerous entire districts, are coloured yellow. These include Gorbals, Tradeston, Oatlands, parts of Bridgeton and Dennistoun, Dalmarnock, Garngad, Shettleston, Plantation, Yorkhill, Scotstoun, Hyndland, Jordanhill, Dowanhill, Kelvindale, Maryhill and all of the suburbs in the western environs of the city.

Areas which have the more serious red and blue colourings include Gorbals, Tradeston, Shawlands, Kelvindale, Blairdardie, the worst being Maryhill, Garscadden and again the western suburbs. The southern suburbs were the luckiest throughout the raids. Only two areas were affected, a parachute mine hitting a row of tenements in Deanston Drive, Shawlands, causing considerable casualties, and a stray bomb destroying a semi-detached villa in Boyd Street, Govanhill. No bombs fell in the city south of these two locations.

A total of 361 streets are listed in the wartime Damaged Properties Index. Some of the more well known of these include Alderman Road, Anniesland Road, Ballater Street, Bellgrove Street, Blairdardie Road, Bridge Street, Buckingham Street, Charlotte Street, Clyde Place, Cloberhill Road, Clarence Drive, Dirleton Avenue, Drumchapel Road, Duke Street, Dumbarton Road, Earlspark Avenue, Finnieston Street, Gallowgate, Govan Road, Great Western Road, High Street, Hyndland Road, Kent Street, Kelvinside Gardens, Knightswoood Road, Lincoln Avenue, Lochlibo Avenue, London Road, Maxwell Road, Moss Road, Nelson Street, Old Dumbarton Road, Peel Street, Polmadie Road, Polnoon Avenue, Queensborough Gardens, Queen Margaret Road, Radnor Street, Roman Avenue, Sauchiehall Street, Scotland Street, Shields Road, Springburn Road, Springfield Road, Sword Street, Tantallon Road, Turnberry Road, Westbourne Gardens, Wilton Street and Yoker Mill Road.

A total of 6,835 houses were damaged and more than 20,000 suffered minor damage. The shipyards of Blythswoods and Yarrows at Scotstoun were badly damaged, 80 workers in the latter being killed when their air-raid shelter received a direct hit.

The raids were to continue sporadically up to 1943, the night of 23 March of that year seeing the last raid on Glasgow. It was as indiscriminate as any of the previous attacks, and the victim this time was Queen's Park Church, one of the splendid works of the famous Glasgow architect, Alexander 'Greek' Thomson.

Soccer matches were curbed during the war years, not just because most of the teams' best players were serving in the Forces, but because it was feared huge crowds could be a potential attraction for a sneak air-raid. Games of a limited nature continued to be played, however, and a sad aspect of these was that despite all the horrors of war in existence at the time, Rangers and Celtic fans continued to behave in what had become a traditional fashion. Liquor was still allowed at matches at the time and bottle-throwing featured in a series of hateful and violent incidents in 1940, 1941 and 1943 – Celtic Park was closed for a month, in fact, after one particularly violent clash between the two clubs' supporters at Ibrox.

Perhaps the great unsung heroines of the war were city housewives. Unlike households in rural areas where there was more likelihood of supplementing rations with some extras from nearby farms, city wives were stuck with the strict terms of the Government rations. The war was only three months old when food rationing was introduced. Food could only be bought on production of your own personal ration book, the butcher or grocer deducting the appropriate amount of coupons, each one dated so there would be no 'saving'. And when your coupons were finished, so too was your shopping – stiff fines or even imprisonment were imposed on anyone flouting the new food laws.

To make the rations go round was a real test of kitchen ingenuity and enterprise. Many items simply disappeared from food shops and were never to be seen again until the war ended. A whole generation of children grew up without ever seeing an orange or a banana along with most other fruits and many vegetables. What was available was on the ration. At first the weekly meat allowance was a frugal 11p per person, which more or less came to 1 lb. But as the war went on, the initial meat portion was to be drastically cut. So too were other items. Bacon and butter started off at four ounces per person and 12 ounces of sugar per week; you got a mere two ounces each of tea, margarine and cooking fat, and cheese fluctuated from two to eight ounces. Sweets and chocolates varied between three to four ounces.

The brave merchant sailors and their convoys bringing food supplies to Britain suffered even more as the war progressed, as they were under constant threat and attack from German U-boats and surface warships, hundreds of merchant ships already having been lost. As supplies got more scarce, this meant further cuts for the housewife and even these meagre rations were cut further, fats (butter, margarine and lard) going down to four ounces, bacon from eight to four ounces. Meat was trimmed to eight ounces a week and eggs were so scarce that at one time the ration was one egg – between two persons per week. Bolstering your diet with the occasional fish supper meant being at your local chippy early for a place in the long queue, hoping you would be served before their limited supplies ran out.

Improvisation was the thing and the women's pages in newspapers and magazines along with radio programmes, devoted much space and time to suggestions for housewives on how they could substitute and improvise. Typical was the popular recipe to make up for the non-existence of bananas . . . a substitute banana sandwich spread. This was made with boiled parsnips mashed cold and flavoured with banana essence. Condensed milk mixed with vinegar was a substitute for unavailable salad dressing. Wonders were performed with dried egg powder. Okay, you couldn't reconstitute a boiled egg with it, but it could be used for a passable omelette. And together with dried milk powder and some flour, amazing surprises appeared from baking ovens. Jam was limited to eight ounces per month, but there was a special allowance of sugar for jam-making and most wives had a go. And the efforts to which others went to produce their own alcohol . . . now *that's* a whole legend in itself.

Shortages being shortages and Glasgow being Glasgow, a whole new breed of suppliers appeared virtually overnight and almost, it seemed, at every street corner, public bar, workplace, meeting-place or anywhere else that people in numbers were to he found. There was a variety of names for them, but invariably they were known as spivs, although most were to take serious objection if you called them that to their face. The word came from the old dialect word spiving, meaning smart. And just as it originally meant these were the smart boys, the wide-o's. Like other commodities in life, they came in a variety of forms, some benign, others malign. Some could get you a little bit of this and that, and said they only did it for a bit of a giggle, 'and a few shillings on the side, like'. While others, more unscrupulous, were engaged in activities which bordered on grand larceny. Ask any of them if you could buy an army motorbike with enough petrol coupons to last you a year and the reply would likely be, 'Give me a week, mate.'

If you had the cash, it wasn't all that difficult, it seemed, to get the goods you wanted. If you didn't know someone, there was always one who knew someone else who would get you that luxury for which you craved, and as the war years continued, and shortages became more acute, luxuries were things like that extra half pound of butter, a bar of chocolate, a quarter bottle of whisky or rum – you could forget about gin – and trendier than Capstan or Players were Lucky Strike, Camel or Chesterfields, or if the supplier was really good, those kingsize Pall Malls.

Short of a few meat ration coupons? No problem. Your local spiv would get you them. Sweet coupons even easier. Pair of nylons to impress the girlfriend, maybe? They'll cost you, friend. But no problem. There's a big American ship in the Clyde and the market's good for nylons, and they're sheer ones at that. Mind you, they'll set you back a couple of quid . . .

Most of the spivs operated without having to commit a felony; well, a serious felony, that is. There was an active trade in all forms of ration coupons, as well as complete books themselves, many of which were bought from the poor who would sacrifice their own and their family's essential means of calories for the sake of a few shillings. A big source of the spivs' supplies was the American servicemen. A large base of their soldiers was stationed at Cowglen, near Pollok – sailors and marines being regular visitors to the Clyde – and the USAAF was based at Prestwick.

Many of their servicemen, in pursuit of local currency or other discretionary favours – more likely the latter – were the most willing suppliers of their own rations of tobacco, spirits and clothing. They were able to get you you any item of food you desired, in fact, even commodities that had still to be introduced to the UK, such as instant coffee from their camp or base's PX (Post Exchange), the American servicemen's equivalent of the British Forces' NAAFI.

Buying such goods, however, was not without its risks, not the least of them being spotted by one of the considerable number of plain-clothes policemen, active in curbing the activities of the spivs. The biggest danger, however, was in some of the illicit alcohol which was on sale. Whisky had become virtually unobtainable, but if you were lucky enough to get some, it would be strictly rationed and only available as a measure from your local pub – and even then they would demand that you were a regular before getting your half. Some of the less principled spivs traded in alcohol from the most dubious sources, such as those who remembered or thought they remembered the ways of their grandfathers and their stills up in the glens or out on the bogs. Such poteen or whisky wasn't so bad, provided you closed your eyes tightly after a good swig and followed it quickly with a more wholesome beer to take the stinging taste away. The thoroughly immoral illicit wartime traders would sell bottles of reputed spirits which had a much more dubious background than backyard poteen. Some bought from sources who made up hooch from raw alcohol, mixing it with other agents such as the spirits in aircraft and ships' navigational instruments, and sometimes even anti-freeze – resulting, needless to say, in a number of unfortunates who ended up either blind or dead as a result of consuming their lethal liquor.

Wartime Glasgow was a whole new experience for its citizens, whether it be through fear of the air-raids, the endurance of housewives daily queuing for food, the absence of so many of the menfolk in the Forces, the incredible cosmopolitan, almost carnival, scene that had become the city centre, crowded with servicemen in uniforms of countless countries, Lord Haw Haw on the radio telling us to give the same welcome to the Germans when they came, food rationing and shortages of all kinds, blackouts and barrage balloons . . . and the spivs.

There were good times: amid the communal risks and deprivations, the determination not to be beaten engendered a welcome spirit of togetherness and mateship. Nevertheless, war was war and it meant death and destruction, and the city was more than thankful when it was all over. Hopefully we will never see its like again.

17

THE IBROX DISASTER

They said it was a tragedy waiting to happen. But, regretfully, that was only afterwards. No one seemed to be saying it beforehand. Or, if they were, no one was listening, no one was taking action. For if ever there was a recipe for disaster, it was the event that took place at the Ibrox football stadium, not far from the very heart of Glasgow, on a cold, dismal Saturday, on 2 January 1971.

It was one of those highlight days in the calendar of a sport which to its keenest followers is the unquestioned truth of that unlikely aphorism . . . that football really *is* something more important than life or death. And to many of these fans, the single match between Rangers and Celtic, known to them as the Ne'erday game and euphemistically termed as Glasgow's footballing derby, is the event of the year. Such is the gusto and ferocity of the play that to some, and doubtless to players, too, the vehemence is such that there's more than a hint of it being a sort of Rollerball on turf. To many of the fans, it's a replay of the Battle of the Boyne, the siege at Londond'ry/Derry – take your pick – or the Easter Uprising. There are even those who say it reminds them of a kind of Nuremberg rally. Maybe they're not far from the drift.

And yet, what happened that fateful second day of the new year of 1971 had nothing to do with the emotions which flow at this football game, invariably a loathsome, disgusting volcano of hatred and detestation of one side for the other, the twin tribes of Scotland. What happened that day occurred because of something else entirely, relating to the attitude of those who ran the sport of football in Scotland and the regard they had for the most important people in the game . . . the fans. For that attitude was one of a disregard bordering on contempt. An attitude that never beggared the question – why should fans be taken into account? There were always fans.

They were always there. They always would be there. So why did they need to be catered for? Let them watch the games in the open, exposed to the kind of weather that Scotland tosses at you from autumn through till spring; let them stand and cling to each other in their 12 x 12 inches of groundroom perched on the steep ash slopes with the storms lashing them; let them have toilet facilities which are brick caverns where they can stand up to their ankles in hot, stinking urine; give them a greasy. luke-warm mutton pie and something alleged to be meat tea and they'll be happy. They don't complain. If they do, so what? They'll be back the next week, and the week after that. The fans! The fans are always there.

It had been that way since the beginning of the game in Glasgow almost 100 years before. Right from the start, this game called football had become a passion of the young masculine blood in Scotland. What better way for wee boys and young men to show their agility and fitness skills, by turning, feigning, weaving, spinning, running, kicking, aiming and shooting that small object they came to work with such expertise. Maybe it would be an old tin can, or perhaps a bundle of rags or newspapers, pressed and squeezed hard then tightly rolled and firmly bound as spherically as possible with a length of string. Perhaps a pock-marked caoutchouc dog's ball or a tennis one, better still. Sometimes the poor boys of the tenement canyons were even lucky enough to have a real footballer's bladder ball, albeit ancient and well battered. And what a great sport this was for them. Whole teams of them could play for hours in streets not yet endangered or polluted with the motor vehicle and where the goals were the pavement space between a lamp-post and the building wall.

Every street had its star and every star had his ambition to play for the kind of team that was wealthy enough to give him his kind of heaven . . . a team shirt, shorts, socks and a game on a Saturday. And by 1971 the sport that had become a game was now an obsessive passion, unequalled in its intensity to any other form of activity in Scotland, except perhaps religion. And, alas, that was on the wane. Their football had, in fact, truly become more important than life or death itself.

And in Scotland's heartland of soccer, one game alone was to them more annually anticipated than any other, the traditional Ne'erday game between the city's two great champions, Rangers and Celtic. They had been playing it, with the odd interruption, since 1894 when it had dawned on the club bosses of the day that instead of their annual Christmas outings to England, their growing army of supporters would love nothing better than to see them play each other. More importantly, there was money in a game like that. Lots of money. And so the Ne'erday game was born.

They had, by tradition, played it on the first day of the New Year but as an exercise in prudence, if not entirely in hope, this had been modified slightly in an effort to assist in the dissipation of the excesses of Hogmanay celebrations which would hopefully produce a slightly more abstemious attendance. The truth, however, was that there was little chance of that happening, since by the second or third day of the New Year pubs were open again and there was plenty of drink available to carry to the game. Sure, there were notices around stadiums saying that alcohol was forbidden, but in 1971 no one paid any attention to them.

Just as it was not the hatred which the fans of these two Glasgow teams of opposing religions show for each other, neither was it the drink taken before or during the game that was to cause the shocking catastrophe, at the time the worst-ever sporting mishap in Britain, and forever to be known as the Ibrox Disaster.

Although the grandfathers and great-grandfathers of that generation knew all about it, it had, ironically, been largely forgotten by 1971 that there had been another great tragedy at this very same arena. And the old-timers remembered it by that same title . . . the Ibrox Disaster. It had happened on another Saturday, on 5 April 1902, when the sport was a mere infant. But what a baby! It had only been going in Glasgow for about 30 years at the time, but within the first few years of the new century Glasgow had three of the biggest stadiums in the world – Hampden, Ibrox and Parkhead.

As it was in 1902, the new Ibrox was the showpiece stadium of Scottish soccer. It was the biggest and best of its kind in the entire country, even if it didn't cater for the comfort of fans, the 80,000 it was capable of holding having to shoulder-to-shoulder it en masse on steep terracings. But that's just how it was, and no one seemed to give such matters further thought.

Perhaps they weren't all that efficient in those days at counting just how many passed through entry gates to get inside their grounds. Or maybe they were just open-hearted, permitting as many who wanted to come along and pay the money the chance to come in and see the game.

Who knows! At any rate, every fan wanted to be there that day at Ibrox for this particular game. For not only was it a chance to be one of the first into this fabulous new stadium, but the game being staged was the most anticipated of British football: Scotland versus England.

There had been a 'roll-up, roll-up folks!' article in the *Daily Record* about the new Ibrox, telling readers, 'We want to see the Rangers' magnificent enclosure paid the highest compliment in the gift of the public by its being taxed to its utmost capacity.'

Well, tax it they did. The crowd that was to turn up was, they said, the biggest crowd ever put together in the one place at the one time in Scotland. More, even, than had endured that horrible day, particularly for one side, at Culloden. More too than were at Bannockburn or Flodden.

The new Ibrox was so magnificent, it even had its own railway station and in the first few hours after midday, 34 trains had emptied full loads of fans, eagerly anticipating the day in a sporting lifetime. Although the game hadn't been due to kick off till 3.30, the turnstiles had opened at midday and they had begun flooding in from then onwards. They had come early to give them plenty of time to find a space, then cram themselves into those few inches of that precious spot which would give them the best possible view of the game of the year.

By three o'clock the density of the huge crowd appeared alarming, but the turnstiles remained open and supporters continued to pour into the park. With only minutes to go before the referee was due to gather the teams, the crowd pressure had become so fierce at the foot of the slopes on the south terracing, that it could no longer contain them. The density and compaction was such that something had to give, and the compressing of the spectators forced thousands from the bottom ranks of the terracing to flood on to the track surrounding the pitch. So many did this, however, that there wasn't even room for them on the track and so they had to seek refuge on the actual playing field. Mounted and foot police then had to shepherd this overflow back from the field to make sufficient room around the pitch for the game to begin unimpeded.

Meanwhile, outside the stadium and just before the game was about to begin, thousands were still milling around desperate to gain entry. Come what may, they wanted to see that kick-off, maybe even, who knows, an early goal. And there was little prospect of that the way these queues at the cash entry points were moving. So hundreds of them gave up the wait and headed for the north end of the park where the only barrier to gaining access was a row of tall, spiked railings. Now, for despairing fans anxious to see every piece of the action and with just minutes before that momentous action was about to kick-off, such an obstruction is of little consequence. Up and over they went, crowding in wherever they could and adding to the unbearably tight crowding of those standing around the park.

No one knows how many were jammed on to the steep spectator slopes of the terracing on the west end of the park. No one knows what fear and horror must have come over the people there when this most dreadful accident took place in that north-west section of their new super terracing. They had been assured it could take any weight with which it was likely to meet; the newspapers had even been reporting that week that the foundations, staging and terracing had all been examined by various engineers who were happy that the structure was thoroughly reliable to support the largest crowds. Or, in the words of one of these reports, 'There is room for thousands upon thousands and no matter where a man may be placed or pushed he will be able to see the game as well from the top storey of the huge erection.'

Unlike traditional stadium terraces made of solid earthscaped bankings, the new one at Ibrox in 1902 was a hollow structure, made of stout beams and girders on to which were fitted wooden staging. It was quite similar, in fact, to the structures they erect in modern competitions, such as Open Golf Championships and the Edinburgh Tattoo – only these ones have seated spectators. This embankment was for an immense, jampacked crowd of standing ones.

The game hadn't reached its first quarter of an hour when the awful calamity occurred. A corner had been awarded against England. The crowd hushed in expectancy, hemmed tightly together on the new banking, pressing forward as a man on their tip-toes to get that extra sliver of a view that would hopefully see the ball being kicked into the English goal. Then, when the shot had been taken, they leaned back again, once more as a man. It was like applying two extra pressure points to a construction which was already straining at its absolute limit.

The almighty crack that followed was as loud as any field gun. The supports had snapped and a vast, fearful fissure, 70ft x 11ft, ripped across the wooden staging, swallowing hundreds of men who plunged, crashing into the twisted lattice of pillars, beams, supports and cross-members before smashing into the ground many feet below. Bodies piled on top of bodies, while others lay gruesomely draped, sustaining hideous injuries, on the crumpled and tangled spars and supports.

While most of the huge crowd had heard the ominous snap and the thunderous clap of the collapsing structure, it was only those in proximity to the scene who were immediately able to appreciate the immensity of the tragedy that had taken place. The others were too engrossed in what was happening on the field to pay too much attention to whatever was going on elsewhere. They had come to see the match of the year and they wanted it to continue.

Play was immediately stopped, however, and the players left the field. They were shocked to discover the extent of the horror of what had occurred, many of the dead and dying being taken into the dressing-rooms and the area around them. The dilemma of the Scottish and English football officials was whether or not to carry on with the match. It was said that they feared there would be real trouble if the game was cancelled and perhaps that might have been the case. But for whatever the true reason, their decision was to play on and the teams returned to the field, still reeling under the horrors of the gory scenes they had just witnessed. Fans, on the other hand, who had fled from the danger area surrounding the fearful void in the terracing, were scrambling *back* there again, ignoring the hazards of the nearby precipice – it was still, after all, a place with a great view of the game. A matter of life or death! Aye, this game was more important than that.

Ibrox's first major disaster and, at the time, football's worst-ever tragedy, grimly overshadowed anything that had taken place on the pitch that day. If there was such a thing as an appropriate conclusion for such an occasion, then perhaps the result of a less than memorable draw was it. The accident was to take a fearful toll of 23 dead and 536 injured, many of whom never recovered from their wounds.

Sadly, it was not the last tragedy to occur at Ibrox Park. Over the years, various improvements were made to the stadium. Huge, all-seater stands were constructed with solid terraces replacing hollow-structured ones. But, like other football parks, for most of the fans it still had the most basic of facilities. Watching their favourite pastime meant having to stand, either herded together on enclosures or precariously swaying among the tight crowds on steep spectator banks. The bigger the football ground, the steeper the bankings. And the steeper the bankings, the more acute the angle of the stairways which had access to them.

Until more recent years, crowd control was an unexplored science: although such formidably steep stairways had every appearance of being hazardous, particularly when hordes of people were descending them en masse, one fumbled footstep sufficient to cause others to tumble, they were accepted without question. Architects and surveyors created them and the various experts of the city building authorities gave them their seal of approval. So who were people like mere punters to say otherwise!

Stairway 13 at Ibrox Park was one such stairway. It was 106ft long and dropped just over 40ft in four flights of stairs. The tread of each step was 11½ to 12 inches. It was the principal staircase to the north-east end of the stadium and that part of the park known by the fans as 'the Rangers end', the home side's very own corner of heaven.

To leave the stadium from that part of the arena, there were two broad summit corridors which fed fans along the ridge of the high banking and channelled them towards the principal egress point, Stairway 13. These stairs had become well known and were treated heedfully by cautious fans over the years – shouts were always going up from those in the know to those not in the know to be careful as they approached the stairway, and even more wary when they eventually got on to it. 'Take it easy, boys . . .' 'Watch the steps, lads . . .' 'Mind the stairs, pal . . .' They were the regular calls from those who feared that on such a steep stairway with the crowd so compressed that it was impossible for an individual to look down and actually see the stairs. Anything could happen. And in the past it had. There had been numerous minor incidents of fans stumbling and others, usually younger ones, being bruised in the packed and seething mass funnelled on to the staircase.

Despite their warnings and many predictions that one day there would be a really serious accident on these very same stairs, they remained as they were until 1961 when an incident of the kind they had forecast occurred. It was a typical match day with the usual huge crowd, and the normal rush to get away from the ground in order to get aboard one of the fan club buses, or catch other transport, or perhaps just to get into the pub before the masses arrived and made getting your first order an ordeal.

Someone had fallen on the stairs which had initiated a crowd jam behind, and the pressure of the still moving mass had built up. When they cleared away the pile of fallen fans, two were dead and the 44 badly injured were rushed to nearby infirmaries. It was a grim warning that this stairway was just as the fans said, a danger area. But that warning was not enough. Six years later there was another similar incident: mercifully, no one was killed on this occasion but 11 spectators were taken to hospital with crushing injuries.

Two years after that, in another January, at another Rangers–Celtic game, someone again tripped. A pile-up began, and two men were seriously injured, another 40 hurt. Stairway 13 had become notorious, and yet it was allowed to remain, virtually as it had always been. Neither the club nor the city building authorities with jurisdiction over such matters were to take appropriate action, although a Rangers official did promise 'a full inquiry'. Whatever was inquired into, the results as it turned out were to be meagre. It was decided to carry out some improvement work on the troubled exit route. More barriers of stout tubular steel were erected on the staircase, dividing it into seven separate passageways, and the side fencing, damaged in the most recent of the accidents, was made higher and stronger, embedding it in thick concrete. Otherwise, however, the notorious Stairway 13 remained as it had always been: steep, daunting and inviting the unknown.

It had been the customary Rangers versus Celtic game that early January day in 1971. The match had been full of the traditional passion, sadly much of the inspiration for that passion being loathing rather than love, abhorrence rather than affection. Just as they always do, they performed the ritual of their usual chants, each of them rendering the one which meant that their team was the best team, the only team and the one they would always support. Then it was into the derogatories: one side denouncing the Pope and Catholics and anything that was green, the others in praise of the land of their father and forefathers, and of its revolutionary army who were again killing British soldiers. Shocking stuff, but nothing new to the regulars who made up most of the crowd. They had heard it all before. They would hear it all again.

It hadn't been the best day for any form of soccer artistry on the field. The ground was rock hard after several nights of below-freezing temperatures and with only minutes remaining in the match, neither side had scored. The first of the fans were already filing from the ground, disappointed that there was yet another undramatic draw in this dramatic game of games. They were not to know, in the soccer-speak of the football commentators, that 'this fast end-to-end play of a game was to end in yet another cliffhanger'.

Just one minute remained of the game's scheduled 90 minutes when Celtic's Bobby Lennox in a last-gasp effort to score, narrowly missed, his volley smashing into the crossbar of the goals and the rebound being picked up by team-mate Jimmy Johnstone, the one they called Jinky, who scored.

A quick scramble on the frozen ground and the game was in motion again after a very brief goal celebration. And incredibly, with just a slim handful of seconds remaining, some kind of retaliatory inspiration had the Rangers players bursting through the Celtic defence, stopping only when the referee whistled for an infringement. Rangers were awarded an indirect, or non-scoring, free kick, within comforting distance of the opposition's goal, and as any soccer man will tell you, that's half a step towards a goal, and it was just the half-step Rangers needed. After a scramble of heads and boots had got to it, the ball got to the foot of their current scoring star Colin Stein, and every Rangers fan leapt to the air in joy. They had scored! Rangers had equalised! And there's no better goal than one like that, the one that rescues your team from defeat!

Many swore it was that last-gasp goal that caused it. Thousands had been making their way from the terraces at the time, many of them moving along the ridge corridors of the high embankment towards the Stairway 13 exit when they heard the shouts and the cheers. Many had reached the stairway and had started to descend when they too heard the commotion, some of them at that point trying to turn back to the arena and share in the joy. This, many were convinced, had been the source of the accident.

Others said that a youth had been carrying his mate astride his shoulders among the crowd going down the stairs and that he had lost his footing which caused their tumble and brought on the disaster. There were reports, too, from some who said there was a man in a near-white raincoat amidst the excited and jubilant fans and that *he* had stumbled, being catapulted from among the heaving mass before falling down again in the middle of them. and it had been this incident which caused it.

Whatever the precise reason, whether one of these incidents, a combination of more than one or some other unknown factor, the result was a pile-up of the most horrendous proportions. In effect, it was like one of those multiple motorway smashes after which the traffic keeps on coming from behind until there's one big mound of rammed cars. The only difference was that on Ibrox's Stairway 13, the traffic consisted of human beings and they kept on coming and coming and coming. The pressure they created was of an order that no human body could withstand. And when the flow of that emerging crowd was eventually halted, there was an ungodly silence: death loves a crowd and it was to have a most wicked feast on this one.

When the first of 330 regular policemen who had been on duty that day were called to sort out what at first appeared to be some kind of minor problem over the exit flow, they were confronted with the most chilling sight imaginable. It was like an army that had somehow been mysteriously frozen in mid-motion, rank after rank of purple-faced men pressed so tightly together it was as if they were one. And they were silent . . . silent because they were either dead, dying or too seriously injured to make any form of noise. Line upon line of them standing still; frozen life figures like the uncovered Emperor's Warriors.

Most of those who had been to that tragic match were fortunately not to use Stairway 13 as their exit point and knew nothing of the immensity of the tragedy until newscasts later in the night. It was all too hard to believe, for they had been there and they had seen and heard nothing of the saddest day in Scottish football.

The first efforts to clear the bodies from that ghastly pile was to be a perilous operation. When they began the task, beginning by pulling out those they could from the bottom of that awful mound, it had the same effect as demolishing a building from its base: it instigated a fearful avalanche of human bodies. Ones who had been standing lifeless came tumbling down part of the steep stairway. This most gruesome of torrents, however, was in its own grotesque fashion responsible for saving some lives, for it had released a few who had miraculously survived uninjured beneath the man mountain. One of the most graphic accounts of this came from a 17-year-old youth from Largs who had been right in the heart of that descending horde when the disaster began.

'I was about three-quarters of the way down the stairs when a gap in the crowd opened in front of me. This caused a sudden surge from those rushing down the stairs. It was to thrust me forward and into the air. When I landed I was amidst a huge pile of fallen fans, lying on my back, my head facing down the stairs with my legs trapped in the tight mass of bodies. All around men were screaming, and dying. Some men nearby tried to pull me out, but it was useless. My legs were so tightly trapped it was as though they were in a gigantic vice. Then the big pile of bodies on top of which I was so firmly wedged slid together down the stairway and I was thrown up in the air again. But when I landed this time I was at the bottom of the pile. I don't know how, but somehow I was still alive at the bottom of that mass while all around me everyone else was either dead or dying. Then, when the pile moved again, I was released and they were able to pull me out. I was taken to hospital with leg injuries, but they did not turn out to be serious.'

The bodies extracted from the human pyramid on Stairway 13 were first of all laid out in neat rows on the edge of the pitch on which just minutes before that climactic scramble of the two teams had been witnessed. The death toll reached 66 and about 150 others were injured, many of them seriously. It had been the worst disaster in Scotland since the war, to be exceeded only by the horror of Pan Am flight 103 at Lockerbie, 17 years later.

At a Fatal Accident Inquiry at Glasgow Sheriff Court the following month, Glasgow Corporation building officials and senior police officers said recommendations about Stairway 13 had been made to the Rangers club prior to the 2 January disaster. In reply, however, the club said it had no recollection of such meetings. Five years later, Rangers embarked on a massive rebuilding programme, the first aspect of which was the bulldozing of the vast north terracing together with Stairway 13. Their new, all-seater stadium now has every facility for the fan and is considered to be one of the most modern and safest in Europe.

18

CAROL X

Once it was the most salubrious of areas, better perhaps than anything that's around today. The mansions were grand and stylish with sweeping driveways, surrounded by acres of well-kept parkland and orchards. Huge staffs tended and trimmed the beautiful acres and catered for the needs of all those who had the good fortune to live in such splendour. Bonnie Prince Charlie visited and courted the daughter of a tobacco lord, Clementina Walkinshaw, when she lived there in the handsome Camlachie Mansion. Burns himself even penned some lines on their daughter, the little Duchess of Albany, and when the area became settled and developed, they named a local street after her.

Barrowfield in Glasgow doesn't look anything like that now. Named after the mansion of one of the founders of the area, Barrowfield was once the name of the entire East End of Glasgow. Only after they built the Rutherglen bridge was it changed, first of all to Brigton, then later to Bridgeton, the locals themselves letting it be known which of these two titles they preferred. The name Barrowfield was to remain, however, but merely as the name of a small enclave within the district.

When Celtic Football Club are playing on their home ground at Parkhead, you can hear the strains of 'Athenry' a mile away, and their roars from much further away when they're winning. But if you live in Barrowfield, such is the proximity of the small scheme to the dominance of the green meccano monster they call Paradise, that you can hear them breathe when there's a game on.

Unless you're a Celtic fan, there's little about paradise in Barrowfield. Being as it is a microcosm of everything that has gone wrong in post-industrial revolution society, Barrowfield only makes the news when some kind of sensational outrage occurs. And in the late '70s and early '80s, sensational outrage was a regular feature . . . a man found with a knife sticking from his skull . . . visiting fire and ambulance crews coming under attack . . . police ordered never to leave any vehicle unattended . . . the community centre burned so many times they had to bulldoze it . . . and regular mobbing and rioting, or as those great euphemists, Glasgow Police, call it . . . 'group disorder'. Despite the headlines such events made, nothing was to have the impact of what was to occur in Barrowfield on the night of Hallowe'en, 1980. Indeed, few happenings anywhere in Scotland have had such historic legal repercussions, culminating in the dismissal of one of the most senior law officers in the land and the instigation of the first private prosecution in Scotland since 1909. Barrowfield had never been such a focus of attention since they were talking about all the goings on at Camlachie Mansion when gorgeous Charlie was there chasing the comely Clementina.

In fact, it was in a place just down from Camlachie Street, named after the big mansion which is at the top end of the Barrowfield scheme, that witnessed the beginning of the horrid events of that Hallowe'en night which was to shock the nation then grip it in its sensational aftermath.

Friday, 31 October 1980: it was just another Glasgow Friday in many ways. Well into autumn, the nights were drawing in. There were only three TV channels at the time, Channels 4 and 5 and satellite television being mere promises of what we would obtain in our living-rooms one day. By a bizarre twist of fate for what lay ahead for one innocent Glasgow citizen that evening, a Hammer House of Horror film was the highlight on the STV channel. Perhaps they thought the viewer ratings would soar on a night like Hallowe'en.

Alastair Burnet and Anna Ford were the duty announcers on ITN that night, their high-rating *News at Ten* on the Independent network featuring the latest events at Leyland, the once-fine truck and car company. It was yet again in the headlines, but not, in 1980, for its output achievement. These were the days of what others called the 'English disease', and industrial strife at Leyland and many other factories, were as much a part of daily news bulletins as the weather forecast. The latest news, said the report, was that the shop stewards were determined to show the bosses this time, and the threat was an all-out strike. The prospect of precipitation sounded much more cheerful in comparison.

Ireland, our forever Ireland, was also in the headlines with the news that a group of IRA men in the Maze Prison had gone into the fifth day of their hunger strike and spokesmen for them were saying they were determined to fast to their death. And death, too, seemed to be nearing for the personable Hollywood star, Steve McQueen, having left hospital following treatment for cancer. They speculated that no more could be done for him. And here in Glasgow city centre police had pounced on a teeny gang of 15- and 16-year-olds – members, it was said, of the Govan Team gang – and relieved them of the kind of accoutrements people like them equate with fashion-label gear, namely nine butcher's knives, four folding knives, one jack-knife, a cosh and two guns.

It wasn't long after the Burnet and Ford team had signed off their news bulletin, that a neat little brunette, just turned 30 and called Carol, made her way home along London Road to her top-flat tenement house in the Barrowfield scheme. She hadn't been in the happiest frame of mind earlier in the evening, since she had fallen out with her boyfriend. It had been a more heated tiff than normal, things being said to each other that may or may not have been the truth, such as the accusation that she had been drinking with a neighbour and that the evening tea hadn't been prepared. The squabble deteriorated, tempers flared and Carol had stormed out of the house. Determined to forget it all, she met up with some pals at the Mecca bar at Bridgeton Cross.

Being on your own in certain areas of Glasgow late on a Friday night, no matter your gender, no matter your fortitude, can be a challenging experience. The streetwise, of course, know where to go, and where not to go, and stay clear of the latter. But often that's not possible: so a sixth sense helps.

There's always, of course, the predictable . . . the ones who have had their great nights at the local, or someone else's local, and want to let the world know about it, even though they have just spent much of their material world for those few hours' escape from reality. But they're the predictable. It's the unpredictable ones who can make that lone city walk even more than a challenging experience.

Coming as she did from the area, Carol knew all about the predictable as well as the unpredictable. She was a graduate of an alma mater where degrees are bestowed on the discerning, honours to the cute and cunning – all vital ingredients of this city's suburban survival kit. That walk home alone posed no great problem to someone who knew the local score.

The wee boys that had earlier in the night gathered round local pubs feebly dressed as guisers hailing all and sundry for Hallowe'en handouts with all the charm of junior muggers – 'Gonnie gie's money for the Guy, pal?' – had all dispersed as Carol hurried from the normally busy London Road, the occasional drunk shouting things that only drunks understand, and turned left into Davaar Street, which at the time led directly into the Barrowfield scheme. The countdown for the nightmare which lay ahead for the hurrying woman on her own had begun.

The news of that late Friday night incident wasn't picked up by the weekend papers. The top story of the day was Jim Watt's successful, flag-waving defence of his world boxing title against Sean O'Grady at the Kelvin Hall. But by Monday, 3 November, when reporters uncovered the grim details, they were immediately in touch with news editors to prepare them for what they were saying would be 'some story'. And some story it was: it led in news bulletins and made a variety of page ones as it told the world of the dreadful incident which had involved a diminutive East End woman, who had been subjected to an ordeal much worse, more evil than anything portrayed on that evening's House of Horror movie on TV.

The headline, 'Hunt For Sex Attack Beasts', perhaps told much, but it needed more than headlines to tell the full story of what had taken place that night. It was worse even than anything the author Alec McArthur had related, or would even have considered relating, in his all-time best seller No Mean City, a book so many derided as being over-exaggerated. For what happened to Carol that night was more savage, more primaeval than any fiction that had ever been written about Glasgow.

The full details of the occurrence as it was picked up by the crime reporters that weekend were too gruesome for that first story which appeared in the Monday morning papers, but there was enough detail to let readers know that this was more than the usual rape case. By coincidence, that most profane crime had figured prominently in the news just days previously with the release of the latest police figures, revealing that two cases a week were now being reported which was more than double the figure of ten years previously.

'We are determined to track down these evil beasts,' said one of the detectives leading the massive hunt for the gang of attackers, said to be four of them, who had beset Carol. He also issued a warning to women, telling them to keep off the streets in the meantime. Two days later, the city was given the welcome news that arrests had been made, and that four youths, aged between 14 and 18, were being detained in custody.

Before their arrests, more details of what had happened to the stricken

Carol were to emerge. It appeared that after the gang had pounced, they took her to a scrapyard just off Davaar Street in Barrowfield where there was an old workmen's cabin, a windowless, former ship's container used for keeping tools and supplies secure. There they had subjected the woman to a *Clockwork Orange* orgy of depraved sex and the most barbaric brutality, slashing her countless times with an open razor.

If ever a weapon was more synonymous with the raw underside of Glasgow or had brought more ignominy to the city than any other single item, it was the open razor. Most thought it had long since been dispensed with, vanished into the pages of pulp fiction, along with the old-time street gangs who had fought their battles with them, often as not flailing them two-handed at each other. But no, there was still some malign hankering for the old cut-throat, that vile antithesis of Excalibur, which slices and slits like a laser, so swiftly and efficiently it can beat the pain barrier and the victim often doesn't know they have been slashed till minutes later when the first sensations of agony are felt with the suddenness of an electric shock.

Nurses and surgeons at the Royal Infirmary were appalled at the severity of the woman's wounds. They were the worst that many of them had ever experienced. Many of the scars she had received in the devilish attack appeared to have been made in the form of some fiendish game of knots and crosses. She had been slashed six times across her cheeks, forehead and nose, which had a deep horizontal scar almost dividing it in two. Her thighs and buttocks were cut open to the bone, the right thigh having three four-inch cuts with a fourth intersecting them, the left with three more cuts each four inches long. Some of the wounds on her face were close to her eyes, one having gone between them.

A slash on her forehead was so wide that the surgeon was able to check with a finger for any fracture of the bone below. The medical team spent hours piecing together her torn and ripped flesh, a job which required a total of 152 stitches to close the wounds.

Carol would appear as just another rape case on the grim and growing statistics which had made such shocking news earlier in the week. But this was no ordinary rape, its perpetrators obviously no ordinary sex-hungry mortals. And the nation waited on the developments and outcome of the usual lengthy process before such offenders are brought to trial and meet their justice (although with a legal system which it appeared went into contortions in order to protect the accused, there was never any guarantee of that).

Of the four youths arrested, three of them, 18- and 16-year-old brothers and another 16-year-old, were eventually served with indictments alleging assaulting Carol by striking her on the head with unknown instruments whereby she became unconscious, dragging her to a cabin in a scrapyard at 10 Davaar Street, removing her clothing and repeatedly raping her. A second charge covered further assaults by striking her repeatedly with a razor to her severe injury, permanent disfigurement and danger of her life. They pleaded not guilty to the charges, one of them lodging a special defence of incrimination, blaming his co-accused, that is, in relation to the second charge. One of the brothers did likewise, as did the third accused. 'Wiznae me . . . wizhim . . .' the courts had heard it all before. So had confused juries, especially when defence counsel hammered it into them that the law of Scotland demanded the corroboration of at least two witnesses in order to convict. And, as so often before, yet another pack of gang members defiantly grinned their way to freedom.

As the city awaited the prospect of what seemed likely to be a most sensational trial, albeit one of the most horrific, Carol was to constantly relive the horrors of that nightmare Hallowe'en. The horrendous experience combined with the extent of her injuries had required the attention of a psychiatrist to help her combat the recurring terror of it all.

Meanwhile, anxious court reporters anticipated what promised to be one of the biggest High Court cases to be held in the city for years. It had now been nearly 15 months since the actual attack and anxious to get details of just when the trial would begin, veteran crime and court reporter Arnot McWhinnie of the *Daily Record* regularly quizzed law officials for details, particularly a date when proceedings would begin to ensure that he would be on duty at the time as he had been closely connected with the case from the beginning.

On Tuesday, 12 January 1982, while making one of these routine inquiries, McWhinnie, to his immense surprise, discovered a development in the story which in a news sense was to prove as sensational as the very case itself. For what McWhinnie's questions were to uncover was that known to only three specified people, but not the victim herself, the Crown Office had decided not to proceed with the charges against the three youths. Their lame excuse, McWhinnie found out, was that the psychiatrist who had been attending Carol had reported that he considered it would be dangerous to her health if she gave evidence. And the Crown Office, in their wisdom, or apparent lack of it in this case, decided not to proceed with the trial. Amazed at what he had just been told, McWhinnie then asked if anyone had been informed about this shocking development in the much anticipated case and was to learn that the information had been passed on to only three people: the three accused.

No one, it turned out, had had the courtesy to consider informing the victim herself that whatever had happened to her on that fateful Hallowe'en and whoever had perpetrated the evil deeds, nothing whatsoever would be done about it.

That this ravaged and unfortunate victim was not informed would have been no great surprise to many who know not only the workings of Scots law, but those involved in it. There still remains that streak of arrogance in our professions which expresses itself in apparent disdain for the very people the qualified practitioners are there to serve. It's an aloofness which grates all the more in Scotland being in such contrast to the normal character of the Scot who bears such attitudes with contempt.

As the law was set out, however, nothing improper had transpired. Those in power had acted with due propriety, if not with humanity. They had not infringed the preciseness of the rules in any way. At the same time, not one of those concerned was to show a jot of consideration for the person who mattered most of all in this unfolding drama, the vexed and violated Carol.

Following his momentous revelations, McWhinnie was a week later to compound the embarrassment of the legal authorities by obtaining details of the Crown evidence which would have been produced had the trial gone ahead. These came to him through an anonymous phone-caller who had arranged a meeting in order to hand over a secret file which revealed conclusively that, in fact, there had been a solid case against the accused. There had been a dramatic confession from one of the boys who had turned Queen's evidence with an eye-witness account of what exactly took place in the workmen's hut. The file also revealed excellent forensic evidence. Because it was considered that the public had a right to this information, all the details of the case were published. It was also surprisingly revealed that when MPs had raised the case with the Lord Advocate, Lord Mackay at the time, later to become the Lord Chancellor of the United Kingdom, he neither knew the details of the case nor of the controversial decision not to prosecute until it had appeared in the press.

McWhinnie's revelations were a sensation, particularly when it was spelt out that not only would there be no court appearance for the three accused, but that never again could the Crown bring charges against them. Our laws are based on precedent, and in a case just four years previously in which an accused had likewise been told they were not proceeding with charges against him, news of it had been reported in the press. A few months later, however, the Crown Office changed its mind and reinstituted the charges against the man. His lawyers appealed, however, and three High Court judges ruled that the Crown had no right to raise further proceedings after stating publicly there would be none. And with that precedent to go on, the three accused of the Barrowfield rape were set to go scot-free forever.

All over the country there was an outcry at the dramatic revelations, but no more so than in Glasgow where there was growing shock that those who had committed such a dastardly crime could go unpunished. It made a laughing stock out of the soaring crime figures; it made a mockery out of the law as being any kind of deterrent; it ridiculed all the hard work done by police and detectives in not only locating and detaining suspects, but all the great effort which had gone into preparing a case to be answered in court; and it brought scorn on the Crown Office, the inner sanctum of our Scots Law which we hold so dear.

In Scotland, there are strict, and much adhered to, rules governing the media in relation to pre-trial publicity. These are known as the sub-judice (before the courts) laws and they expressly forbid any detail, comment or photographs of accused and witnesses being used once charges are made and a case is pending. However, now that the charges had been dropped against the three accused, there was no case before the courts and therefore no technical legal objection to the full story now being told of what had happened to Carol. And, likewise, she too was free to speak and tell the world of her ordeal.

The story she was to tell so graphically to journalists angered the nation even more than it would have done had it been reported in the normal court fashion. For this time they were being told that no one would be punished for the crimes reported in what they were reading. And perhaps the most shocking aspect of the story was the fact that despite the advice given by the psychiatrist to the Crown Office, Carol revealed that she had, in fact, wanted the case to go to court, even though she had made two suicide attempts. She had wanted to be there and give evidence against them. 'But they haven't let me,' she sobbed nervously when recounting her feelings and the trauma she had undergone.

Detail by dreadful detail, Carol related the chilling events of that night in October, which until now were prohibited from being discussed outside of court because of the strict sub-judice laws. She spoke about the earlier part of the evening with her boyfriend, later to become her husband; their quarrel; the storming from the house afterwards; her meeting with other friends at the bar at Bridgeton Cross; then leaving them to walk the near-mile further east to her house in Barrowfield.

'It was about ten o'clock at night and I was walking home after having a drink. I remember a young boy came over to me and asked if I could give him a light for his cigarette. I went into my bag to get my lighter. Suddenly I was struck on the head from behind and I don't remember much after that. The next thing I remember was a boy leaning over me. All I remember was the glint of a blade. I said "You don't have to use that, surely", and he said something like "You are getting it." I was fighting back with my hands and they were being cut. He chopped the top off one of my fingers.

'The next thing I remember was coming to and running out of this dark hut. I didn't know where I was. I ran to a main road and then knew where I was and ran up the road to our flat. As I ran I felt wet, down below. Then I realised I was naked from the waist down and barefoot. I put my hands on my thighs and discovered blood was running down me.

'When I got to the flat my hands were so badly cut I couldn't knock on the door properly; I could only faintly tap on it with the side of my hand. My boyfriend didn't hear me and so I ran across to a friend's house nearby and they called an ambulance and the police. The police actually followed the trail of blood from that house to my boyfriend's and told him what had happened.

'When I got to the Royal Infirmary the hospital couldn't stitch the wounds right away because of the dried blood and dirt so I couldn't have an operation until ten the next morning- When I saw my wounds for the first time I was horrified.'

Her boyfriend, comforting her as she bravely recounted those terrifying moments, interrupted at that point to say that when he had seen her in hospital before the operation she had been so bad, he had fainted. After a brief pause, Carol resumed her story.

'I spent a week in hospital and a few days later I had to take part in an identification parade at Tobago Street police office. I was still stitched up and I couldn't even walk up the steps. Two policewomen had to carry me along the line-up of youngsters. I only recognised one. I was shaking like a leaf when I pointed to him; just seeing him again brought it all back to me. I collapsed after picking him out and had to be carried into a side room and given tea. It was really horrible seeing that face again.'

Four months later, Carol took a drug overdose and was found by her boyfriend who rushed her to hospital. Then in October, around the anniversary of the attack, she became depressed again and only the intervention of her boyfriend had prevented her from trying to leap out of their top-flat tenement window. 'But it's all behind me now,' she said. 'That won't happen again . . . now I'm just bitter.'

The reporters interviewing her described how she had ugly visible scars across her forehead, running down from her left eye over her cheek and across her nose. Other visible scars scored her body and both legs.

'I can't even bear to look in the mirror when I brush my hair and every time I take a bath it still shocks me. I can't even walk down the street alone. If I see a young boy I run.'

With the story now making national headlines, the pressure grew on the Lord Advocate, Scotland's senior law officer, to make a statement, but he wasn't immediately available on 20 January, the day following the sensational revelations, because he was in Strasbourg on European law business. The growing criticism over the Crown handling of the case spilled into the House of Commons and Mrs Thatcher herself was quizzed by MPs demanding a review of the law. MP Donald Dewar, later to become Scottish Secretary, and himself a lawyer, was the Labour Party's Legal Affairs spokesman in Scotland at the time, and he joined in the chorus of protest and outrage, likewise demanding a full explanation from the law authorities.

The headquarters of the law in Scotland is at the Crown Office in Edinburgh. At its head is the Lord Advocate, the law supremo in Scotland and something of a deified figure who is answerable to no one, save the Queen herself and Parliament. He is aided by his assistant, the Solicitor-General. They command a huge team of prosecutors stationed at the various sheriff courts throughout the country, at the High Court in Edinburgh and when it goes on circuit. Those stationed at sheriff courts are known as procurators-fiscal, those prosecuting in the High Court known as advocates-depute. All vital decisions affecting criminal trials in Scotland are taken at the Crown Office, and the Lord Advocate, who sits in the House of Lords, is responsible to Parliament for decisions on whether or not to prosecute. Otherwise, however, his power is such that he need give no reasons for his decisions. Nevertheless, most prosecution work is delegated to the Solicitor-General and his 12 advocates-depute.

The sensation was escalating with every aspect of the affair, now being widely referred to as the Glasgow Rape Case. Yet more staggering news emerged a few days later with the forced resignation of the Solicitor-General. He was the well-known Member of Parliament, the late Nicholas Fairbairn, wit, raconteur, bon viveur, fop and sniffer of snuff. He was not merely one of the most colourful characters in the legal profession, but when he wasn't the dolled-up dandy up to his customary dalliances, he was also the star performer as defence counsel in countless criminal cases. Not only had the department he headed at the Crown Office failed to proceed with the case against the three accused, but Solicitor-General Fairbairn had compounded that misjudgement by making a statement to the press about it before his boss, the Lord Advocate, had made his own announcement to the House of Lords. This is an unforgivable parliamentary sin for which he was summoned to the office of Prime Minister Margaret Thatcher and told he must go, via the usual courteous route, of course, namely by tendering his resignation. Later, when asked in a TV interview whether he had jumped or had been pushed, a humbled Fairbairn paused for the apposite answer, and then with the customary aplomb replied, 'I fell.'

Continuing with his inquiries as to what developments could now take place in the case, reporter McWhinnie spoke to Ross Harper, one of the city's best-known criminal lawyers at the time. When he inquired if this really was the end of the legal road for Carol, Harper immediately came up with the idea of a private prosecution. 'This would be the ideal solution in a situation like this,' he said, going on to explain an almost defunct legal procedure

One of the rarest forms of seeking justice in Scotland if the authorities don't do so, is by the ancient enactment of raising a private prosecution. These are so rare that many associated with the law in 1982 had wrongly assumed they were a thing of the past. And who could have blamed them for, in fact, the only time this century that a private prosecution has succeeded was back in 1909 when a company raised an action by this method to prosecute a coal supplier for fraud. Other attempts to raise such prosecutions had all been unsuccessful.

The process of raising such actions is a complex one and is instituted by making an application to the courts. This is quaintly known as a Bill for Criminal Letters and the application on behalf of Carol was couched in similar antiquated language. It read that it urged the court to punish the three youths with the pains of law, claiming 'Albeit by the laws of this and every well-ordered realm, assault and rape are crimes of a heinous nature and severely punishable, yet true it is and of verity that the said accused are guilty of the said crimes'.

The Glasgow Rape Case was now top-billing stuff, breaking into the remote and rarified territory of antiquarian law with the eyes of the nation tightly focused on every twist, every turn of every eventuality. The Bill for Criminal Letters was listed for hearing in the highest court, to be debated and decided on by the most senior judges of the High Court of Justiciary.

Rarely had their been such an all-star cast assembled in the courtroom: Lord Emslie, the Lord Justice General, along with Lords Cameron and Avonside on the bench; the private prosecution team was led by Charles Kemp Davidson, QC, Dean of the Faculty of Advocates, Alistair Cameron, QC, Kevin Drummond, advocate, and Ross Harper, solicitor; the defence was led by Hugh Morton, QC, Donald Macaulay, QC, George Penrose, QC, and solicitors Desmond Finnieston, Frank McCormick and Brian Fitzpatrick; and representing the Crown was Lord Mackay, the Lord Advocate, who had already aired his views on the application by refusing to endorse it. Although this was his prerogative, he had no right of veto and the court would be the final arbiter.

It was now March 1982, more than 16 months since the rape had shocked the nation, and the case was now set for the next stage in the long process towards justice. This was the hearing on whether or not the private prosecution could proceed to its next stage, to a criminal trial, and it was scheduled to last for four days. The main points to be argued would be, firstly, that while it was the prerogative of the Lord Advocate to initiate all criminal prosecutions in Scotland, would it be permissible, should he decline to do so, for a private citizen to raise one? And, secondly, if that indeed were permissible, would all the nationwide publicity given to the case affect the chances of a fair trial?

The sparks flew right from the opening arguments: the defence counsel predictably attacked the vast press coverage which had already been attributed to the case, demonstrating they were not going to miss a point on this score by handing over to the three judges thick files containing photographed copies of articles from the *Daily Express*, *Sunday Times*, *Glasgow Evening Times* and *Daily Record*, emphasising that the most significant story had been the one revealing details from the original Crown prosecution, including an alleged confession.

The incisive Queen's Counsel Donald Macaulay posed the question, 'How can documents of that kind get into the hands of the press? It seems rather remarkable and extraordinary to say the least that the defence solicitor's statement could have got to the *Record* to put their clients into jeopardy. It reflects that the reporter has been given access to police notebooks.' He considered that it also meant that the three youths would be unable to get a fair trial anywhere in Britain.

News coverage on radio and television was also brought up, as QC Macaulay then went on to read to the court for more than an hour and a half extracts from various broadcast bulletins concerning the case.

QC Hugh Morton, representing one of the three teenagers, took another tack. He claimed the three were now facing prosecution by the back door, after which he astutely turned to the point of legal aid when the Scottish Secretary indicated sympathetic consideration to such a request from the alleged victim.

'If the position is that the Crown is barred from a public prosecution by sending three youths letters saying there would be no further proceedings, then it would be grossly unfair of the State to get round that by the back door by paying someone else to take up the prosecution. It would be grossly oppressive for the Crown to continue to prosecute by financing the means of doing it.'

The Lord Advocate, Lord Mackay, took issue with that point, immediately rising to address the three judges on the allegations, telling them that his position might have been impugned. 'It was open to the construction that I was doing something unfair. I am doing my best to serve the ends of justice as fairly as I can,' he said.

Lord Emslie then answered the point of a 'back door prosecution', saying that there was no suggestion of the Crown trying to do this, whereupon QC Morton apologised for having impugned the Lord Advocate's position in any way.

On 1 April 1982, just two weeks after the end of the four-day hearing, the three judges announced the verdict which was to make legal history. Namely that Carol would be free to instigate a private prosecution against the three teenagers originally accused of her rape, and that the trial would be set for the following month in the High Court in Edinburgh. In their lengthy and unanimous verdict, which took almost an hour and a half to read out, they said they had only decided to grant the private prosecution because it was 'a quite exceptional' case, but at the same time issued the warning that this case did not necessarily open the doors for similar actions in the future. The judges rejected the claims by defence counsel that the youths could not get a fair trial anywhere in Britain because of the colossal publicity the case had already received.

On the point of private prosecutions, Lord Emslie was to make it clear in his judgement that the rights of a private prosecution in Scots Law had grown up alongside those of the Lord Advocate.

'These rights still exist and there seems to be no good reason in principle for saying they should not be available in any case in which the Lord Advocate has, for any reason, declined to prosecute an offender to a conclusion.'

It had been years since a trial had attracted such attention as that of the three teenagers accused of the razor and rape attack on Carol which opened at the High Court in Edinburgh on Monday, 24 May 1982. There were few niceties in the Bill for Criminal Letters heaving with its articulate argumentation versus skilful speech, its calm and formal debate and the ornate courtroom resounding with the eloquent silver tongues of the finest law brains in the country as they tested out and probed rare and unexplored territories in the mechanics of jurisprudence.

This time it was back to the hurly-burly of everyday criminal trials where normal courtroom voices blend to make up our 'them and us' society: the guttural and the glottal, the up-a-close appearances, the street corner attitudes conflicting with those of the behavioural refinements that are the usual products of the Merchant schools and fine universities. It was back, too, to the pages of *No Mean City* when the first of the evidence unfolded with all the drama and sensation that had been so anticipated.

A 19-year-old witness called Stephen Cameron – NB the name – gave evidence against his three friends on the night of the attack, alleging that he saw one of them brandish an open razor and shout, 'I have ripped the lassie.' That was just a foretaste of what had happened to Carol on that evening in hell.

Cameron, who had originally been charged with the three others but was later released and granted immunity from prosecution, went on to allege that one of his pals had shouted that particular obscenity after having had sex with the victim in the scrapyard's hut. He had then looked on as the other two also raped the woman.

Earlier, when he had been drinking with one of the accused, another of the group had arrived to announce he had a 'bird' in the scrapyard. When they got there, one of the accused was lying on top of the woman and they took it in turns to have sex with her, one of them with a razor in his hands. There was blood everywhere.

In his defence, one of the accused said he had been too drunk to have sex that night, another that while he did have intercourse with the woman, she had not objected. It was little wonder that the trial judge, Lord Ross, had to warn the jury not to allow their judgement to be biased in any way by feelings of disgust, horror and revulsion as the evidence unfolded. But, having said that, there was little to be heard in the succeeding days of the trial that wasn't just that . . . disgusting, horrific and revulsive.

Carol herself, ever-so tiny as she took the witness stand, her face clearly showing the devastation of the razor attack, reiterated the story she had earlier told the press. She trembled visibly as she was asked to examine a set of coloured photographs which had been shown to the jury earlier. It was the most trying part of her evidence because since her appearance had become so fearful, Carol had stopped looking in mirrors. She had even learned to put on make-up and comb and fix her hair without their use. Imagine the sheer terror she was then experiencing when the court official handed over the batch of colour prints showing the wounds to the various parts of her body when they had just been stitched by the surgeons at the Royal Infirmary – and worst of all, the transmogrified vision which had once been her face.

There wasn't really much more to the story. It was as simple, squalid and sordid, as Carol had told it herself first of all to the press, then in the High Court. The wretched woman had undergone a night of unimaginable depravity and it had taken 19 months before the due processes of Scots Law was to hear the verdict of a jury of seven men and eight women.

Joseph Sweeney, aged 18, was sentenced to 12 years' imprisonment. His young brother Gordon, 16, and their friend John Thomson, also 16, all with addresses in Barrowfield, were cleared earlier of the charges of slashing Carol, and were convicted on the considerably reduced charge of indecent assault for which they were placed on deferred sentence for one year. It was believed to be only the third successful private prosecution in Scotland in about 400 years. Appeals against the convictions were made by Joseph Sweeney and Thomson, but both failed.

The Glasgow Rape Case had a series of reverberations in the years to come. Reporter McWhinnie received a prestigious British Press award for his journalistic endeavours.

In August and December 1983, the year following the trial, the tragic Carol was involved in two further attacks, one in an attempted rape after being dragged into a Gallowgate close-mouth, another when she received injuries after four men burst into the house in which she was staying in Roystonhill.

A year and a half later, in April 1985, Gordon Sweeney, one of the two 16-year-olds put on a year's deferred sentence at the trial, died in the Royal Infirmary after being found with severe head and neck injuries in Stamford Lane, Barrowfield. Stephen Cameron, who had given evidence at the Rape Case trial, together with his two brothers James and Gordon, appeared in the High Court in Glasgow four months later and denied having murdered Sweeney. But another fearful element emerged from their trial, and it was the fact that Stephen Cameron had become an outcast after testifying in the

Glasgow Rape Case trial. He said he had been tagged 'a grass', threatened, chased and shunned in the pubs of the East End. His life had become so unbearable that he was forced to ask police to help get him a house out of the area.

But the long shadow of the sensational rape case was to return and haunt him when he moved back to the family home and had ended in violence when an armed mob led by Gordon Sweeney attacked him. Bricks, bayonets, a baseball bat and swords were the weapons mentioned in the eight-day trial which concluded with Gordon Cameron, 24, being jailed for 14 years, and his brother Stephen, 22, for 12 years, both on reduced charges of culpable homicide, the Scottish term for manslaughter. A third brother, James, was found not guilty.

Scots Law was to benefit considerably from the Carol X case, by changing Crown Office procedure in cases of murder and rape. The Lord Advocate now personally examines every case in these categories and makes the final decision on whether charges should be dropped. If no proceedings are taken in a rape case, the victim is now given the civilised courtesy of being informed.

Of the principal characters in the Glasgow Rape Case, Carol X, marked for life by that night of depravity, still lives in the city; the reporter Arnot McWhinnie went on to run his own press agency; the lawyer Ross Harper, who so courageously took up Carol's case and instituted the private prosecution, became a distinguished Professor of Law and President of the International Bar Association; the QCs Charles Kemp Davidson, Hugh Morton and George Penrose became High Court judges; Lord Mackay became the Lord Chancellor; Donald Macaulay a life peer; Lord Ross became the Lord Justice Clerk; Alistair Cameron, the Home Advocate, the Crown Office's third most senior figure; and the advocate Kevin Drummond was made a Sheriff.

And Barrowfield? In appearance it hasn't changed all that much in the late '90s. Like much of the East End, it bears all the ugly scars of post-industrial wasteland. The factory owners and manufacturers who once needed it and its people have moved on. There is no singular reason why this part of the East End became what it did, just as there is no simple solution. Either side of the political divide has its explanations for the likes of Barrowfield, and each is in direct contrast to the other, which, perhaps in itself, is one of the reasons why such places exist. But at least there is hope. Under the aegis of the Camlachie Housing Association, enlightened forces are at work.

Through Scottish Homes, a new partnership incorporating residents is creating a project similar to that which has already upgraded and transformed parts of Castlemilk, one of the early post-war schemes on the south side of the city. They confidently expect that in ten years time the area will be unrecognisable in attitude as well as appearance. Few places better deserve the break.

19

KEARNY

෧෧

There's a Glasgow in Kentucky, named by one of its founders after his old home-town. It wasn't so much that this part of the world, bluegrass or not, had him reminiscing about the dear green place, but when you're as far from home as he was, it's comforting to have reminders – which is why there are another seven or so Glasgows scattered around the United States. There's one in Virginia near the Blue Ridge Mountains, and in Missouri there are even two, one of which is called Glasgow Village, a suburb of St Louis, which has adopted Glasgow's bird, tree, bell and fish coat of arms as its own. Others in Connecticut, Illinois, Montana and Delaware make up the North American collection of communities with our placename, not forgetting a couple up in Canada too.

In reality, however, there was really only one town in North America that might have been called Glasgow for what it meant and represented; a place that in so many ways actually resembled bits of Glasgow; where the common accent in the streets was that of Glaswegians; where Scots in their thousands were attracted to it because of what it offered them. This was a town that was different from all the other American Glasgows because it really was a place known to citizens of that city, although it never did get its name. It was called Kearny instead, pronounced Carny and almost invariably misspelled as Kearney.

Kearny is in New Jersey, the fourth smallest state in the Union which hugs New York city as though longing to be part of it. From one end of Kearny's main street you can see a most dramatic skyline, building after building fingering the heavens. Just standing at that end of the street you soon appreciate why this is *the* Glasgow town. The accents will tell you that for a start.

Ever since the last war, more people from Glasgow as well as many surrounding places came to this little outer suburban town than to any other single place in the United States.

At the peak of the post-war migration from Scotland, you would not have found another place in the world with such a large concentration of Glaswegians in such a small area. And if the accents don't convince you of the town's Scottish connections, the shops and clubs certainly do.

One of the great meeting-places is Graham's Bar at the junction of Kearny and Bergen Avenues. I've even heard bus drivers stop just by the pub and shout 'Paisley Cross', not so much for a laugh as to let passengers know exactly where they were on the Avenue. Inside Graham's there's no mistaking the Glasgow affiliation when you take a look at some of the decorations fixed to the gantry behind the bar. Among the treasured collection there's the almost mandatory full-group picture of the latest Scottish international team, the signed portrait of the great eternal hero, Jim Baxter, some Scottish one-pound notes, and a variety of those little notices whose sentiments are a mixture of jings and jingoism, such as 'I'm Glad I'm Scots' and 'God Made the Scottish'. And by the looks of some of the faces fixed in that seriously intentioned mode of the Glasgow male with a couple of glasses in front of him, this is not the kind of place to make any casual jokes about Scots or Scotland. Even with a big happy smile on your face.

Kearny wouldn't win any beauty or environmental awards or even be listed in any of those grandiose championship designations which citizens of the US love for their communities, such as 'The Place To Which Most Americans Would Like To Retire'. But it hardly matters to locals when there is an intersection on Kearny Avenue that is not unlike the point where Eglinton and Bedford Streets meet in the Gorbals: there's a comforting feel about sights like that when you're 3,000 miles from home. And there are plenty of other similar reminders for those with hearts so often in far-off and dearly loved places.

Take a wander along Kearny Avenue till you get to the Fire Station, then go down a lane opposite which takes you into Paterson Avenue, neat and leafy with its line of splendid sycamores and trim, clean-cut, clapboard houses, and continue a little way along to Highland Avenue and you come to one of the places that for years has been a haven for thousands of Scots in New Jersey, the Scots-American Athletic Club. There you are greeted with the club's coat of arms, the Lion Rampant flanked by two thistles, and if they don't recognise your face, they'll certainly recognise your accent, or lack of it.

The gantry at the comfortable bar is stacked with all the old favourites, like Bell's, Teacher's and Grant's Standfast. The lager is Tennent's on draught and they drink more of it here than in any other place in the States, having spared no efforts in their endeavours to arrange a regular quota – the nearest supplier is more than 1,000 miles away in Florida, but that's just a minor problem in the US. Obviously the beer also travels well by the way they knock it back in the St Andrew's Lounge of the club.

The club was founded back in 1931 in very humble circumstances. A few Scots got together, pooled their money and bought a room-and-kitchen which they used as their first club premises. It was just the kind of place every new migrant in a foreign land craves: somewhere to swap his new world experiences, meet familiar faces, hear familiar accents and feel the comfort of something very precious to them, a little piece of home. The old room and kitchen was to become a congenial, spacious and well-appointed function/club rooms with bar, dance hall, billiards, big screen TV and, more importantly, a genuine home from home for the countless Scots who were to use it over the years. That club and many others like it in town were the venues to meet countless sports stars and personalities regularly invited over from Scotland to share special memories of the far-off place they still thought of as home, even though many had lived in their adopted land much longer.

The entertainers came just as regularly; the most welcome ones were those who gave them precisely what they wanted by belting out their timeless favourites like 'The Last Mile Home', 'Auld Scots Mother of Mine' and 'The Star o' Rabbie Burns', to which their adoring audiences would unashamedly weep. And by the time they got to such emotional classics as 'There's A Wee Hoose 'Mang The Heather', they would be ripped apart, and tears would flow in oceans.

It was the late and much Kearny-beloved Glen Daly, a great favourite in the clubs here, who said of such nights, 'No entertainer anywhere in the world could get a more fantastic and emotional audience. Maybe it all sounds too mushy and sentimental, but when we meet up in Kearny, we all have a good greet together; it produces such a feeling of warmth that I just can't describe it.'

Then Glen would snap them out of their sentimentality with that favourite repartee of his – glottal stop and all – which never missed those digs at Ibrox, life on the Provi cheque and wee fat wives going the messages along Govan Road. He was a knockout in Kearny.

It was much the same scene at the other popular clubs like the Irish-American, the Ulster and the Antrim and Down with their various special nights. A big attraction at the Scots-American at one time was the Sunday morning delivery of the *Sunday Mail* and *Sunday Post*, which really put that special Scottish something into the Sabbath at hundreds of surrounding homes. These Scots had everything they needed: their Tennent's, the Sunday papers and dinner, no doubt bought from one of the town's most popular suppliers, like Cameron's Scottish Market or the Royal Market. Both these butcheries had a vast array of those endearing old favourites like steak pies, Scotch meat pies, beef links, black pudding, Ayrshire middle cut and Belfast ham and all the other things Scots tend not to think about till they're 3,000 miles from home, like Tunnock's caramel wafers, Walker's shortbread and Tetley teabags. And when you could get all that, who needed the Gallowgate, Brig'ton or Paisley Cross?

A stroll along the main drag from Graham's bar would leave you in no doubt that this is a town that bared it's chest to the New World: if they could have places like Little Italy, the Jewish Quarter and Chinatown, then why not a Macsville or a Scotstown (even though they called it Kearny).

There's the Argyle, which doubles as a gift shop and restaurant, and when it comes to fish and chips, this one equals all the glories of the Unique back in Glasgow's Govanhill. They do a cracking Scottish breakfast, too, on Saturdays from 8 till 11 a.m., a fry-up guaranteed to help you recover from the worst Friday night's indulgences. Or is it nostalgia more than the nosh that does it? Then there's the shop called Pipers' Cove with books like *Teach Yourself to Play the Great Highland Bagpipe* and gewgaws like Bonnie Prince Charlie in glass. Wall plaque faces of Harry Lauder can be bought, along with those tapes of Kenneth McKellar, and who can make you pine for Granny's Hie'lan' hame more than him! In Molly's Cafe snack shop there a 'Scots, Do It Better in the Kilt' sign and Mars bars and Irn Bru on sale. And there's a solicitor's office nearby named Gillespie, Gillespie & Jablonski – all great sights for families and friends from home to see who would come out every summer on the bargain charter flights.

On a more poignant note, they could also be shown the Kearny War Memorial further down that same street, inscribed with the 11 names of the men who fell in the Korean War in 1950–55: out of that 11 there's a John Dougan, Jr, Alex McMillan, James Green, James Gordon

Davidson, Alexander Deans, John Reid and Samuel Turnbull. Make no mistake about it – you're in Scots territory.

New Jersey is one of the oldest settled states in the Union. The Dutch arrived as far back as 1668 when the low-lying flats on either side of the Passaic and Hackensack tributaries of the Hudson were forested with fine cedars which were quickly removed, not so much for the quality and grain of their hard-wearing wood, but because they were being used as hideaways by river pirates, among them the notorious Captain Kidd himself. The settlement on the curving bend of the Passaic which was to be called Kearny was named after the Civil War hero, General Philip Kearny, who had been something of a military adventurer: he served with Garibaldi in Italy then with Napoleon III in Algeria, before being killed early in the war at home while fighting on the Union side in the battle of Chantilly, Virginia, in 1862.

The Scots connection with the area had its origins in the British manufacturers who began eyeing the burgeoning markets and demand for supplies which had been growing furiously even before the new nation was afflicted by its disastrous Civil War. By the mid-nineteenth century, the export of thread to the United States from Paisley represented 75 per cent of the Scottish mills' production. Realising the fabulous market potential in the New World, Andrew Coats, son of thread mills founder James Coats, sailed for America in 1839 to assess the market and strengthen the company ties there. He was to lay the foundations for their expanding empire, becoming the general agent for the J. & P. Coats Spool Cotton business.

In Coats' footsteps a few years later, the other major Paisley thread firm also acted on the great opportunities over the Atlantic, despatching George A. Clark, one of the senior members of the family, to be the pioneer in the former colony for his company. He settled in New York around the same time as Andrew Coats. Both realised it made more sense to produce in America rather than to export there, and Clarks announced in December 1864, that they would invest in a mill at Newark, New Jersey – Kearny's southern neighbour just across the Passaic – which was followed by a second mill nearby. Coats did likewise, building their mill at Pawtucket which went into production in 1870.

Other Scots companies had similar ideas to the Paisley firms, like the Nairn linoleum manufacturers from Kirkcaldy. Michael Barker Nairn went to New York in the early summer of 1886 and bought land for the establishment of a factory at Kearny. Production began in midsummer 1888 and was so successful that in just under four years, it had paid off its establishment costs, a success story for the company that was to continue for many years to come. An enormous plant called Congoleum Inc still exists there, but no longer has any connection with Nairn Floors Ltd.

Between the major thread and floor-covering enterprises, thousands of Scots families crossed the Atlantic for work and a better chance for the future which was promised them there. In the ten-year period from 1921–31, almost 400,000 Scots followed in the footsteps of those early pioneering Scots, those hardy and courageous ones who had shared in the carving of this New World. President Woodrow Wilson sang their praises when he said, 'Every line of strength in American history is a line coloured by Scottish blood' – which explains not only why all these towns over there are called Glasgow, but also the eight Aberdeens, eight Edinburghs, eight Scotlands, dozens of towns called Campbell, Cameron, Douglas and Crawford, and over 100 beginning with Mac.

By the Second World War, however, migration quotas for British migrants had been drastically slashed and in the main post-war period of migration between 1945–1950, just over 16,000 Scots left for the US. But the Scots connection with New Jersey had been firmly rooted, and in Kearny itself that concentration continued to be Scots from Glasgow and surrounding areas. They had no particular connection with thread or lino production, but flocked there because of the favourable reports from earlier settlers who encouraged them to come as it was the kind of place they were sure to feel at home.

And, sure enough, they felt at home no matter how poorly they arrived, as earlier arrivals rallied round to help just as they had been helped themselves, providing them with clothes, furniture and temporary accommodation till they got work, which invariably never took long.

Exile, regardless of the reason, is always something of a calamity; to some a little death, even. But workaday places like Kearny, even though one visiting comedian labelled it 'an appallingly ugly toilet of a town', could convert that calamity into something of a triumph. They could be new Americans in their variety of workplaces by day, then go home at night to a place that was a little part of Glasgow – whether they played a game of pool or sat around the bar in the Scots-American, or even just sat down to an old-fashioned steak-pie-and-peas dinner bought from Cameron's the butcher. Kearny was their protective enclave where they could retain the old culture. Kearny was their buffer to being dumped headlong into the American mainstream. It gave them breathing space as they took in all the various customs of their new and adopted land, much of which was so strange and foreign – whether it be in manners, clothes, technology or all those things that were new to them. Home, after all, is where you are happy, and Kearny, whether by kitsch or clannishness, offered them that happiness.

It also offered them work with renumeration and opportunities, the like of which hadn't been on the agenda for them in Glasgow and Scotland. They had left a Britain in post-war, hangover years when so much, it seemed, was about drudgery and shortages, primitive housing and poor wages. Yet after arriving in Kearny, they were earning money virtually overnight that they would only have dreamt about at home and were already talking about getting themselves a house that had at least two bathrooms and a car the length of a block.

These Scots settlers adapted well, and were quick to take on American attitudes: when they saw someone pass in an expensive car before, there would be a mental snarl, whereas now their thoughts would be about getting one that was even better. They would talk about their possessions, just as Americans do, since that was the way you let folk know how well you had done. They were, after all, in a country where minds were set on success.

A carpenter who went out with his family from Webster Street in Bridgeton told me that the first wage he got in Kearny had been eight times what he earned in Glasgow. 'No kidding, I could hardly believe it. How could you *not* love a place where you earned money like that.' In the space of a year, the family had an enormous Pontiac station-wagon and a house with every ingredient and luxury of modern-day living. As the carpenter's wife told me: 'See my kitchen, it's bigger than my whole house was in Webster Street.' The Beach Boys had yet to happen, but they were already getting the Good Vibrations about Kearny and the States.

But just as it's Lochaber no more, Linwood no more and charter flights no more, it's now virtually Kearny no more, in the Scottish sense, that is. For in the same way that the immigrants of other nations initially flocked to be beside their countrymen, so the Scots migrants and their descendants have also moved or are moving on. Where there were once over 21,000 Scots living in this small New Jersey town, it's now reckoned there are only 1,000. Friends of mine who lived in Davis Avenue and Elm Street have all gone too, most of their houses now occupied by Portuguese families, the newest grouping of migrants to find their home in Kearny. No doubt, in time, they too will move on.

These new Portuguese settlers are real movers. They began arriving back in the '80s and many of them were specialists in stonework and excellent tradesmen, like the Italian masons before them. They invested first of all in the plant they required and some early arrivals did deals on new driveways around Kearny during one of the periods when I was visiting. A Scottish family in Davis Ave told me how they had come to their house the day before and within minutes of them doing a deal on a price for a new driveway, a squad of them descended with earth-moving machines and other new equipment, and by that night the work was complete. 'Boy, can these guys sell and move things,' said my friend, highly impressed with his very smart and most expertly built, new driveway.

Many of the shops and other businesses formerly owned by Scots in Kearny have also been taken over by other Portuguese families. The traditional pattern of American immigration unfolds; the fledgling arrivals group together for the security and comfort of familiarity; they would then immediately seek work in the same trades they had in the country they had left, save prodigiously and, at the same time, fiercely maintain the old culture, whether it be churches, clubs or cafés. But as time passed and they came to terms with their new surroundings, their new freedoms and perhaps the US's greatest beauty – its ideas – the migrants, and certainly their offspring, singled out new challenges, new frontiers. Just like those immigrants from so many other nations, the Scots moved and are moving on. Many have gone to more affluent suburbs in New Jersey, some to better areas of New York, others to sunnier locations, such as Florida and California.

New York's Little Italy is a prime example of such migrant progression. Once it was jampacked with the the sons and daughters of the Mezzogiorno who had gone to live there after being cleared at Ellis Island.

To all intents and purposes, it's as though they are all still there, with its multitude of Italian businesses in and around Mulberry, Mott and Hester Streets. There are dairy stores like Di Paulo's, selling ricotta, mozzarella and latticini tutti freschi; the Piemonte Ravioli Company has every conceivable pasta, all of which is home made; and Italian working men's clubs and restaurants exist in abundance, like Florio's, Umberto's and La Puglia. But most of New York's Italians don't live in Little Italy any more, having moved out long ago in the age-old pattern of migrant movement.

Likewise with Kearny. The clubs still remain, having relaxed their membership rules to keep up numbers, and many of the food shops and restaurants still survive and will undoubtedly continue to do so for the benefit of those who will always return. But for the many thousands who experienced the early years there, Kearny, New Jersey – the real Glasgow town of the United States – will always have a special place in their hearts.

He doesn't live there any more, but one person whose heart has a very special place for Kearny is Glasgow man, Alex Thomson. The Glasgow part of his life is that he was born in Scotland's biggest city and began his career as a young working man there. But for most of his life he has lived, and loved living in the town that has been his home for over 40 years. Alex is a typical Glasgow-to-Kearny story.

Alex Thomson fell in love with the New Jersey town the moment he set foot there. 'I felt I was on holiday the very minute I arrived in Kearny,' says Alex, who during the four decades he has lived in New Jersey has become one of the best-known and liked characters in the town, and that's not just because he can tell more jokes than anyone else. If you catch him without a smile on his face then you know there's something really wrong.

For years, Alex was one of the most jovial of the regulars at the Scots-American and Irish-American clubs, of which he is a gold card member. He was their MC at countless socials, dances and the other regular functions patronised by local ex-pat Scots. He also belonged to that breed of Glasgow Scots to whom Kearny meant another New World success story: the former Govan beat policeman went on to become a highly paid sales executive with one of America's biggest meat companies.

The Alex Thomson story is archetypal of many of the post-war settlers in New Jersey. It was in the spring of 1954 that Alex left Glasgow on a £57 one-way ticket on board the SS *Georgic*, one of the old transatlantic workhorses of the Cunard Line. Lots of ships crossed the Atlantic far more quickly than the *Georgic*'s nine days, but their fares were more expensive. The long voyage was compensated, however, by the heightening of that unique sight which is the New York skyline appearing on the horizon followed by the sail up the Hudson.

Alex Thomson recalls those moments as though they were yesterday. 'It was Monday, 3 May 1954, to be precise, and a day I'll never forget.'

Glasgow, at the time, continued to endure the severe agonies of post-war withdrawal syndrome. Food rationing was still enforced, although the very week Alex left for the US the Government announced that in just over two months time they would be abolishing restrictions on meat sales. From that July onwards, for the first time in 15 years, housewives would have complete freedom in the food they purchased.

Alex had lived at 64 McNeil Street, in the heart of the old Gorbals, the bleakest and blackest and most densely populated of all the old slum tenement areas in the city. The ancient, crumbling tenement houses reeked with decay and dereliction, having been neglected by indifferent landlords for decades. The war and its problems were only a convenient excuse to spend as little as possible on them.

When people speak nostalgically of the old Gorbals, they are strictly referring to that aspect of the area which pulsated with personality and individuality and had a caring concern which is burned into the hearts of all who lived there. Other than that, the living conditions in its latter years were little worse than hellish. Toilets were stairhead-communal and baths non-existent, except at the public bath-house.

The events of those last days in Glasgow before he migrated are time-warped in Alex's memory. He doesn't dwell on them, but occasionally they flow back in a sweet, nostalgic jumble . . . Jack Radcliffe and Stanley Baxter in the perennial *Half-Past Eight Show* at the Alhambra, seats from 10p; Blackpool holiday landladies offered full board at 75p a day, including a television in the lounge and beds with the very latest comfort, interior springs; Celtic were top of the league with a team which included legends such as Bonnar, Collins, Fallon, Tully and Mochan while Rangers had their Woodburn, Waddell and Liddell – and to see them play each other in the Charity Cup at Hampden cost 12p for the terracing, 25p for a seat in the Centre Stand.

After his father died, Alex Thomson's mother and sister emigrated to Kearny and the glowing reports of life in New Jersey were to entice he and his wife Cathy over. 'They said there would be no problem getting a job, and nothing could have been more true. I arrived on the Monday and started work in Louden's the butchers on Kearny Avenue on the Tuesday morning. Before joining the police force in Glasgow, I had served my apprenticeship as a butcher . . . Anderson's, 666 Eglinton Street, to be sure. Anyway, when I left, my wages as a constable in Govan were £8 a week, which was not bad money in Glasgow at the time. My first wage in Kearny was $85 a week, and the rate of exchange being what it was at the time meant that it equated with around £50. Sure, I could have been a policeman here in New Jersey; my Scottish qualifications would have got me in okay. But they didn't pay enough. That was the great thing when we came out here: there was choice for you in work. And between that and the money, they were pretty good reasons to quickly fall in love with America.'

Eight months after his arrival, Alex got a much better job, this time with Swift, one of America's biggest meat companies. It was the start of a career in buying which was to take him on to an income and lifestyle he says he could only have dreamt of back in Glasgow.

'Kearny was the kind of place you just couldn't help but like,' says Alex of his first impressions there. 'For instance, the main drag, Kearny

Avenue, is a nice broad street lined with trees – with all the Glasgow and other Scots people around, you just felt at home all the time. You spoke the same language as at home, you dressed the same way, you could go to football games, enjoy yourself in the great clubs like the Irish-American and the Scots-American. I never once felt alienated here. Never.'

Over the years, however, there was an imperceptible drift away from the town, as the Scots followed the American mode that as you prospered, you moved.

Some, as they got older, followed that other American pattern by heading for warmer climes, places such as California and Florida; others went to the Carolinas. Many moved to be nearer their children, mainly first-born Americans who had sought out their own fortunes elsewhere in the US. Alex's own son, Alex junior, is a qualified psychologist who settled in Rutherford, a more upmarket part of New Jersey.

'These last few years, though, the movement out of Kearny by the Scots has been really noticeable,' said Alex. 'At the same time, the Portuguese, the new wave of migrants, have appeared and adopted Kearny just like the Scots had done all those years ago. Now when you walk down Kearny Avenue it's more like a walk down some street in Lisbon. Signs in Portuguese in the windows of shops and stores, people everywhere speaking Portuguese, Portuguese foods and supplies. It's different. But lots of the Scots shops are still here, like Cameron's, Stewart's, the Royal Market and restaurants like the Argyle and Thistle.'

Since many of the Scots moved on to more upmarket parts of New Jersey and New York, they regularly return to indulge in everything that reminds them of home: they visit the clubs, see the Scottish soccer match of the day on TV, have one of the best fish and chip meals and collect the weekend supplies like potted meat, black pudding, links and steak pies from the Scots butchers. Just like them, Alex Thomson, now retired, and his wife Cathy also regularly return to Kearny from their new home at Leisure Village in Lakewood, 65 miles away in southern New Jersey and just ten minutes from the sea. In fact, many former Kearny Scots live nearby in this more unhurried part of the Garden State. But even there it doesn't seem all that far from Scotland – the Thomsons' new address is Hamilton Circle and the surrounding streets are called Argyll Circle, Dumbarton Drive, Aberdeen Court, Fife Court, Hamilton Court, Balmoral Court, Thornhill Court and Inverness Court.

'But we will always have that very special place in our hearts and minds for Kearny, our very own home from home in the US. It was a great place.'

20

THE BATTLE OF
GEORGE SQUARE

It's hard to imagine fully armed Scottish soldiers with heavy machine-gun units occupying Glasgow city centre with tanks being tuned up nearby, ready to help keep order; with army officers studying our best buildings to decide which would be the most suitable to set up gun emplacements where they would have the maximum effect on the gathering angry crowds; police being openly attacked by the angriest mobs in the streets; public transport being openly and wilfully sabotaged and brought to a halt.

All Britain was agog at what was going on in Scotland's biggest city and fearful Government officials were wondering if this was the beginning of a revolution. Yet it was all happening within living memory in the very centre of Glasgow.

The Ne'erday celebrations a few days previously were about the only happy memory amidst the poverty and unrest of that week in late January 1919 as the city braced itself for what many feared was going to be a bloody civil war. All the signs pointed ominously to some kind of major upheaval just around the corner. An apprehensive Government steeled itself for the worst, the Cabinet meeting in special session debating which Army regiments would be the 'most appropriate' to send north.

So what brought about such desperate events, the day remembered in the history annals of the city as Black Friday, which the workers labelled Bloody Friday?

Until the First World War, the politics of Glasgow had traditionally been Liberal, but by 1914 and the outbreak of hostilities, that was changing rapidly. Because of prevailing conditions, there was no more fertile soil than Glasgow and Clydeside for the only movement which promised any kind of hope and salvation for the worker . . . socialism and the trade unions. The latter had been introduced into the workplace in the closing years of the previous century, and was firmly established by the outbreak of war. In Glasgow alone there were 20,000 members in the largest union, the Amalgamated Society of Engineers.

World War I, the war given the dubious title of the Great War, had ended only months before those eventful days of early 1919. As the war memorial in George Square testifies, the city had provided 200,000 men – volunteers and conscripts – who served in the Forces from 1914 to 1918. That means that one in every 40 taking part in the war had been a Glaswegian. No other city contributed so many sons and daughters in the service of the country. And yet in no other city were there so many opposed to the war, willing to speak out and demonstrate against the warmongers. To them it wasn't the 'just war' that the Government had so often preached it was and it had been equally facetious to label it the war to end all wars.

Regular meetings were held throughout the city denouncing the war. It was a capitalists' war not a workers' war, that was their theme. The fury and scale of the anti-war protestors concerned the authorities who made full use of special legislation drafted to curb them, cracking down on their leaders, arresting and jailing several of them.

It wasn't just the war itself that had stirred the protestors. Soaring costs had instilled a more intense response from the workers to various actions called for by their unions. Living costs had begun escalating within weeks of the outbreak of the earliest battles, food climbing by 50 per cent after the first year. Prices of the day seem lamentably insignificant by today's levels, but then wages were pitiful, measured in shillings not in pounds. It was therefore crippling to wives' budgets when ordinary household items cost the earth. It hurt the menfolk equally when the luxury of their beer nearly doubled in price.

The trade unions, through a vigilance organisation which came to be known as the Clyde Workers Committee, became more actively engaged in the general welfare of workers and laudably demonstrated their strength when rents were added to the growing list of increases. By 1915 they had shot up from 12 per cent to as much as 23 per cent, placing an intolerable burden on thousands of suffering families, many of them the wives of serving soldiers. A rent strike had been organised and landlords countered with predictable warnings of evictions – and just to show that they meant what they threatened, 18 city tenants were summoned to the Small Debts' Court. But what happened next startled the authorities. Thousands of the city's workers took immediate and direct action, huge deputations marching from the shipyards and munition factories to join the 15,000 who demonstrated outside the court building on the day the rent cases were called. Their message was that unless the court action was dropped, thousands more would stop work in support of the rent strikers.

'Red Clydeside again,' muttered frustrated Government ministers in London when confronted with this new and potentially dangerous situation in Glasgow. There were hurried consultations with the court authorities which resulted in no order being made by the Sheriff on the back rent demands of the landlords. The Government took note. The next day it was announced that legislation would be instigated to freeze all rents at their 1914 level, and although they hadn't actually organised the rent strike, it was the Clyde Workers Committee which got the deserving kudos for it.

For the remaining years of the war, the unions grew in strength, agitating for better conditions for their members who were being continually faced with lowering standards because of spiralling prices. They were not afraid to challenge the authorities, despite the stiff censures thrown at them, such as DORA. DORA was no lady: it was the acronym for the Defence of the Realm Act, a hardline law with draconian measures to curb anyone or any organisation the Government considered to be stepping out of line. DORA, thought the Government, would be the answer for these troublemakers. They used the full potential of their power and ordered troops in Glasgow, for instance, to invade the offices of *Forward*, a workers' newspaper.. The journal was suppressed and copies impounded. William Gallacher and two other men associated with the publication were arrested under DORA laws and charged with publishing material 'calculated to cause mutiny, sedition or disaffection among the civilian population and to impede progress and restrict the production of war material'. Gallacher, a former merchant seaman and shop steward at the Albion Motor Works, along with a second man were jailed for a year and the third to three months' imprisonment. But it would take a lot more than that to scare off the activists.

A few days later, James Maxton, a young schoolmaster newly converted to Socialism and in later years to become the legendary MP for Bridgeton, gave a fiery anti-war speech in Glasgow Green, for which he and two other anti-war campaigners received sentences ranging from 12 to 18 months. And David Kirkwood, who had gone from errand boy to skilled engineer to shop steward at Beardmore's famous Parkhead Forge, together with five other prominent trade union militants, were pounced on by armed detectives and taken into custody before being handed a unique sentence permissible by the dreaded Defence of the Realm Act: they were to be deported. The order against them said they were free to go anywhere they wished, except for one place . . . Glasgow. Kirkwood opted for Edinburgh, the others headed south, to England. The deportation order was to last for a year.

Such was the tinderbox mood in the city, that Glasgow Chief Constable James Stevenson had discussions with the authorities about the use of military assistance should there be any widespread trouble. He was convinced matters would deteriorate and feared an insurrection of the kind which would be beyond the powers of his constables to contain. Whatever reassurance he was given, the details did not emerge until the trouble he forebode was actually to break out.

It was against such a background that tens of thousands of servicemen and women were being demobilised. The propagandists had promised them their brave deeds in battle would not be forgotten and Prime Minister Lloyd George glibly assured them that when the war was over that they would return to a land which was fit for heroes. But the reality was they were coming home to a Scotland where living conditions were as deplorable, and in many instances worse, than what they had left four years before. Most of them were going to homes with neither baths nor toilets. Meagre dole money, only recently introduced, was only available for the first six weeks of the unemployment which so many were to face. Women workers who had replaced men during the war were ungraciously sacked, forcing them into sweated labour jobs.

Typical of the wages and conditions at the time were those being paid by a chain of Glasgow cafés. Waitresses and kitchen staff working 12-hour shifts earned 60p a week. If a girl accidentally broke a plate, 5p was deducted from her wages; a cup and saucer, and the fine was 7½p; a wineglass, 10p. And if you were a few minutes late for starting work in the morning you lost 1½p from your 60p week's wage. Thousands of females were forced into prostitution – a survey at the time revealed the shocking statistic of 17,000 girls plying the trade in the city hoping to earn something for their families.

Even before demobilisation, unemployment had been mounting as orders for ships, munitions and other engineering products fell off. Peace was bad news for industry. It was even worse for returning soldiers who were to discover the shocking truth that there was no work for them. Over 100,000 workers had already been dismissed from their jobs, and they took their place in the unemployment queues which were swelling by trainload after trainload of returning war veterans.

Something had to be done and the Clyde Workers Committee together with the Trades Council, presided over by Emmanuel Shinwell, the son of an immigrant Jewish clothes dealer and former Co-op shop assistant, decided to campaign for a cut in the working week as a measure to ease unemployment. There had been growing agitation for years to have work hours reduced which was hardly surprising since the regular working week for the majority meant starting at six in the morning and finishing at 5.30. Saturday was a half day. The engineers' union had been negotiating for a reduction from 54 to 47 hours a week, but the demand now was for a reduction to 40 hours – and to strike for it if necessary. The workers backed them, and all the talk in the city in the dying weeks of 1918 was the pending strike for the 40-hour week. It was called for on Monday, 27 January 1919.

That morning the workers had a meeting in the St Andrew's Halls, now the home of the expanded Mitchell Library. More than 3,000 crammed inside the hall which had never experienced anything like it before. Before the platform party began their speeches, the huge crowd broke into song, but it was no inspirational or revolutionary chorus. Instead it was a popular ballad of the day, a simple and sentimental little tune that went: 'My ain wee hoose . . . there's no place in all the world like my ain wee hoose.' And they sang that ballad over and over again.

The crowd needed no lectures, or homilies or harangues from the speakers. They were in the mood for one thing and one thing only – to strike. And when one of them proposed a mass picket, a course of action they had never taken before, there was unanimous agreement. They would go from the Halls to the factories and march from one to the next and on to the next until everyone was on strike. But there was no need. The word was out about the meeting and tools were downed at workplaces almost simultaneously. The strike was utterly spontaneous, and the workers demonstrated a new solidarity, undoubtedly inspired by the achievements of their comrades in Russia. Although some of the larger shipyards continued their operations, a total of 40,000 remained idle as the strike went into its second day. By Wednesday, 29 January, power workers had joined in, although by agreement with the strike committee sufficient supplies were to be maintained for hospitals, lighting and transport, electric tramcars being the city's main form of public transport.

Their confidence boosted, the Strike Committee then ordered the City Magistrates to halt the tramcars, knowing that in doing so, they would bring the city to a standstill. In their ultimatum, the strikers gave the councillors a week to comply with their demand. But their call was indignantly ignored. The situation degenerated and became so potentially dangerous in the city that there was a meeting of the War Cabinet in London on Thursday, 30 January. They considered calling in 2,000 special constables for full-time duty to bolster the city's police force, depleted by 500 of its men who still had to return from service in the Forces. It was suggested they be given urgent release, but Winston Churchill, Secretary of State for War, said it would be impossible to arrange this as they were scattered in diversified units of the Services. But he did recommend that they continue to apply the force of DORA and seize some of the strike leaders – then wait until some 'glaring excess' had been committed before taking stronger measures, such as the use of troops. He did say, however, that the War Office would take all necessary steps to meet any eventuality and arrangements would be made for troop movements to Glasgow. Churchill's orders were acted on and men in various barracks throughout Scotland gathered their battle gear and made ready for a new front line . . . the city of Glasgow.

George Square had been the workers' rallying point all that week and on the morning of Friday, 31 January, it was full to capacity, everyone seeking information and copies of the one (old) penny daily *Strike Bulletin*. Much of the talk that morning had been about the magistrates' refusal to halt the tramcars. It was a sore point with the strikers and later in the day it became the spark inflaming the worst disturbances the city had known for years and has ever seen since.

The general mood became uglier the more they debated the magistrates' refusal to stop the trams and it became obvious that some kind of tumult was just waiting to happen. Just then a tramcar loudly trundled from South Frederick Street into George Square and protestors leapt on board. One of them climbed to its top deck where he unhooked the rooftop trolley umbilically linking the vehicle to the electric system. Their behaviour was too much for an off-duty soldier, probably home on leave and unaccustomed to such indiscipline, and he lashed out at one of the men. That was all they needed. The riot was on. Churchill's moment of 'glaring excess' had arrived.

Nervy police reacted by drawing batons and charging the first of the skirmishes. Soon there were pitched battles between police and protestors throughout the square and in many of the streets adjoining it; military-like charges by the protestors, then counter-charges by police with flailing batons. Having recently returned as ex-soldiers, many of the demonstrators were used to more ferocious and deadly warfare than a police charge. Compared to the horrors of France, this was a bit of a picnic to them and undaunted, they retaliated, forming ranks to make their own charges and send the police scurrying for cover.

Missiles were thrown and a pub in North Hanover Street invaded, but not for simple looting. They wanted bottles to throw at the police. Constables ran up North Frederick Street to try and surround them but were met by other strikers in Cathedral Street and another battle taking place there. Flying bottles dotted the air, one hitting Chief Constable Stevenson as he took command. Then Sheriff Mackenzie got up to read the Riot Act. He didn't get far into his reading, however. Strikers rushed him and the official papers were torn from his hands. He, too, was struck by a bottle.

In an effort to calm the riot, respected shop steward David Kirkwood appeared at the balcony of the City Chambers. He appealed to the crowds to disperse and go instead to Glasgow Green. They readily obeyed, but the police were waiting there and another riot broke out. This time the strikers found better weapons than beer bottles, however, as a long row of iron fencing was ripped from the ground and its spiked railings used as spears. Batons were no match for that, and the Bobbies beat a hasty retreat.

Late in the afternoon, trouble spread to other parts of the city. Hundreds of tramcars were immobilised and there was widespread traffic chaos. Two policemen trying to prevent attacks on trams in the Saltmarket were rushed by the crowd and stripped of their uniforms. They had to flee for their lives, naked. Looters went into action, but mainly against jewellers shops.

The strike leaders were in the thick of the battle – two of them, Gallacher and Kirkwood, were badly injured, the latter being brutally bludgeoned as he left the City Chambers. Twenty of them were seized by police and taken into custody, and alarmed authorities requested help from the Army.

'Glaring excess' was met with glaring reaction, as the first of the troops arrived at Buchanan Street Station that night and others poured into the city the following morning, arriving at Queen Street Station. They included the Seaforths, Gordons and other Highland regiments, and with shouldered rifles they marched through the streets, some headed by regimental pipe bands and followed by long convoys of ammunition wagons. It was no mere show of strength, as the soldiers were quickly displaced for action. Machine-gun emplacements were positioned on top of buildings and platoons of troops were stationed at the most vital ones; some, armed with rifles, patrolled the streets, while others hurriedly unrolled coils of barbed wire to encircle the City Chambers; a howitzer gun was readied at the main door; and, most fearful of all, six huge battle tanks were warming their engines in their temporary garage at the Meat Market just off Gallowgate.

That was enough for the protesting workers. They astutely took the point and dispersed. Slowly they returned to work and ten days later their strike was officially ended, its leaders having been in court and charged with the most serious offences. They were convicted of forming part of a riotous mob and 'overawe[ing] and intimidate[ing] the police, to forcibly take possession of the Municipal Buildings and the North British Station Hotel'.

Shinwell, Gallacher and Kirkwood were further charged with inciting a mob of 20,000 'riotous and evilly disposed persons'.

Three months later at the High Court in Edinburgh, 12 of the leaders stood trial, further charges against them of looting and theft having been dropped. Kirkwood, the shop steward, was acquitted. Shinwell, the Trades Council president, was sentenced to six months, and Gallacher, the other shop steward, to three months. The three stalwarts were not forgotten, and went on to become the most distinguished and memorable Members of Parliament: Kirkwood was the MP for Dunbartonshire for almost 30 years before becoming the first Baron Kirkwood of Bearsden; Shinwell, a legendary Parliamentarian, became a Minister of Fuel, a Secretary of State for War and Minister of Defence before becoming Lord Shinwell of Easington; and Gallacher, who had met Lenin, and was an equally legendary figure, became President of the Communist Party and the outspoken and unforgettable MP for West Fife for 15 years.

And what of the strike-participating workers? Their bold actions did not go unrewarded. Their strike ended ten days after the riot they now called Bloody Friday, and employers agreed to a 47-hour week. But it wasn't for more than a quarter of a century later, and after another world war, that 40 hours was to be accepted as the average working week.

SELECTED BIBLIOGRAPHY

Glasgow 1919: The Story of the 40 Hours Strike. Introduction by Harry McShane (The Molendinar Press)
Glasgow. David Daiches (Andre Deutsch)
Glasgow at War. Paul Harris (Archive Publications)
Glasgow Art Deco. Rudolph Kenna (Richard Drew Publishing)
A Glasgow Collection: Essays In Honour of Joe Fisher. No Mean Writer. Sean Damer (Glasgow City Libraries)
The Heart of Glasgow. Jack House (Hutchinsons of London)
The Second City. C.A. Oakley (Blackie)
Glasgow's Giants: 100 Years of the Old Firm. Bill Murray (Mainstream)
The Old Firm: Sectarianism, Sport and Society in Scotland. Bill Murray (John Donald Publishers, Edinburgh)
Blood on the Thistle. Douglas Skelton (Mainstream)
Ireland for Beginners. Phil Evans and Eileen Pollock (Writers and Readers Publishing Co-operative Society Ltd)
The Irish in Scotland. James E. Handley, (John S. Burns and Sons)
Ireland's Civil War. Calton Younger (Frederick Muller)
Ireland – A History. Robert Kee (Weidenfeld and Nicolson)
The Good Auld Days. Gordon Irving (Jupiter Books)
Music Hall Memories. Jack House (Richard Drew Publishing)
The Cinemas of Cinema City. T. Louden
Pictures Past. Janet McBain (Moorfoot Publishing)
Workshop of the British Empire. Michael S. Moss and John R. Hume (Heinemann)
The Angry '30s. Julian Symons (Eyre Methuen, London)

The Golden Age of Shipping. Robert Gardiner, Ambrose Greenway (Conway's)

The Rise and Fall of British Shipbuilding. Anthony Burton (Constable)

No Gods, Precious Few Heroes. Chris Harvie (Edinburgh University Press)

Crisis on the Clyde. Jack McGill (Davis-Poynter)

Tony Benn, A Biography. Jad Adams (Macmillan)

Reflections of a Clyde-built Man. Jimmy Reid (Condor)

Reformism on the Clyde, the Story of UCS. Stephen Johns (Plough Press)

The UCS Work-in. Willie Thompson and Finlay Hart (Lawrence and Wishart, London)

A Legacy of Fame. Colin M. Castle (Murdoch Carberry Publishing)

Comrade John Maclean, MA. Tom Anderson (Glasgow, 1930)

John Maclean. Nan Milton (Pluto Press)

Prisons and Punishment in Scotland. Joy Cameron (Canongate, Edinburgh)

The Making of Urban Scotland. Ian H. Adams, (McGill-Queen's University Press, Montreal and Croom Helm, London)

The New Scots. Bashir Maan. (John Donald, Publishers, Edinburgh)

Oscar Slater: The Mystery Solved. Thomas Toughill (Canongate)

The Big Yin. Johnathan Margolis (Orion)

Billy Connolly – The Athorised Version (Pan Books)

Gullible's Travels: Billy Connolly. Michael Joseph (Pavilion)

Ministry of Health Plague Report, 1900

Daily Record/Sunday Mail, The Herald, Evening Times, Scottish Catholic Observer